TEACH YOURSE

COLLOQUIAL ARABIC

It is generally supposed that a single language is spoken throughout the Arab world. But it is only written Arabic that is more or less common to the individual countries, and the spoken language can differ as widely as Spanish and Italian. This book has been prepared for those who wish to make everyday use of the living language of modern Egypt and for those who would like to add a colloquial Arabic to their knowledge of languages. Its subject is Cairene Arabic, the form of Egyptian colloquial Arabic spoken in Cairo which sets the standards for modern Egyptian usage. After working carefully through this book, the student should be able to carry on simple conversations fluently and accurately.

TEACH YOURSELF BOOKS

COLLOQUIAL
ARABIC

The Living Language of Egypt

T. F. Mitchell

Professor of English Language and General Linguistics,
University of Leeds

ST. PAUL'S HOUSE   WARWICK LANE
LONDON EC4P 4AH

First printed 1962
Sixth impression 1975

This volume is published in the U.S.A.
by David McKay Company Inc.,
750 Third Avenue, New York, N.Y. 10017.

ISBN 0 340 05774 2

Printed and bound in Great Britain
for the English Universities Press Ltd
by Richard Clay (The Chaucer Press), Ltd., Bungay Suffolk

ACKNOWLEDGMENTS

I am most grateful to the Shell Petroleum Company for generously allowing me to draw freely upon material contained in my *Introduction to Egyptian Colloquial Arabic* (Oxford, 1956).

My sincere thanks are also due to Dr. Mohamed Ahmed Abu Farag for his invaluable help in the preparation of Part IV.

T. F. M.

CONTENTS

I. THE LINGUISTIC BACKGROUND

There is a great deal in a name, sometimes a great deal of confusion. It is commonly supposed that *Arabic* designates a single language uniting in ties of mutual comprehension speakers from countries as widely separated as Iraq, Egypt, and Morocco, but this is not so. It is only *written* Arabic, that is the Classical language of the Koran and early literature and the grammatically similar neo-Classical or Modern Arabic of contemporary literature, journalism, broadcasting, and public address that is more or less common to the Arab world. Speaking and writing are essentially separate aspects of linguistic activity and the first has always preceded the second, both in the process of man's evolution and in the sequence by which the individual child acquires a complicated set of listening and speaking habits long before he sets hand and eye to paper. As a result of the normal processes of linguistic development, the colloquial Arabic which lives in the several Arab societies to-day and by which they mostly live, differs as widely between Arab countries as do those languages which nowadays go under the different names of Italian, Spanish, and Portuguese. Within the Arab world, the comparatively static and uniform written Arabic acts in a wholly desirable way as a kind of limited Esperanto, providing a means of communication between educated men of whatever nationality ; as a spoken medium, it is an example of that paradox known to linguists as a *Schriftsprache* and might aptly be named *pan*-Arabic. The nearest contemporary European parallel to this use of a written language as a " control " for purposes of spoken communication is provided by the *Hochdeutsch* used between speakers of otherwise mutually unintelligible varieties of German, but a closer parallel is the historical one of Latin in the Middle Ages before the emergence of the several Romance languages. Even in English, of course, there are differences of grammar and vocabulary between the written and spoken language but the degree of such difference is far less than that between the artificial pan-Arabic and the living colloquial of any Arab country. Moreover, both written and spoken English are recognized in English-using societies as belonging to one living language and are both systematically taught and maintained by authority; colloquial Arabic, on the other hand, is largely ignored by its users and, what is more, unlike colloquial English, may not freely be written.

The educated Egyptian, then, uses pan-Arabic to talk, on as wide a range of topics as the present state and degree of unification of the written language allows, to equally literate Iraqis, Saudis, Moroccans, and even Europeans. No reasonable man, however, in whatever homogeneous society, is anxious to talk like a book, much less like a newspaper or a public orator, and the language that the same educated Egyptian uses on return to the bosom of his family or generally with his compatriots is quite other than that in which he addresses non-Egyptians. This second language is wholly Egyptian and it is exclusively with it that this book is concerned.

Egyptian Arabic is a vigorous, living language and, like all languages, which are inseparable from the men, women, and children who use them, it is, and has been over the many centuries of its evolution, subject to constant change. It is naïve to believe, as some do, that it is possible, let us say in the interests of Arab political and economic unity, to suppress all national forms of Arabic and to impose in their stead, either gradually or overnight, a new form of Arabic identical with or closely related to the present written language. What is needed in the present somewhat schizophrenic conditions is both development of pan-Arabic in order to increase its scope and at the same time the institution of *national* written languages. There are signs that an Egyptian written language is struggling to emerge; the dialogue of some playwrights, for example, is deliberately contrived to conform to both written and colloquial usage, but this is a half-measure at a time when nothing less is needed than the complete freedom in which, for example, a hypothetical thriller-writer is as much at liberty as Agatha Christie in England to include colloquial forms in his work and the educationist is able to write a grammar of English for use in Egyptian schools in which colloquial English is faced squarely by the colloquial Egyptian of the school-child's day-to-day experience. Egypt, favourably placed as she is culturally, politically, geographically, and demographically, and with the consciousness of " own language " that so many of her people enjoy, has a splendid opportunity to give the lead in this vital matter to the rest of the Arab world. The authoritative grammars, dictionaries, and other law-giving books must be written and compiled by Egyptians themselves, for they alone are masters of their own language.

Some may say that to do as has just been suggested would be to run counter to the ideal of Arab unity in the economic, political, religious, and cultural spheres, but surely such action would be to serve this ideal, for it is only by bringing differences out into the open that, when occasion demands, they can be avoided. Moreover, the parallel drawn above between pan-Arabic and Latin (now dead) is by no means a complete one, since vital factors are present in the modern situation which were absent in the Middle Ages. Pan-Arabic is not the pre-rogative of a single class of society, and not only is education to-day more widespread but the mass media and jet aircraft of the times make the world a small place indeed.

The question may reasonably be posed as to which form of Arabic the foreign learner should first be taught and the right answer in the current situation is undoubtedly pan-Arabic. But thereafter he may wish to learn one of the many living forms of Arabic and the question again arises, which ? In the absence of any indication as to the particular country most likely to interest him, there can be no doubt about the answer. Egyptian films are seen and the Egyptian radio heard in every Arab country and Egyptians teach in schools from Kuwait to Libya ; it is hardly surprising, therefore, that the Egyptian colloquial is much better known than any other. In addition, it has advanced further than other colloquials along the road to linguistic independence, for there exists a clearly recognizable norm to which educated Egyptian usage conforms. Standards are set in Egypt by the cultured classes in Cairo.

There are numerous forms of Egyptian colloquial Arabic, just as there are many dialects of English. Divergence may be considerable, as for example between Cairo, Qena in Upper Egypt, and the Bedouin area west of Alexandria, or it may be less marked as, say, between the towns and villages of the

Delta. Moreover, differences of educational standard and class correspond to speech differences in a single district. An educated Egyptian, however, has very definite ideas on what constitutes a " prestige " pronunciation, turn of phrase, etc., and the dominance of Cairo is not surprising, since the part played by capital cities in establishing a norm is well known. In England, London, as the centre of government, commerce, literature, law, etc., attracted in the past people from many parts of the country who helped fashion the dialect of English which was to become so widespread and which, in its present form, is spoken by most educated Englishmen to-day. It is, then, cultured Cairene Arabic that is the subject of this book.

Finally, a word of warning. In the present situation the student must be prepared to meet the attitude, common enough in European centres of learning, that written language, preferably literary, is alone worthy of study. The student of Arabic is as certain to encounter bigotry on the part of linguistically unsophisticated people—and how many of us are truly without prejudice in linguistic matters ?—as he is to hear the dogmatic expression of views which, based on obsession with " Classical " and written form, are opposed to the statements of grammar and pronunciation made in this book. To such statements he should turn a deaf ear, concentrating rather on listening to what his informant is saying and how he is saying it. The pronunciation hints which follow are intended to help him to this end.

II. HINTS ON PRONUNCIATION

There is a minimum of phonetic courtesy to be achieved in learning to use any language ; moreover, the advantages that proficiency in pronouncing Arabic confer on the English speaker are self-evident : among them, the respect of the Egyptian is not the least. The general hints contained in this book should suffice for practical purposes and provide a firm foundation on which to build a more detailed study of Egyptian pronunciation.

The system of writing used in the book is a transcription of colloquial pronunciation ; it is neither a transliteration of Arabic written forms nor an orthography, which would require a constant shape for a given word, whatever its pronunciation in context. It is not, however, that kind of phonetic transcription which aims at representing as many features of consonant-and vowel-sound as possible, but rather one whose object is to suggest an acceptable pronunciation, with the minimum of frills and without losing sight of grammar and lexicon.

The transcription comprises the following consonant-letters, vowel-letters, and diacritics :

(a) *consonants* : b, d, ḍ, f, g, h, ḥ, k, l, m, n, q, r, s, ṣ, t, ṭ, w,
x, y, z, ẓ, ς, ʃ, ʕ, γ
(b) *vowels* : a, ɑ, e, i, o, u
(c) *diacritics* : acute accent, hyphen, breve (˘)

Other consonant symbols, sporadically used and relating to loan-words in the colloquial, are included in the Addenda to the following section.

In the case of ḍ, ḥ, ṣ, ṭ, ẓ, ς, ʃ, ʕ, and γ, the letter-shape is strange and, with the exception of ʃ (= *sh* in *ship*), its strangeness relates to special pronunciation difficulty. In addition, it will be found that q and x are used with very different values from those associated with them in English orthography. Vowels occur both long and short ; long vowels are shown by doubling the letter, i.e. long a by aa, long i by ii, etc. Capital letters are not used in the transcription.

PRONUNCIATION OF CONSONANTS

(a) Little difficulty is offered to English speakers by the sounds written with : f (as in English *film*), b (Eng. *bad*), s (Eng. *sit*), z (Eng. *zeal*), ʃ (Eng. *sheen*), k (Eng. *king*), g (Eng. *gear*), m (Eng. *mat*), n (Eng. *nap*), w (Eng. *win*), y (Eng. *yes*). t and d, too, do not present insuperable obstacles but care should be taken to ensure that the tongue is in contact with the teeth as well as with the ridge behind the teeth, since in most contexts it is exclusively with this ridge that contact is made in pronouncing the corresponding English sounds (cf. Eng. *tag* and *dam* and contrast Arabic taag *crown* and damm *blood*). s, z, t, d must always be distinguished from ṣ, ẓ, ṭ, ḍ.

(b) The following will require more careful attention :

ʕ : the glottal stop or catch. A common enough sound in English dialects, cf. a Cockney pronunciation of the *t*'s in *a bit o' butter*, and one which occurs frequently in Standard English pronunciation between words beginning and ending with a vowel, e.g. *Jaffa* ʕ*orange*, *sea* ʕ*eagle*, and also when we wish to give emphatic stress to a word beginning with a vowel, e.g. *it's* ʕ*absolutely* ʕ*awful*. Arabic examples are : ʕiktib *l write !*, ʕumm *mother*, ʕult *I/you said*, daʕiiʕa *minute* (time), haʕʕ *right*.

h : a sound which will not be found difficult when it begins a word or syllable as in haat ! *bring, fetch !*, muhimm *important*, but one which must be carefully pronounced in the same way when, in an un-English way, it ends a word or syllable, e.g. ʕabúuh *his father*, ʕáhwa *coffee* ; beware, however, of an English tendency to make h sound like x (see below) in these contexts. It sometimes helps in the early stages to put in an extra " ghost " vowel following h, i.e. ʕáhawa (for ʕáhwa) and to aim at eliminating it gradually. In the speech of many educated Egyptians final h, e.g. ʕabúuh, is often not pronounced but the beginner is advised to practise its inclusion.

l : in almost all contexts the " clear " l of *leaf* as opposed to the " dark " l of *feel*. Imagine you are going to pronounce the word *leaf* but keep the tongue in the " l "-position, prolonging the sound and without uttering the " -eaf " portion ; contrast the sound with that of the l at the end of *feel.* The pronunciation of Arabic **fiil** *elephant* and **milk** *property* in the manner of English *feel* and *milk* would be woefully inadequate. Most Irishmen, it may be noted, use the right kind of *l* in all English contexts : most Americans and Scots use the wrong kind even in *leaf.* An important exception to the general rule is that the " dark " *l* of *feel* is used in **ṣalláah** *God* and derivative forms as **ṣinṣálla** *I hope* ; **ṣa** of **ṣalláah** is elided if preceded by a vowel and, if this vowel is **i**, then **ll** is pronounced with the " clear " *l* of *leaf*; e.g. **ṣilḥámdu li-lláah** *praise be to God.*

r: English initial *r* in words like *rugged, rock,* and *rascal* will never do. The rolled Scottish *r* of *burn* is what is wanted. Many English people make the right kind of " r " in words such as *very* and *thorough* ; if you do, try to isolate it in order to control it, if you do not, try to pronounce a very quick " d " in place of " r " in these words. Pay particular attention to the need to pronounce Arabic **r** when final : **ṣamíir** *prince* sounds nothing like *a mere.* A quick flip or tap of the tip of the tongue against the ridge behind the teeth is the basis of this sound and it is also the basis of the trilled or rolled " r ", which consists of a number of intermittent taps and which is the sound of Arabic **r** when doubled (**rr**). The trilled " r " may take some time to master if the student cannot make it already, but with practice it will come, even if only after a month or so of perseverance. Arabic examples are : **raml** *sand*, **bard** *cold*, **bárra** *outside*, **barr** *land, country*.

ṣ
ẓ
ṭ
ḍ : so-called " emphatic " consonants, to be distinguished from " non-emphatic " **s, z, t, d** respectively. For the emphatics, the tongue must be broad (laterally expanded) and " thick ", filling the mouth : for the corresponding non-emphatics, the tongue is narrow (laterally contracted) and " thin ". The lateral expansion and contraction of the tongue may be practised when looking in a mirror. In addition, the front of the tongue is very much lower and the whole tongue much flatter in the mouth for the emphatics ; for the non-emphatics the front of the tongue is raised and the back depressed much as it is for

the pronunciation of the vowel i (see below) : the difference
is easily perceptible in moving from, say, the t-position to
the ṭ-position and vice versa while maintaining the
necessary contact at the teeth or junction of teeth and
gums. It sometimes helps to practise hollowing the tongue
from front to rear and to retain the hollowing when pronouncing the emphatics ; the mirror is again helpful in
this connection. The position of the lips is also important ;
for the emphatics, they are held neutral or slightly
rounded and protruded : for s, z, t, d they are spread. It
may be noted that l of Ṣallāaḥ (see above) is characterized
by emphatic articulation.

The features described above combine to produce in the
emphatics a characteristic " hollow " resonance ; the hiss
of ṣ, for example, is of much lower frequency, much more
indeterminate than the high-frequency, clear-cut sibilance
of s. In this particular case, it is also helpful to pronounce
s with considerable tension in the tongue and lips.
Examples of difference between emphatic and non-
emphatic are :

tiin *figs*	ṭiin *mud*
baat *he spent the night*	baaṭ *armpit*
seef *sword*	ṣeef *summer*
bass *only*	baṣṣ *he looked*
dall *he directed*	ḍall *he lost his way*
baṛd *after*	baṛḍ *some*
záayir *visitor*	ẓáahir *clear*
mafrúuz *selected*	maḥfúuẓ *learnt by heart*

x : not a difficult sound. Feel back along the roof of the
mouth with the tip of the tongue until the *soft palate* is
reached ; the soft palate and the *uvula* (the extremity of
the soft palate ; it can be seen in a mirror, hanging down
at the extreme back of the mouth) must be made to
vibrate for x as, for example, when breathing out heavily
during snoring. It is much the same sound as in Scottish
loch or *och aye* and German *achtung*. Arabic examples are
xáfab *wood*, baxt *luck*, muxx *brains*. More practice may be
necessary when the sound occurs before or after i (or ii),
e.g. baxiil *miser, miserly*, xígil *he was ashamed, confused*.

ɣ : x with the vocal cords vibrating, that is to say with the
     buzzing introduced into x that is made when passing from
     s to z, i.e. sss-zzz, xxx-ɣɣɣ. If difficulty is encountered,
     " dry gargling " should do the trick. ɣ is also the familiar
     sound of French " r " in Paris and Northern France.
     Examples are ɣaffir *watchman*, ɡuɣáyyɑr *small*, ʃuɣl *work*,
     riɣíif *loaf*.

q : a sound made in a somewhat similar manner to k but of
     very different acoustic impression, made in fact in the
     same place as x and ɣ, at the uvula. Make a k as far back
     as possible ; again the mirror is of some help. This sound
     is used by educated speakers for " classicisms " in the
     colloquial ; used in the right places, it is perhaps the most
     important single sign of educated speech. Examples are
     qárya *village*, ʕilqurʕáan *the Koran*, ḥuqúul izzéet *the
     oilfields*.

     q is a " Classical " sound to which colloquial ʕ usually
     corresponds ; there is, however, no simple equation
     classical q = colloquial ʕ. Words keep habitual company
     with other words and their total associations with par-
     ticular contexts and styles of discourse. No doubt
     ʕadíima and qadíima are in some sense the " same word "
     in fi máṣr ilʕadíima *in Old Cairo* and in f-ilɾuṣúur ilqadíima
     in olden times but it would be quite wrong to substitute one
     form for the other and the difference between the forms is
     charged with meaning.

ḥ : a sound articulated (like ɾ) in the pharynx, the throat
     region above the windpipe ; to master it, it is necessary to
     " get the feel " of this region. Look in a mirror and see
     what happens to the Adam's apple when one swallows ;
     it will be seen to rise considerably and then descend again
     to its position of rest : if an attempt is made to keep it at
     the top of its run instead of allowing it to descend, the
     discomfort felt will be in the region in which it is necessary
     to make ḥ. To pronounce ḥ, adopt a posture as if about to
     retch, then release the tension in the pharynx just
     sufficiently to allow egress of air from the lungs ; the
     result should be a satisfactory ḥ. Try to make the root of
     the tongue fill the throat for the sound, which, it must be
     emphasized, is not in the least like x or h and must at all

times be ·clearly distinguished from them. It is· quite
possible to make a sound which combines features of ḥ and
x and this is often· a stage through which the· beginner
passes on the way to mastery of ḥ. Examples are : ḥáaga
thing, ḥilw *sweet, nice,* naḥl *bees,* ráḥḥab· *to welcome,* riiḥ
wind, malḥ *salt.*

ع: the voiced sound corresponding to ḥ, i.e. as y is to x (see
above) so ع is to ḥ. Follow carefully thé instructions for ḥ
and simply introduce the necessary buzz of voice ; do not
do anything else. It has to be remembered that the tongue
is made up of many muscles and is capable of movement
in its parts as well as in its whole, so that it is quite
possible for the root of the tongue in the pharynx to be
correctly disposed for ع (and ḥ) and for the front of the
tongue to perform unwanted action ; when practising,
therefore, open the mouth fairly wide and keep the part of
the tongue visible in a mirror flat on the floor of the
mouth. Having mastered the basic sound by following the
above instructions, the student is likely to experience
difficulty in controlling these two sounds in context, in
" turning them on and off " at the right moments in the
stream of speech ; it is quite possible to imbue speech with
the sound of ع throughout—the effect ·is somewhat
" strangled ". Such an effect is unfortunate in Arabic and
in the early stages practice in " turning on and off " will
be necessary, especially after vowels but also before vowels
to some extent; practice the sound, therefore, inter-
vocalically, short and long, i.e. aa-ع-aa, aa-ع-uu, aa-ع-ii,
uu-ع-aa, uu-ع-uu, uu-ع-ii, ii-ع-aa, ii-ع-uu, ii-ع-ii, a-عع-aa,
a-عع-uu, a-عع-ii, etc. Finally, beware of a common
tendency to confuse ع with ق. Arabic examples are :
عáada *custom, habit,* عádad *number,* عeen *eye,* عiid *festival,*
عumr *life, age,* baعdéen *afterwards,· later,* buعd *distance,*
sábعa *seven,* sabعíin *seventy,* báعat *he sent,* gaعáan *hungry,*
biعíid *far,* buعáad *far* (plural), láaعib *player,* záععaق *he*
shouted, dáfaع *he paid,* wiقiع *he fell,* niعnáaع *mint,* sabع *lion.*

Doubled consonants

Any Arabic consonant may be doubled. Except when final,
a doubled consonant must be pronounced at least twice as

long as its single counterpart and is characterized by greater muscular tension in the articulating organs It is infinitely preferable to pronounce a doubled consonant occurring between vowels extremely long rather than not long enough ; many English speakers do not pronounce doubled consonants with sufficient length when they occur at some distance from the accented syllable, e.g. naʃʃaliin *pickpockets* (sing. naʃʃáal). The contrary tendency is also observable among English speakers, who often pronounce a single consonant too long when it occurs after a short stressed syllable, as t and s in kátaba *clerks*, kásar *he broke*. Consonants which are pronounced long occur in English at the junction of words or of affixes and words ; for example, *black king* (contrast *blacking*), *misspelt, unnecessary*, but, of course, the double letters of English spelling in such words as *better* and *butter* are pronounced as single sounds. The single-double distinction is a very important feature of Arabic and the ss of kássar *he smashed*, for example, must always be pronounced considerably longer than s in kásar *he broke*. Other examples are ʕissámak (*the*) *fish*, ʃayyáal *hardworking*, dáffaʕ *he charged* (*money*), fáddʒa *silver*, ʃayyaliin *porters*, baṣṣ *he looked*, muhimm *important*. Doubled consonants are usually pronounced shorter when final.

Addenda

(a) The sound written *v* in English sometimes occurs for f in the transcription, e.g. lofẓ *pronunciation*, but has no independent status except in very rare loan-words such as se(e)rv *service* (*tennis*), vitíss *gear-lever* ; it has not, therefore, been included above. Similar remarks apply to the sound written generally as *p*, which sometimes occurs for transcribed b, e.g. yóom issábt *Saturday*, but again has no independent status except in loans, e.g. piláaj *seaside resort*. Less sophisticated speakers tend to replace v and p in such loans with f and b respectively, e.g. balf *valve*, biiba *pipe*. j, as in English *jeep*, also occurs in loan-words, e.g. jakétta *jacket*, jóoki *jockey*, julúuji *geologist*.

(b) The sounds of English *th* in (i) *thin* and (ii) *then* belong to a " Classical " pronunciation of Arabic and occur sporadically when reading written language aloud. Examples occur in the book and the symbols used are as follows : θ (as *th* in *thin*), **ð** (as *th* in *then*). An emphatic counterpart of **ᵤ**, symbol **ð̣**, also occurs in this style of pronunciation.

PRONUNCIATION OF VOWELS

General

Of the six vowels (**a, ɑ, e, i, o, u**), three (**i, e, a**) are articulated in the front of the mouth and three (**ɑ, o, u**) in the back: the tongue becomes flatter in the mouth or at a greater distance from the roof of the mouth as it moves from **i** through **e** to **a** and, conversely, moves towards the roof of the mouth in the back series from **ɑ** through **o** to **u**; the degree of opening, measurable roughly by the distance between the top and bottom teeth, is greatest for the open vowels (**a, ɑ**) and least for the close vowels (**i, u**). The lips are spread for **i** and **e**, neutral for **a** and **ɑ**, rounded for **o** and (especially) **u**.

Vowel-length

Vowels occur both short and long; when pronouncing a long vowel, give it at least twice the length given to its single counterpart; cf., for example, **ṣádaf** *sea-shells* and **ṣáadif** *he chanced upon.*

Two principal rules govern the occurrence of long vowels:

(1) they occur only in prominent or stressed syllables, cf. **máasik** *holding* but **masíkhum** *holding them;*
(2) they do not occur in closed syllables, i.e. type CVVC, where C = consonant and VV = long vowel, unless the syllable is final, cf. **manadíil** *handkerchiefs* but **manadílha** *her handkerchiefs.*

Note

It will be seen that if a vowel is pronounced short, then it is written short, even where grammar and lexicon would suggest a long vowel.

Contrary to rule (1), long vowels sometimes occur in non-prominent syllables in loans from written Arabic, e.g. **ɣadátan** or **ɣaadátan** *usually*, **Ṣilqahíra** or **Ṣilqaahíra** *Cairo.* The vowel in such cases is not as long as in prominent syllables (cf. **ɣáamil** *workman*) but is distinctly longer than the short counterpart. This possibility of incremental length has been indicated where-

appropriate in the transcription by the use of brackets, i.e.
ɣa(a)dátan, Silqa(a)híra. Loans from the written language also
account for a few exceptions to rule (2). Most educated
speakers make a difference of vowel-length between ɣámmi *my
uncle* and ɣáammi *ignorant* (a " learned " form) and also
between ɣamm *uncle* and ɣaamm *public, general* (cf. ɣaam
year); in neither ɣáammi nor ɣaamm is the vowel pronounced
as long as in, say, ɣáamil, where it occurs in an open syllable.
Again, contrary to rule (2), a vowel which is generally short
and corresponds to a long vowel in related forms is sometimes
pronounced very long when the word containing it is singled
out for special emphasis, e.g. **di yáalya gíddan !** *that's terribly
dear !*, cf. the more usual **yálya** (masc. **yáali**). Taking the
language as a whole, however, exceptions to both rules are
extremely rare.

Finally, it may be noted that the style of utterance on which
the transcription in this book is based is *slow colloquial*; in
rapid style, vowels are commonly pronounced long only before
a pause.

Vowel-quality

In English we " slur " the vowel-sounds in the majority of
syllables which are non-prominent or unstressed. Consider the
vowels italicized in " th*e* Queen *o*f England " or " fr*o*m head t*o*
foot ". This must be avoided at all costs in Arabic ; each
vowel should be clearly pronounced, each syllable given its due
rhythmic weight. For this among other reasons, do not try to
speak too rapidly at first—the formation of good habits early on
will save a lot of trouble later. Vowels will now be considered in
turn from the point of view of the quality to be associated
with them.

a : between the vowel sounds of " Standard " English *hat* and
hurt or *had* and *herd*. Try to isolate the vowel in *had* and
then make it sound a little like the vowel in *herd* ; if the
complete word *hat* is taken as a starting-point and made to
sound something like *hurt* without going the whole way, the
result should be an acceptable rendering of the Arabic
haat ! *fetch, bring !* Other examples are : **dáras** *he studied*,
baab *door*, **kátaba** *clerks*, **kitáaba** *writing*. Remember to

beware of any tendency to "slur", for example in the
second or third syllable of **kátaba**.

a : when short and in a closed syllable, between the vowels of
"Standard" English *hut* and *hot*; when in an open
syllable or when long, as the vowel of English *heart*.
a occurs especially in the vicinity of the emphatic consonants, e.g. **ṣaff** *row, line*, **ruṣáaṣ** *lead (metal)*, **ḍárab** *he hit*,
fáḍḍa *he emptied*; *silver*, **ḥáaḍir** *certainly*, **baaṭ** *armpit*,
baṭn *stomach*, **ẓann** *he thought, believed*, **maẓbúuṭ** *exact(ly)*.
The vowel also commonly occurs in association with **r**,
e.g. **raff** *shelf*, **raaḥ** *he went*, **ráagil** *man*, **ḥúfra** *hole*, **bárra**
outside, **barráad** *fitter*, **naar** *fire*, but contrast the occurrence
of **a** in, say, **ráayiḥ** *going*, **ráagiʕ** *returning*, **bard** *cold*, **wárra**
he showed, **fíráan** *mice*. **a** is also regularly associated with **q**,
e.g. **qárya** *village*, **ʕilqa(a)híra** *Cairo*, **ʕaqsáam** (*administrative*) *departments*. It is not essential for the vowel
immediately to precede or follow **ḍ**, **ṣ**, **ṭ**, **ẓ**, **r**, or **q**; cf.
máṭbax *kitchen*, **xáaliṣ** *very, completely*, **lafẓ** *pronunciation*,
ṭurumbáat (*petrol*) *pumps*, **ʃarabáat** *socks*, **mabrúuk** *congratulations !*, **ʕilqurʕáan** *the Koran*. The consonant context,
moreover, is not an infallible guide to the quality of an
associated open vowel, cf., for example, **hábhab** *it barked*,
máyya *water*, etc., and numerous loans from foreign
languages, as **lámba** *lamp*, (**sámak**) **bakaláa** *cod*; cf., too,
ʕámar *he ordered* but **ʕámar** *moon*. Moreover, back vowels
may be used with non-emphatic consonants which themselves must be clearly differentiated from emphatic
counterparts, e.g. **xáddar** *he anaesthetized* but **xáḍḍar** *he
trimmed (hair)*; *watered (seedlings)*; although the vowel in
the first syllable of **xáḍḍar** tends to be nearer than its
counterpart in **xáddar** to the vowel of English *hot*, nevertheless both these Arabic vowels are back vowels and to be
distinguished not so much from each other as both of them
from **a**, cf. **ʕándah** *I call*, **lukánda** *hotel*, **ʕándaf** *cleaner*.

The distribution of **a** and **a** varies between men and
women (see below), to some extent also between individuals,
and notably between dialects. Cairene **xaaf** *he was afraid*,
for example, corresponds to **xaaf** in Upper Egypt. A "Classical" pronunciation anywhere in the country conforms to
the practice of Al-Azhar Mosque and University in Cairo

and requires **a** in association with **x** and **γ,** and also invariably with **r,** e.g. **xaal** (*maternal*) *uncle*, **γáayib** *absent*, **fi(i)ráan** *mice*. Thus, a man using his " Classical " style at an appropriate time may be heard to say **xáadim** but will certainly use **xáadim** *servant* on normal colloquial occasions.

The difference **a : a** (usually in association with the consonantal distinction emphatic : non-emphatic) tends to relate to difference between the speech of men and women respectively. **garráah** *surgeon*, for example, is typically a woman's form, to which **garrúah** would usually correspond in men's speech.

e : a vowel approximately mid-way between the vowels in *bet* and *beet*. Pronouncing the vowel of English *bit* energetically and with spread lips usually produces the right result. The sound is common enough in English dialects, for example in Devon and Southern Ireland. Take care not to pronounce **e** like the " ay " sound in *day* or *bait*. Examples : **beet** *house*, **beeḑ** *eggs*.

When short, **e** is difficult to distinguish from short **i** in the speech of many people, especially in rapid style (cf. **bétna** *our house* and **bitna** *we spent the night*), but most educated speakers appear to make a slight difference and even in dialects where no distinction is made it would for most purposes be desirable to retain the transcribed difference between **bétna** and **bitna** in order to facilitate identification of the forms.

i : when short, as in English *bit*, e.g. **bint** *girl, daughter* ; when long or final, approximately as in English *beet* but with more tension in the tongue and greater spreading of the lips, e.g. **ʃiil** *remove !,* **tamálli** *always.* An example which illustrates both qualities is **kibíir** *big, old.* Before **-yya,** the vowel tends towards the quality of **e,** e.g. in **maṣríyya** *Egyptian* (fem.).

ii, pronounced short in accordance with the rules of vowel-length, tends nevertheless to retain the quality described for **ii,** not non-final **i** ; the qualities of **ii** and **i** in **ʃiil** *remove* (masc.) *!,* **ʃilhum** *remove* (masc.) *them !,* **ʃiili** *remove* (fem.) *!,* **ʃiliih** *remove* (fem.) *it* (masc.) *!,* are substantially the same.

o : between the vowels in *hawk* and *hook.* Pronounce the vowel of *hawk* with greater rounding and protrusion of the lips and an acceptable o should result. The sound is again common enough in English dialects, but neither the usual *o* of *no* nor the *ow* of *now* will do at all. Examples : fooʕ *above*, *upstairs*, *on top*, miṣóogar *registered*.

As between e and i, the difference between short o and u (see below) is greatly reduced in the speech of some, especially in rapid style.

u : when short, as in English *put*, e.g. kútub *books* ; when long or final, approximately as *oo* in *food* but with greater tension and stronger rounding and protrusion of the lips, e.g. ʃuuf *see !*, yinsu *they forget*. duxúul *entrance, entry*, illustrates both qualities. Before -wwa, the vowel tends towards the quality of o, e.g. in húwwa *he, it*.

Like ii (see above), uu may be regularly shortened in accordance with the rules of vowel-length, e.g. ʃuuf but ʃúfha *look at her !* In parallel with ii, u in ʃúfha may be pronounced as uu in ʃuuf, but equally, and in contrast with the usual practice concerning ii, u may be pronounced with the quality described for short non-final u above.

Diphthongs

A diphthong is a combination of two vowel sounds in the same syllable. English contains many diphthongs (cf. the pronunciation of *bay, by, boy, bough, bow* (ribbon), also *bear, beer,* and *boor*) and is sharply differentiated from Arabic in this respect. Diphthongization may occur notably in Egyptian Arabic when, following a vowel (especially a and ɑ), y and w are either final or precede another consonant, circumstances in which they are often pronounced respectively as final i and u. As diphthongal elements, however, y and w should not be pronounced " lazily " as in the typical southern English pronunciation of, say, *hay* and *how* but, on the contrary, with energv and perceptible tension in the articulating organs ; at the same time seek to make y as much as possible like the *y* of *yes* and to pronounce w with strong lip-rounding and protrusion—indeed, with many speakers, the sounds are so characterized by such features as to be consonantal rather than vocalic. Examples : law *if*, mawgúud *present*, yíwṣal *he arrives*, ʃaay *tea*, ṭayyáar *aeroplane*.

THE PROMINENT SYLLABLE

Turning now to the diacritica of the transcription, and first to the acute accent, we find that just as in English words, e.g. *phótograph*, *photógrapher*, *photográphic*, a given syllable stands out to the ear above the others, the first, second, and third syllables respectively in the examples, so Egyptian Arabic words contain a similarly prominent (*or* accented *or* stressed) syllable. In contrast with English, however, the facts concerning the placing of this syllable can be formulated within a few rules, since prominence in Egyptian Arabic depends on the structure of the word in terms of its constituent syllables. Taking every syllable to begin with a consonant and to contain a vowel, there are five syllable types : CV, CVC, CVV, CVVC, CVCC (C = consonant, V = vowel, VV = long vowel) ; e.g. maẓbúuṭ CVC-CVVC, katábt CV-CVCC, manadíil CV-CV-CVVC, Ṣáabiḷ CVV-CVC, kátab CV-CVC, kátabit CV-CV-CVC. CVV rarely occurs final except in loan-words and as a variant possibility for CVVh, where -h is the third person singular masculine pronominal suffix ; it will be remembered that vowel-length and prominence are concomitant and that, therefore, any CVV syllable is by definition prominent.

The following rules show how prominence depends on the quantitative syllabic pattern of the whole word :

(1) If the ultimate syllable is long (CVVC, CVCC), that syllable is always prominent, e.g. fanagíin *cups*, fihímt *I/you understood*, ḍarabúuh (or ḍarabúu) *they hit him*. CVV must be considered long in ultimate position in loans such as tintirárii *dyer's, cleaner's*.

(2) If the ultimate syllable is not long (CV, CVC), then, in relation to the pattern of remaining syllables, either the penultimate or the antepenultimate syllable is prominent as follows :

(a) If both the penultimate and antepenultimate syllables are short (CV), e.g. kátaba *clerks*, kátabit *she wrote*, and, in the case of words of four or five syllables, the pre-antepenultimate is not a further short syllable, e.g. Ṣinkásarit *it* (fem.) *was broken*, then the antepenultimate is prominent ;

(b) in all other cases, i.e. in the overwhelming majority of

Egyptian words, the penultimate syllable is prominent, e.g. muɽállim *teacher*, maknása *broom*, dáawa *he treated, cured*, Ꞩitwágaꞑ *it was found*, mahiyyíti *my pay*, fihmúuha *they understood her*, ɗarabítu(h) *she hit him*. It will be seen that whereas the operative distinction in relation to the ultimate syllable was between *long* and *not long*, the distinction that has to be made in respect of other positions is in terms of *short* and *not short*; the difference in prominence between ɗárabit and Ꞩinkásar, ɗarabítu(h) and Ꞩinkásarit, relates to the difference between short (CV) and not-short (CVC) in the first syllables.

Notes

(a) It will have been clear from the examples given that the rules of prominence apply to suffixed and unsuffixed forms alike.

(b) There are two exceptions to the rules, both of which concern the pattern CVCVCV(h) which, in contrast with usual antepenultimate prominence, has the penultimate prominent in :

   (i) The third person singular feminine perfect of weak verbs of the ráma-type when associated with a vowel-beginning pronominal suffix, e.g. rámit + u(h) = ramítu(h) *she threw it*;

   (ii) the plural forms ɗubúɽa *hyenas*, subúɽa *lions*, dukúra *males*, libísa *underpants*, yiríba *crows*, hiṣína *horses*, in which the rare sequence of close vowels (u-u and i-i) in the first two syllables is associated with penultimate prominence and which thus contrast with, say, kátaba *clerks*, búxala *misers*, ɽínaba *grape*, etc. This pattern is commoner in other dialects than in Cairene and in the case of i-i the alternative forms Ꞩilbísa, Ꞩiyríba, Ꞩihṣína, are, in fact, more usual than the forms given.

(c) Although on the face of things xamast in the numeral-noun construction illustrated by xámast iyyáam *five days* contains a long final syllable which is non-prominent, it will be found at the appropriate place in the grammatical section that there are a number of special features about this type of grammatical structure and that the -t of

xamast, arbitrarily allotted to the numeral, is in fact a feature of the whole complex.

(*d*) It frequently happens, of course, that in phrases and sentences a word is pronounced without prominence in relation to adjoining words. Standing alone, both **kitáab** *book* and **faríid** *Fareed* (proper name) have their prominent syllable, but in **kitab fariid** *Fareed's book* it is possible for the prominent syllable of the second word only to stand out; no long vowel appears in a non-prominent syllable, it will be remembered, hence **kitab.**

ELISION

Elision concerns the omission under certain conditions of the short vowels **i** and **u**, on the one hand, and of **ʕ** (with or without an accompanying vowel),[1] on the other. Where elision of a vowel ± **ʕ** occurs at the junction of words or of a particle and a word, the feature has been marked in the writing by a hyphen.

1. *Elision of short* **i** *and* **u**

The close vowels **i** and **u** differ in status as syllable-makers from the open vowels **a** and **ɑ**; in parallel contexts, **i** and **u** are elided, **a** and **ɑ** are not. Contexts of elision of **i** and **u** may be subdivided according to whether elision is within the word or at a word-junction. It is only the latter that is indicated by the hyphen in the transcription.

(*a*) *Intra-word*

Elision relates exclusively to suffixation and, strictly speaking, is a term of comparison between suffixed and unsuffixed forms. The conditions necessary for the elision in a suffixed form of a short vowel present in the final syllable of the corresponding unsuffixed form are:

(i) The suffix must begin with a vowel;
(ii) the final syllable of the unsuffixed form must be of structure -CiC or -CuC;
(iii) the penultimate syllable of the unsuffixed form must be open, i.e. CV- or CVV-.

Examples:

ɣáawiz (m.s.) + **a** = **ɣáwza** *wanting* (f.s.), **ʕáabil** *he met* + **u** = **ʕáblu** *they met* or *he met him*, **yáaxud** *he takes* + **u**

---

[1] Never of the **ʕ** which corresponds to Classical **q.**

= yáxdu *they take* or *he takes it*, wiḥiʃ (m.s.) + a = wiḥʃa *unpleasant* (f.s.), fíhim *he understood* + it = fíhmit *she understood*, yitwígid *it is found* + u = yitwígdu *they are found*.

Contrast the facts when the suffix begins with a consonant, e.g. ʃáabil + hum = ʃabílhum *he met them*.

Contrast, too, the non-elision of open vowels in comparable contexts, e.g. ḍárab *he hit* + it = ḍárabit *she hit*, ʃitwágad *it was found* + u = ʃitwágadu *they were found*.

Finally, contrast the case of non-elision when the penultimate syllable of the unsuffixed form is closed (CVC), e.g. fáhhim *he explained* + u = fahhímu *they explained* or *he explained to him*.

Exceptions:

(i) Final -CuC in the unsuffixed form is comparatively rare and u is not elided in the case of the pattern CuCuC, cf. kútub *books* + u(h) = kútubu(h) *his books*.

(ii) i of the suffix -it (3rd pers. sing. fem. perfect tense) is never elided when a further suffix is added, cf. kátabit + u(h) = katabítu(h) *she wrote it*, rámit + u(h) = ramítu(h) *she threw it*. Contrast, for example, ʃáalit + u(b) = ʃalítu(h) *she said it* with ʃáabil + u(h) = ʃáblu(h) *he met him*. Contrast, too, -i- of the suffix -it of the feminine noun in construct, which, in contrast with the i of the verbal suffix, is regularly elided, e.g. tigáara + u(h) = tigártu(h) *his business* (not *tigarítu(h) ; cf. tigaríthum *their business*).

(iii) Elision is not a feature of the " Classical " language and is accordingly absent from " classicisms " in the colloquial. This is particularly noteworthy with participial forms; educated speakers will prefer, for example, munfáɣil (m.s.)/ munfáɣila (f.s.)/munfaɣilíin (pl.) *angry, upset*, to the less sophisticated minfíɣil/minfíɣla/minfiɣlíin.

(b) *Inter-word* (word-junctions)

The ability to link in one syllable as a result of elision the end of one word and the beginning of the next is absolutely essential to the attainment of fluency in the language and considerable attention should therefore be paid to the feature of elision from the beginning.

A vowel appearing elsewhere in an initial (short) syllable of a word is elided when

(i) the syllable in question is of type Ci- or Cu-;

(ii) the syllable is non-prominent;
(iii) the preceding word ends in a vowel.

Examples:

ʕinta + tiʕibt = ʕinta-tʕibt *you are tired*, ʕana + fihimt = ʕana-fhímt *I understood*, ʕiddíini + huduumak = ʕiddíini-hdúumak *give me your clothes*, ʕabu + ḥuseen = ʕabu-ḥséen *Husein's father*.

Contrast once again the non-elision of open vowels in parallel contexts, e.g. ʕinta katábt *you wrote*, ʕana ḍarábt *I hit*, ʕiddíini ʃaráabak *give me your socks*, ʕabu faríid *Fareed's father*.

Contrast, too, the case when the initial syllable is prominent, e.g. ʕabu ʕúmar *Omar's father*, fáḍḍa ʕílabu(h) *he emptied his boxes*.

Notes

(a) Elision also concerns the vowel of particles, notably of fi *in*, bi *by, with*, li *to, for*, and wi *and*, as well as that of the verbal prefix bi-, e.g. ʕiʃtaréetu-b káam ? *How much did you buy it for?*, huwwa-f máṣr *he's in Cairo*, huwwa-byilʕab *he's playing*.

(b) In emphatic utterance which is characterized by the deliberate enunciation of each syllable, elision will not occur; compare yáa xuṣáara uttered in this way with the more usual ya-xṣáara ! *what a pity !*

(c) Although the vowel u is elided as expected in, say, ʕandi + ḥumaar = ʕándi-ḥmáar *I have a donkey*, nevertheless ḥ is often pronounced with the lips rounded as for u.

(d) Contrary to rule, a is elided in a few common forms in which ḥ or ʕ follows the vowel, e.g. ʃufti + maḥammad = ʃúfti-mḥámmad ? *did you* (fem.) *see Mohamed ?*, ma + maʕiiʃ = ma-mʕiiʃ *I haven't* (got) *any*.

2. Elision of ʕ

In principle, utterance in Arabic may not begin with (i) a vowel or (ii) two consonants. Initial ʕ is often no more than a means of obviating these inadmissible features and, as might be expected, is frequently elided when the word to which it belongs no longer begins the utterance.

There are two major subdivisions of the contexts in which ʕ is elided when no longer initial; following a consonant and following a vowel. It should perhaps be noted that if a pause is made before the word in which the consonant is initial, then notwithstanding any of the rules given subsequently, ʕ is not elided.

(a) Preceded by a consonant

ʕ is very commonly elided when following a consonant unless the word with which it is associated elsewhere is singled out for emphasis. Thus ʃúyl íbnak *your son's work* is a commoner form than ʃúylī ʕíbnak, which might, however, be used to mark a contrast, say with ʃúylak ínta *your work*; again, ɣamalt ééh ? *what have you done ?* is doubtless more frequent than ɣamáltī ʕééh ?, which may be used to indicate surprise, indignation, sarcasm, etc. A word like ʕábadan *ever, never*, is hardly, if ever, used other than emphatically and as a result ʕ is very rarely elided. Generally speaking, elision is more frequent in the speech of less educated people; the most important categories and forms involving elision of ʕ in educated usage are as follows:

(i) 1st pers. sing. imperfect tense (e.g. ʕáktib *I write*); imperative forms (e.g. ʕíktib *write !*); the perfect tense of derived forms of the verb (e.g. ʕitbáɣat *it was sent*, ʕiftákar *he thought*, ʕistáɣlim *he inquired*); verbal nouns of the derived forms (e.g. ʕistiɣláam *inquiry*, ʕintixabáat *elections*).

(ii) More particular forms as follows: the article ʕil; the pronouns ʕána *I*, ʕínta *you* (m.s.), ʕínti *you* (f.s.), ʕíntu *you* (pl.), and ʕíḥna *we*; the nouns of relationship ʕabb *father*, ʕumm *mother*, ʕibn *son*, ʕaxx *brother*, ʕuxt *sister*; the " deictics " ʕaho/ʕahe/ʕahum and ʕáadi *there is/are*; the interrogative particles ʕeeh *what*, ʕímta *when*, ʕánhu *which*; the phrase- and clause-introducing particles ʕilli *that (relative), which (ditto)*, and ʕinn *that (conjunctive)*; a few common nouns such as ʕism *name*.

(iii) ʕ is variously elided or not in the comparative form of adjectives (e.g. ʕil + ʕakbar = either lákbar or ʕilʕákbar *the bigger, biggest*) and in one or two broken plural patterns of nouns, notably ʕaCCaaC (e.g. ʕil + ʕayyaam = either ʕilʕayyáam or liyyáam *the days*, also ʕiʕfáal ilʕabwáab or ʕiʕfáal libwáab *the locks of the doors*). On balance, educated

practice tends towards non-elision ; this is also particularly true of (noun) patterns which contain only two consonants other than ʕ, e.g. ʕizn *permission* (contrast ʕibn
and ʕism above), ʕakl *food*, ʕúgra *rate, hire*, ʕamíin *trust-
worthy*, ʕasáami *names*, ʕagáaza *leave*, ʕasáasi *basic*,
ʕiháala *retirement*, ʕiṣáaba *injury*, ʕizáaza *bottle* ; ʕ is far
better not elided in these forms.

Notes

(*a*) ʕ is not elided when it is the initial radical (see below) of
certain verbal forms, e.g. ʕámar *he ordered*, ʕáxxar *he
delayed*.

(*b*) ʕ is similarly retained in the quadriliteral form (see below)
ʕárnab *rabbit*.

(*c*) ʕ of ʕeeh is not elided following **h** in fiih ʕéeh ? *what is
there ?, what's going on ?*, nor after **yy** in záyyi ʕéeh ?
such as ?

(*d*) ʕ corresponding to " Classical " **q** is never elided, e.g. ʕifl
lock, ʕirʃ *piastre*.

(*e*) Elision of ʕ which is not accompanied as below by the
elision of a vowel is not marked in the transcription except
by the omission of ʕ.

(*b*) *Preceded by a vowel*

When a vowel precedes, not only may ʕ be elided as indicated
above but so, too, under certain conditions, may the preceding
or following vowel. Contexts are broadly divisible into those in
which the vowels flanking ʕ are the same and those in which
they are different.

Same vowels.—Except under conditions of strong stress, one
of the vowels is elided together with ʕ, e.g. ʕinta + ʕáḥmar
= ʕint-áḥmar *you are red*, fi + ʕíidu(h) = f-íidu(h) *in his hand*
(in the transcription, the first vowel has regularly been
omitted) ; the forms ʕinta ʕáḥmar and fi ʕíidu(h) occur when
special emphasis is given to ʕáḥmar and ʕíidu(h). From the
single sentence ʕana ɣawz-áakul *I want to eat*, it will be noticed,
it cannot be said whether a man or a woman is speaking since
ɣaawiz + ʕaakul and ɣawza + ʕaakul may both give the same
result.

Different vowels.—Some subdivision is necessary under this heading. Generally speaking, when the vowels preceding and following ʕ differ, both vowels and ʕ remain, e.g. ʕismåha ʕéeh ? *what's her name ?*, biyiɣmílu ʕéeh ? *what are they doing ?* The following contexts, however, and especially the vowel i, need special notice :

-V ʕi-

ʕi is elided whatever the vowel that precedes, e.g. da + ʕilli + ʕinta + ɣawzu(h) = dá-ll-inta ɣáwzu(h) *that's what you want*, ʕissana + ʕilli + fáatit = ʕissána-lli fáatit *last year*, ʃuufu + ʕilli + ʕuddamku = ʃúufu-lli ʕuddámku *look* (pl.) *who's in front of ~ you*, ʕana + ʕiddethaalu(h) = ʕana-ddetháalu(h) *I gave it* (f.) *to him.*

-i ʕa-

-i, as well as ʕ, is elided before a or -a, e.g. bi + ʕaktib = báktib *I write, am writing*, naawi + ʕaruuħ = náaw-arúuħ *I intend going*, xalliini + ʕarawwaħ = xallíin-aráwwaħ *let me go home*, ɣali + ʕafandi = ɣál-afandi *Ali Efendi.*

-a ʕu-

A rare junction, frequent only in the vocative context and treated in the manner of -a ʕi-, i.e. with elision of ʕu-, cf. ya + ʕumm in yá-mmŭ kalsúum ! (O) *Umm Kalsum !* ; notice the back quality of the open vowel, at any rate in men's speech— yá-xti (= ya + ʕuxti) (O) *my sister !* usually corresponds in the pronunciation of men to yá-xti in that of women.

Notes

(a) ʕalláah *God* is treated exceptionally, ʕa being elided after any vowel, e.g. li + ʕallaah = li-lláah *to God*, yarħamkumu + ʕallaah = yarħámkumu-lláah *may God have mercy on you*. In passing, it may be noted that, in spite of appearances, yarħamkumu is not an exception to the rules of prominence which have been given ; yarħámkumu-lláah is a borrowing from the Classical language and the apparently word-final u does not belong to the first word but is a feature of the junction.

(b) The special treatment of the noun plural pattern ʕaCCaaC in rather less educated speech has been already noted under 2 (a) (iii) above (cf. liyyáam as a variant of ʕilʕayyáam *the days*) and is also relevant in the present

context. The elision of ς̣a- (cf. ς̣alláah above) may be
encountered in, say, fi + ς̣afráan = fi-fráan *in ovens*, to
which fi ς̣afráan more generally corresponds in educated
usage.[1]

(c) The hyphen in the transcription marks the elision of a
vowel (± ς̣); it is not specifically intended to mark the
place at which the vowel occurs in corresponding contexts
of non-elision (cf. ς̣ana-f xidmítak *I'm at your service*
= ς̣ana + fi, etc., huwwa-byílς̣ab *he's playing* = huwwa
+ biyílς̣ab) but does so incidentally in the case of elision of
(vowel + ς̣) or (ς̣ + vowel).

(d) Notice the regular elision of i but retention of ς̣ in ς̣abu
+ ς̣imaam (proper name) = ς̣abu-ς̣máam *Imam's father*.

(e) In disyllabic forms (notably ς̣illi) in which ς̣i is initial in the
prominent syllable in contexts of non-elision, ς̣i may be
elided according to rule but the prominence associated with
the syllable may remain to mark the junction with a preceding vowel-ending form, e.g. ς̣aná-lli ḥarúuḥ *I'm the one
who'll go* = ς̣ána + ς̣illi + ḥarúuḥ.

(f) The prepositional particles min *from* and ς̣ála *on* require
special notice in the matter of elision when they precede a
noun prefixed with the definite article; not essentially but
extremely commonly, the total portions -in and -la of
the particles are elided, e.g. m-ilmáktab *from the office*
= min + ς̣ilmaktab, ς̣a-ṭṭarabéeẓa *on the table* = ς̣ala
+ ς̣iṭṭarabeeẓa.

THE " EXTRA " OR ANAPTYCTIC VOWEL

Three successive consonants are inadmissible in Egyptian
Arabic. Such successions could potentially occur when a word
ending in two consonants is followed by a consonant-beginning
word or suffix, but the pattern is avoided by the introduction
of an " extra " vowel between the second and third consonants;
this vowel, often pronounced very short but which may equally
be the vowel of a prominent syllable according to the rules of
prominence, is written in the transcription with the breve sign,

[1] fi-fráan should perhaps be related to a form ς̣ifráan rather than
ς̣afráan.

i.e. ĭ, ă, ŭ. In the vast majority of contexts the quality to be associated with this vowel is that of short non-final i as already described; preceding the pronominal suffixes, however, the vowel is regularly ŭ (before -ku(m) and -hum) and ă or ɑ (before -ha).

Examples :

bíntĭ maḥmúud *Mahmoud's daughter*, ma fíʃ ḥáddĭ-hnáak *there's nobody there*, ma rúḥtĭʃ *I didn't go*, ʕultílu(h) *I said to him*, ḥaʕʕúhum *their right*, ʃuftắha *I/you saw her*. ŭ occurs sporadically in other contexts, e.g. after ʕumm in, say, yú-mmŭ kalsúum (O) *Umm Kalsum !*

CONCLUSION

The pronunciation of isolated sounds and words, however useful, is only half the battle. The stringing together of words and phrases into the sentences required for speech purposes needs constant practice from the outset. Moreover, as to some extent we have seen, the sentence brings out features of pronunciation not apparent with the word in isolation but which must be observed if accuracy and fluency are to be achieved. The secret of success is constant practice. Learning by heart, with the aid of an Egyptian, not too great a number of the sentences which are given in this book will help considerably, for it is surprising how little material is necessary in order to exhaust the difficult sequences which occur in a language. Insist with the Arabic speaker on the need for patience and careful correction, then listen to and repeat each phrase and sentence over and over again, trying to remember every detail, including the rise and fall of the speaker's voice. Imitate him slavishly and do not feel embarrassed about it ; the chances are that the more outlandish you sound to yourself, the nearer you are to the mark. Practice must include as much listening for the sake of listening as possible, for not only must the tongue be trained to utter Arabic but also the ear to catch what is going on in the language.

III. GRAMMAR

ROOTS AND RADICALS

Perhaps the most striking characteristic of all forms of Arabic is that the great majority of words are built on a framework of three consonants and that by ringing the changes with affixes, vowel-differences, etc., on a given base it is possible to obtain a great variety of related forms, e.g. on base **k-t-b**, the series **kátab** *he wrote*, **yíktib** *he writes, will write*, **káatib** *clerk*, **kátaba** *clerks*, **kitáab** *book*, **kútub** *books*, **maktúub** *written*, **máktab** *office, desk*, **maktába** *library*, etc. The base, **k-t-b** in the example, is called the *root* and each consonant of the root a *radical*. The terminology is equally applicable when bases are of more or less than three consonants.

Many such patterns as those illustrated in the preceding paragraph are grammatically specialized, cf. for example, the characteristic prefixes **ma-** and **mu-**, the presence of vowel **i** or **a** in the second syllable and, in some cases, of a suffix **-a**, in the so-called nouns of place and instrument, e.g. **máglis** (pl. **magáalis**) *council, council-room* (root g-l-s), **maʕáṣṣ** (pl. **maʕaṣṣáat**) *scissors, shears* (root ʕ-ṣ-ṣ), **muftáaḥ** (pl. **mafatíiḥ**) *key* (root f-t-ḥ), **maknása** (pl. **makáanis**) *broom* (root k-n-s).

NOUNS AND ADJECTIVES
GENDER AND NUMBER

Gender and number are important because they relate not only, indeed not so much to the form of individual nouns, adjectives, verbs, etc., as to their agreement when occurring together. At present nouns and adjectives only will be dealt with but differences of gender and number are equally important elsewhere, notably in respect of verbs, pronouns, and demonstratives.

Two genders have to be distinguished, masculine and feminine. As a rule final **-a** (or **-ɑ**) [1] marks a noun or adjective as feminine singular, whether or not there exists a corre-

---

[1] Variation between the open vowels **-a** and **-ɑ** is a purely phonetic matter.

sponding masculine form. Examples, masculine form first:
málik-málika *king-queen*, kibíir-kibíira *big, old*, ʕagnábi-
ʕagnabíyya [1] *foreign(er)*, máktab-maktába *desk, office-library,
stationer's*, kitáab (m.) *book*, ʃírka (f.) *company*. The commonest
exception to the rule that final -a/-ɑ is a feminine sign is
provided by the plural forms of many nouns, for example
riggáala *men*, rúyasa *supervisors*; there are, too, a few
invariable adjectives ending in -a/-ɑ, of which ʃítra *clever* is an
example. Conversely, some nouns which do not end in -a/-ɑ
are none the less feminine; these include (i) words of female-sex
reference, e.g. sitt *woman, lady*, bint *girl, daughter*, fáras *mare*,
(ii) names of towns and countries, e.g. maʂr *Cairo*, ʕissuwées
Suez, libnáan *(the) Lebanon*, (iii) some parts of the body, viz.
ʕiid *hand*, rigl *leg*, widn *ear*, ʕeen *eye*, raas *head*, daʕn *chin*, baʈn
stomach, (iv) some miscellaneous nouns, including ʕarḍ *earth,
floor*, naar *fire*, ʃams *sun*, márkib *ship*, bálad *town*, filúus *money*.

With a few extremely rare exceptions provided by " classicisms " in educated colloquial usage, gender distinction relates
to the singular only in Egyptian Arabic. There is thus, for
example, only one (common) plural form rufayyaʕíin *thin*
corresponding to rufáyyaʕ (masc. sing.) and rufayyáʕa (fem.
sing.). Generally speaking, such a threefold differentiation of
forms as rufáyyaʕ-rufayyáʕa/rufayyaʕíin is characteristic of
adjectives rather than nouns, but certain forms in Arabic are
used both nominally and adjectivally.

There are two types of plural formation relating to both
nouns and adjectives. These are
 (i) straightforward addition of certain suffixes to the singular;
 (ii) *internal* difference in relation to the singular, e.g. ʂaħn/
    ʂuħúun *plate/s, saucer/s*, kibíir/kubáar *big (one/s)*.[2]
Plurals of the second type, traditionally known as " broken "
plurals, are very numerous.

Plural by suffix

The plural suffixes are -iin, -aat/-ɑɑt and, to a lesser extent,
-iyya. These are distributed as follows :

[1] If the masculine ends in -i, then a corresponding feminine form
ends in -iyya or -ya.
[2] The fact of internal difference does not exclude the possibility of
further difference *external* to the root, cf. suʔáal/ʔasʔíla *question/s*.

(a) **-iin** is úsed for the plural of

    (i) nouns and adjectives of the pattern illustrated by
sawwáaʕ-sawwáaʕa/sawwaʕíin *driver/s*, kaddáab-
kaddáaba/kaddabíin *liar/s*, malyáan-malyáana/
malyaníin *full*;

    (ii) active and passive participles (see below), as ʕaarif-
ʕárfa/ʕarfíin *knowing*, maftúuḥ-maftúuḥa/maftuḥíin
open(ed);

    (iii) adjectives of the pattern of kuwáyyis-kuwayyísa/
kuwayyisíin *nice, good*, ʕuṣáyyar-ʕuṣayyára/ʕuṣay-
yaríin *short*;

    (iv) most derivative nouns and adjectives of which the
singular is characterized by a suffix -i or -aani,
e.g. ʕasbáani-ʕasbaniyya/ʕasbaniyyíin *Spaniard/s,
Spanish*, díini-diníyya/diniyyíin *religious*, barráani-
barraníyya/barraniyyíin *outer, exterior*.

(b) **-aat/-aat** is suffixed to nouns having only one singular form
which is characterized for the most part by final **-a/-ɑ**. The
use of **-aat/-aat** is distributed among

    (i) a number of patterns in which the final radical is pre-
ceded in the singular by the long vowel **-aa/-ɑɑ**;
ḥáaga/ḥagáat *thing/s*, ḥisáab/ḥisabáat *account/s,
bill/s*, ʃaháada, ʃahadáat *certificate/s*, ʃammáaʕa/
ʃammaʕáat *(clothes-)hanger/s*;

    (ii) many loan-words, e.g. duséeh/dusehâat *file/s*,
ʕutubíis/ʕutubisáat *bus/es*, baskalítta/baskalittáat
bicycle/s;

    (iii) nouns of the pattern CVCVCV, where V = a/ɑ, e.g.
báraka/barakáat *blessing/s*, ḥáʃara/ḥaʃaráat *insect/s*;

    (iv) nouns which in the singular end in **-iyya**, e.g.
ḥanafíyya/ḥanafiyyáat *tap/s*, masʕulíyya/masʕuliy-
yáat *responsibility/-ies*;

    (v) certain m-prefixed patterns, with gemination of the
second radical and final **-a/-ɑ**, e.g. mixádda/mixaddáat
pillow/s, magálla/magalláat *magazine/s*;

    (vi) the " counted " or " little plural " form of collective
nouns (see below), e.g. búṣal *onions* (coll.)/baṣaláaya
an onion/baṣaláat *3–10* or *a few onions*;

(vii) verbal noun plurals (see below), e.g. ʃistiɣráaḍ/
ʃistiɣraḍáat *parade/s.*

(c) -iyya is used for the plural of

(i) those nouns of trade or occupation which are characterized in the singular by a suffix -gi or, less often, -i,
e.g. makwági/makwagíyya *laundryman/-men,* ɣarbági/
ɣarbagíyya *gharry-driver/s,* makaniiki/makanikíyya
mechanic/s ;

(ii) certain military and police ranks, e.g. ʃawiiʃ/ʃawiʃíyya
sergeant/s, ʃumbáaʃa/ʃumbaʃíyya *corporal/s.*[1]

" Broken " plural

Although there is considerable regularity of correspondence
between singular and plural patterns, it is nevertheless not
always possible to forecast from singular to plural or vice versa.
Both singular and plural forms of nouns and adjectives should,
therefore, be learned as they are met. The following are
common plural patterns (C = consonant) :

(i) ʃaCCáaC and ʃiCCáaC: ʃálam/ʃiʃláam *pen/s, pencil/s,*
ʃakl/ʃaʃkáal *shape/s,* loon/ʃalwáan *colour/s* ;

(ii) CuCúuC and CiCúuC: ṣaḥn/ṣuḥúun *plate/s, saucer/s,*
beet/biyúut or buyúut *house/s* ;

(iii) CíCaC and CúCaC: ɣilba/ɣilab (*small*) *box/es,* ʃánṭa/
ʃúnaṭ *bag/s, briefcase/s* ;

(iv) CuCáaC: kibíir/kubáar *big, old,* ṭawiil/ṭuwáal *long, tall* ;

Note

This is the pattern of certain common adjectives, with
the feminine singular formed in the usual way with -a.[2]

(v) CuCCáaC: ɣáamil/ɣummáal *workman/-men,* ʃáaṭir/
ʃuṭṭáar *clever, intelligent* ;

Note

Nouns and adjectives of pattern (v) are always of
personal reference. The singular form is as that of the
active participle of the simple verb-form (see below).

(vi) CúCaCa: ʃaríik/ʃúraka *partner/s,* xaṭiib/xúṭaba *orator/s* ;

[1] The names of most such ranks have recently been modified
(" arabicized ") by decree.

[2] Phonetic variation between -a and -a is henceforth taken as read
and -a is used to symbolize an open vowel generally.

Note

This pattern, in contrast with (v), is of nouns only and is again exclusively of personal reference. The pattern CuCaCáaʕ, e.g. **xuṭubáaʕ,** is sometimes used by educated speakers.

(vii) CaCáaCi : **kúrsi/karáasi** *chair/s*, **ʃákwa/ʃakáawi** *complaint/s*, **ṣiníyya/ṣawáani** *tray/s* ;

(viii) ʕaCCíCa and ʕiCCíCa : **suʔáal/ʔasʔila** *question/s*, **gawáab/ʔagwíba** *answer/s*, **sábat/ʔisbíta** *basket/s* ;

(ix) CaCáaCiC : **máktab/makáatib** *office/s*, *desk/s*, **gárdal/garáadil** *bucket/s*, **márkib/maráakib** *ship/s*, **sitáara/satáayir** *curtain/s*, **ginéena/ganáayin** *garden/s* ;

(x) CaCaCíiC : **fingáal/fanagíil** (or **fingáan/fanagíin**) *cup/s*, **ṭarbúuʃ/ṭarabíiʃ** *tarboosh/es*, **mandíil/manadíil** *handkerchief/s*, **fanúus/fawaníis** *lamp/s*, **niʃáan/nayaʃíin** *medal/s, decoration/s.*

Note

Singular patterns containing four consonants regularly correspond to one of the plural patterns (ix) or (x), depending on the length of the vowel between the third and fourth consonants of the singular, viz. short vowel—(ix), long vowel—(x). Singulars containing three consonants with a long vowel between the second and third, and with the ending -a, correspond to plurals of pattern (ix). Etymologically, the singular type illustrated by **fanúus** and **niʃáan** under (x) relates to forms containing a long vowel in the first syllable, i.e. **faa-** and **nii-.**

Addenda

(i) The following are examples of frequently occurring nouns for which the type of singular-plural relationship is comparatively rare : **gámal/gimáal** *camel/s*, **gábal/gibáal** *mountain/s*, **wálad/wiláad,** or **ʕawláad** *boy/s, son/s, young man/men*, **kitáab/kútub** *book/s*, **madíina/múdun** *city/-ies*, **saʕf/ʕúsʕuf** *ceiling/s*, **ṣaṭḥ/ʕúṣṭuḥ** or **ṣuṭúuḥ** *roof/s*, **raas/ruus** *head/s*, **sána/siníin** or **sanawáat** *year/s*, **ráagil/riggáala** *man/men*, **duktúur/dakátra** *doctor/s.*

(ii) In some cases a given singular form may correspond to more than one plural, e.g. **gawáab** *answer* ; *letter/*ʕ**agwíba**

answers ; **gawabáat** *letters*, **másal** *proverb, saying* ; *example/*
ʕamsáal *proverbs* ; **ʕamsíla** *examples*, **líʕba** *game* ; *toy/*
ʕalʕáab *games* ; **líʕab** *toys*.

(iii) A few nouns form their plural by the straightforward
addition of a suffix -aan, e.g. **ḥeet/ḥeṭáan** *wall/s*, **yeet/**
yeṭáan *field/s*. This suffix also appears in association with
internal difference of the " broken " type, e.g. **faar/firáan**
mouse/mice, **gaar/giráan** *neighbour/s*, **toor/tiráan** *bull/s*,
yazáal/yizláan *gazelle/s*, **ʕamiiṣ/ʕumṣáan** *shirt/s*.

(iv) Nouns of relationship are often of special shape. The most
important are **ʕabb/ʕabbaháat** *father/s*, **ʕumm/ʕummaháat**
mother/s, **ʕaxx/ʕixwáat** *brother/s*, **ʕuxt/ʕixwáat** *sister/s*,
ʕibn/ʕabnáaʕ *son/s*, **bint/banáat** *daughter/s*, **ʕamm/**
ʕaʕmáam (*paternal*) *uncle/s*, **ʕámma/ʕammáat** (*paternal*)
aunt/s, **xaal/xiláan** (*maternal*) *uncle/s*, **xáala/xaláat**
(*maternal*) *aunt/s*, **gidd/gudúud** *grandfather/s*, **gídda/**
giddáat *grandmother/s*. Note **ʕíbnï ʕámm/xáal** (*male*)
cousin and **bíntï ʕámm/xáal** (*female*) *cousin*.

Dual

The distinction already made between singular and plural
will be familiar enough to those with a " western " linguistic
background. It is also necessary, however, under the general
heading of *number* to distinguish other categories, the most
important of which is *dual*. Unlike singular and plural, dual
relates to nouns only. Dual nouns are characterized by the
suffix **-een**, e.g. **betéen** *two houses*, **kitabéen** *two books*. When
compounded with any suffix, feminine nouns which elsewhere
end in -a contain -t- in place of -a, e.g. **ṭarabeeẓa** *table* + **een**
= **ṭarabeẓtéen** *two tables*. -t- is preceded by the vowel i (similar
in function to ï) when otherwise a sequence of three or more
consonants would result, e.g. **ʃirka** *company* + **een** = **ʃirkitéen**
two companies (cf. elsewhere below, say, **ʕarabíyya** *car* + **na**
= **ʕarabiyyítna** *our car*, **tigáara** + **na** = **tigarítna** *our business*).

Nouns of personal reference, with the exception of nouns of
relationship, do not occur with the suffix **-een** but are associated
with the numeral **ʕitnéen** *two*. Thus, **ʕitnéen sawwaʕíin/**
ʕasáakir/muʕallimíin/ʕarbagíyya/ʕummáal/ʃúraka *two drivers/*
soldiers/teachers/gharry-drivers/workmen/partners, but **ʕaxxéen/**
ʕuxtéen/waladéen/bintéen/ragléen/maratéen *two brothers/*

sisters/boys (or *sons*)/*girls* (or *daughters*)/*men* (or *husbands*)/
women (or *wives*).

The dual form of nouns relating to certain parts of the body
occurring in pairs will correspond to an English plural in
translation, e.g. **rigléen** *legs,* **Ɛidéen** *hands,* **ɛenéen** *eyes.*

Collectives

With regard to certain nouns, termed *collectives,* it is sometimes necessary to distinguish between *five* categories of
number. The form **ʃágara**[1] *tree,* for example, is regularly
related to **ʃágar** (*a lot of*) *trees, trees* (*in general*) by the addition
of the (feminine) suffix **-a** ; equally relatable to **ʃágar,** by the
addition of **-aat,** is **ʃagaráat** (*a few*) *trees,* a form which occurs
most commonly in association with a numeral form from " 3 "
to " 10 ". Threefold differentiation of the type **ʃágar/ʃágara/**
ʃagaráat is characteristic of all collectives, but in the case of
ʃágar, there is not only the regular dual form **ʃágara + een**
= **ʃagartéen** *two trees,* but also the broken plural form
ʃaʃgáar (*different kinds of*) *trees* to be considered. The designation *singulative* is more appropriate than *singular* to the
form **ʃágara,** and **ʃagaráat** may be termed the *counted* or *little
plural* form. Thus, *in toto* we have **ʃágar** (collective), **ʃágara**
(singulative), **ʃagartéen** (dual), **ʃagaráat** (counted or little
plural), **ʃaʃgáar** (plural or big plural). The majority of
collectives, however, lack a (big) plural form. The little plural
is characterized by the suffix **-aat** (rarely **-ayaat**) but the
singulative suffix is frequently **-aaya,** not **-a** ; cf., for example :

Collective	Singulative	Little plural
xoox *peaches*	**xóoxa**	**xoxáat**
lamúun *lemons*	**lamúuna**	**lamunáat**
burtuƐáan *oranges*	**burtuƐáana**	**burtuƐanáat**
básal *onions*	**básala** or **baṣaláaya**	**baṣaláat**
gázar *carrots*	**gázara** or **gazaráaya**	**gazaráat**
baṭáatiṣ *potatoes*	**baṭatṣáaya**	**baṭatṣáat**
Ɛúuṭa *tomatoes*	**Ɛuṭáaya**	**Ɛuṭáat** or **Ɛuṭayáat**

The singulative and little plural forms of certain collectives
are characterized not by the suffixation of **-a(aya)** and **-aat** but

---

[1] Or **ʃágara.**

by the association of the collective form with one of the specific words ḥabbáaya/ḥabbáat, ḥítta/ḥítat, lúʕma/lúʕam, raas/ruus, ṣubáaɣ/ṣawáabiɣ, i.e. :

faṣúlya *beans*	ḥabbáayit faṣúlya	ḥabbáat faṣúlya
bisílla *peas*	ḥabbáayit bisílla	ḥabbáat bisílla
súkkar *sugar*	ḥíttit súkkar	ḥítat súkkar
láḥma *meat*	ḥíttit láḥma [1]	ḥítat láḥma
ɣeeʃ *bread*	lúʕmit ɣéeʃ	lúʕam ɣéeʃ
toom *garlic*	ráas toom [2]	rúus tóom
sugúʃʃ *sausages*	ṣubáaɣ sugúʃʃ	ṣawáabiɣ sugúʃʃ

The dual is formed on the appropriate special word, e.g. ḥittitéen súkkar *two lumps of sugar*.

GENDER AND NUMBER CONCORD

Singular patterns

The following examples illustrate the typical noun-adjective sequence, in which the adjective follows the noun :

Masculine	*Feminine*
béet kiblir *a big house*	ginéena-kblira *a big garden*
ʕamííṣ wísix *a dirty shirt*	maɣláʕa wísxa *a dirty spoon*
ráagil ṭawíil rufáyyaɣ *a tall, thin man*	sítti ṭawíila-rfayyáɣa *a tall, thin woman*

These examples illustrate the most frequent pattern of concord, in which it will be seen that gender difference relates to the presence or absence of final -a, especially in adjectival forms.

The sequence of noun preceding adjective will be familiar to those with experience of, say, the Romance languages; less familiar will be the fact that in order to get concords right in Egyptian Arabic, it is necessary to know the sub-class of both the noun and adjective involved. Thus, in contrast with the adjectives in the examples above, adjectives of origin and nationality, which end in -i (masc.) and -iyya (fem.), show gender distinction only when the preceding noun is a noun of personal reference. siggáada ɣaríiḍa *a wide carpet* is like maɣláʕa wísxa in the feminine example above but only siggáada

---

[1] *A slice or piece of meat.*
[2] *A clove of garlic.*

ɣágami *a Persian carpet* is possible, not *siggaada ɣagamiyya; conversely, in association with a noun of personal reference, the adjectival form in -iyya must be used where appropriate, e.g. sitti ɣagamíyya *a Persian lady.*

Certain adjectives of colour, similarly formed by the addition of a suffix -i, for the most part to a noun of material reference, are wholly invariable, e.g. búnni *brown, coffee-coloured,* ruṣáaṣi *grey* (lit. *leaden, lead-coloured*), rumáadi *grey* (lit. *ashen, ash-coloured*), banafsígi *purple,* burtuSáani *orange(-coloured),* fáḍḍi *silver(-coloured), silvery,* dáhabi *gold(en),* lábani *pink* (lit. *milky*). Other forms, appearing elsewhere as nouns, are used as invariable adjectives of material, e.g. sáaɣa dáhab *a gold watch,* ɣúmla fáḍḍa *silver coins,* ṭarabéeʒa xáʃab *a wooden table,* ʃánṭa gild *a leather bag,* béeʃa dantílla *a lace veil,* ʃarabáat ṣúuf *wool(len) socks.* Other noteworthy invariable forms are sáada *plain* and ɣítra *clever* as in, for example, ráagil ɣítra *a clever man.*

Knowledge of the nominal and adjectival classes concerned is also necessary when more than one adjective follows the noun, in order to place the adjectives in the correct order. When the noun is of personal reference, the position of the adjectives is immaterial; we may say, for example, either ráagil ṭawíil ingilíizi or ráagil ingilíizi ṭawíil *a tall Englishman,* but in association with other classes of noun, an adjective of origin must immediately follow the noun, e.g. Sissiggáada lingilíizi-lɣarííḍa *the wide English carpet,* unless there is also present an adjective of material, in which case the latter immediately follows the noun and immediately precedes an adjective of origin, e.g. siggáada ṣúuf ingilíizi *an English wool carpet,* ʃáal haríir híndi-kbíir *a large Indian silk scarf.* Examples containing adjectives of material but not adjectives of origin are karaváṭṭa [1] haríir zárSa *a blue silk tie,* fustáan ṣúuf xafíif *a light woollen dress.* In the earlier examples above, viz. ráagil ṭawíil rufáyyaɣ and sitti ṭawíila-rfayyáɣa, the adjectives are neither of origin nor of material and therefore their sequential order is immaterial. It may be noted in passing that somewhat similar positional variation in association with other differences is observable in English, as between, say, *hard black eyes, black silk stockings, jet-black hair, a black, glowering look.* The particle wi *and* in Arabic often corresponds to the comma of the last

---

[1] Or karafítta.

English example, cf. ʕóoḍa háwyɛ-w wásɛa *a large, airy room*
(lit. *airy and spacious*).

There is in Arabic a special regular paradigm of nouns and
adjectives of colour (excluding the invariable forms in -i noted
above) and physical defect. Examples are ʕáḥmar (m.s.)-
ḥámra (f.s.)/ḥumr (pl.) *red*, ʕáxḍar-xáḍra/xuḍr *green*, ʕáṭraṣ-
ṭárṣa/ṭurṣ *deaf*, ʕáxraṣ-xárṣa/xurṣ *dumb*, etc. ʕíswid-sóoda/suud
black, ʕábyaḍ-béeḍa/biiḍ *white*, ʕáɛwar-ɛóora/ɛuur *one-eyed*,
ʕáɛma-ɛámya/ɛumy *blind* are somewhat irregular and it may
help in learning them to realize that ee and oo usually correspond to Classical Arabic ay and aw respectively and ii and uu
to the pronunciation of *iy* and *uw*. In certain contexts and
notably in combination with fáatiḥ/fátḥa/fátḥiin *light* and
γáamiʕ/γámʕa/γamʕiin *dark*, adjectives of colour of this
special pattern are used in the masculine singular form even
when the noun they accompany is feminine, e.g. karafítta
ʕáḥmar fáatiḥ *a light red tie*, bádla ʕázraʕ γáamiʕ *a dark blue suit*.
fáatiḥ and γáamiʕ can only appear in the masculine singular
form in this context but, in association with the invariable
colour adjectives in -i and provided that the noun is feminine,
they may optionally be used in the feminine forms fátḥa and
γámʕa, e.g. karafítta-rṣáaṣi fátḥa (or fáatiḥ) *a light grey tie*,
bádla búnni γámʕa (or γáamiʕ) *a dark brown suit*.

Plural patterns

Singular concord involved principally the distribution of
corresponding adjectival forms with and without final -a, in
association with a preceding noun of singular form; plural
concord concerns the association of the plural form of nouns
variously with the plural form of the adjective or with its form
in -a. The latter form is identical with that of the feminine
singular, so that if one gives to this form the designation
feminine and if in the traditional way one considers gender to
relate exclusively to the noun rather than to the total context,
then it may be said of a noun like ʕamíiṣ/ʕumṣáan *shirt/s* that
it is masculine in the singular (cf. ʕamíiṣ wísix *a dirty shirt*) but
feminine in the plural (cf. ʕumṣáan wísxa *dirty shirts*).[1] The

---

[1] The words " feminine in the plural " conflict with the later statement (top p. 47) that there is no gender distinction in the plural.
One might, therefore, amend the form of words to read, say, ". . . but
in its plural form is associated with the feminine singular adjective."

plural form **wisxíín** is only used with the plural form of nouns of personal reference, so that once again it is necessary to know the class of noun with which one is concerned in order to get concords right. It is equally necessary again to know the category of adjective involved. Not only do adjectives of origin and invariable adjectives generally behave as in singular patterns, cf. **sagáayir ingilíízi** *English cigarettes*, **náas báladi** *low-class people*,[1] **ʃarabáat sáada** *plain socks*, but those adjectives of which the plural form is of " broken " pattern, e.g. **kibíir-kibíira/kubáar**, are variously in *either* the plural *or* the form in **-a** when the noun they accompany is not one of personal reference; cf. **biyúut kubáar** *or* **kibíira** *big houses*, **ganáayin kubáar** *or* **kibíira** *big gardens*. Where alternative possibilities exist, the form in **-a** is on the whole the more usual.

The following rules may be helpful:

(i) The adjective accompanying plural nouns, other than nouns of personal reference, almost always has the form of the feminine singular adjective. Those adjectives having a broken plural may be in either the plural or, more commonly, the feminine singular form;

(ii) the plural form of adjectives, whether broken or in **-íin**, is used with nouns of personal reference; some adjectives which never accompany such nouns, rarely occur in plural forms, e.g. **matíin** (m.s.)**-matíina** (f.s.)/**mutáan** (pl.) *strong, durable*.

Adjectives of nationality following nouns of personal reference do not always behave in the manner of other **i**-ending adjectives, cf. **náas ingilííz** *English people*, **banáat ʃalmáan** *German girls*, but, as expected, **náas maṣriyyíin** *Egyptian people*, **banáat ʃasbaniyyíin** *Spanish girls*.

Differences of plural concord, therefore, do not parallel those of the singular. The difference between **ṭawíila** and **ṭuwáal** is relevant to plural concord but not to the difference between, say, **riggáala** *men* and **sittáat** *women* as the difference between **ṭawíil** and **ṭawíila** was relevant to the difference between **ráagil** *man* and **sitt** *woman*; cf. **riggáala-ṭwáal rufayyaʃíin** *tall, thin men* and **sittáat ṭuwáal rufayyaʃíin** *tall, thin women*, and

---

[1] **magáalis baladíyya** *local councils* is exceptional and may perhaps be regarded as a loan from the written language. Similarly, **ʃingilizíyya** is used with **baḍáayiʃ** *goods* but **ʃingilíízi** is also possible.

contrast the earlier singular examples. It may therefore be convenient for practical purposes to say that there is no gender distinction in the plural, but, as has been shown, concordial differences of a similar kind relate as much to plural as to singular associations of noun and adjective.

Other patterns

Dual.—The plural form of the adjective is essential with the dual form of the noun, e.g. ḥetéen kubáar *two big houses*, ʕamiṣéen wisxiin *two dirty shirts*. Even rare plurals are necessary in this context, e.g. ʕamiṣéen mutáan *two strong shirts*.

Collectives.—The adjective accompanying the collective form of a collective noun is in the (masculine) singular, e.g. wáraʕ kuwáyyis *good paper*, xóox ṣáabiḥ *fresh peaches*.[1] Plural adjectives usually accompany the "little plural" form of collectives, e.g. tálat xoxáat ṣabḥiin 3 *fresh peaches*, tálat ʃagaráat ṣuyayyariin 3 *little trees*, but the feminine singular form of those adjectives which are "broken" in the plural may optionally be used, e.g. tálat xoxáat kibíira (or kubáar). Contrast the compulsory use of the singular form of the adjective ɣáali-ɣálya/ɣalyíin in, say, ʃahadáat ɣálya *high qualifications*, where the ending -aat is not that of the "little plural"

Co-ordinate nouns.—The plural adjectival form is necessary in association with co-ordinate sequences of singular nouns, e.g. sikkíina-w ʃóoka wisxiin *a dirty knife and fork*, fúrʃa-w miʃʃígdáad *a new brush and comb*.

DEFINITION

Concord operates between noun and adjective in Arabic in respect not only of gender and number but also of what may be called "definition" or "definiteness". béet kibíir *a big house* is *indefinite*, ʕilbéet ikkibíir *the big house* (lit. *the house the big*) is definite. In the definite pattern the article ʕil[2] is prefixed to the adjective as well as to the noun.

---

[1] An exception is baṭáaṭiṣ maʕlíyya *chip potatoes, crisps*.

[2] The *l* of the article is pronounced as the following consonant before t, d, s, z, ṭ, ḍ, ṣ, ẓ, n, r, ʃ, k, and g, and as l before all other consonants: e.g. ʕil ráagil = ʕirráagil *the man*, ʕilṣúfra = ʕiṣṣúfra *the dining-table*, but ʕilmáktab *the office, the desk*, ʕilfilúus *the money*, etc.

Nouns may be defined in a number of ways:

(i) By the prefixation of the article, e.g. ſigginéena *the garden*;

(ii) by the addition of a pronominal suffix, e.g. banáat *daughters* + u(h) *his* = banáatu(h) *his daughters*;

(iii) by belonging to the category of proper noun, which is only associated with definite concord, e.g. maşr *Cairo, Egypt*;

(iv) by close association with a following noun which is itself defined, e.g. báab ilbéet *the door of the house*. Feminine nouns when so defined have the ending -(i)t in place of -a (see under *Dual* above), e.g. ginént (or ginéenit) ilbéet *the garden of the house*;

(v) by association with the vocative particle ya, e.g. ya wálad ! *boy !*, ya şúmar ! *Omar !*

Nouns defined in the manner of (i)–(iv) must be accompanied in the noun-adjective phrase by adjectives which are also defined by the prefixation of the article, e.g. ſigginéena-lwarraníyya *the back garden*, banáatu-lḥilwiin *his pretty daughters*, máşr ilſadíima *Old Cairo*, ginént ilbéet ilwarraníyya *the back garden of the house*. Nouns defined in the manner of (v) are accompanied by adjectives with which ya is also associated, e.g. ya wálad ya ṭawíil ! *I say, the tall young man !*, ya şúmar ya-şyáyyar ! *young Omar !*

It will be seen that a noun may not bear more than one defining characteristic; for example, the article is precluded from association with banáatu(h) by the presence of the pronominal suffix, from similar association with ginént by the fact of the following defined noun, and may not precede şuyáyyar when şuyáyyar is preceded by ya in ya şúmar ya-şyáyyar ! (cf. şúmar işşuyáyyar *young Omar*).[1] It is in this light that the inclusion of the particle li (elsewhere = *to, for*, etc.) is to be seen in, say, dárbu l-ilwálad *his hitting (of) the boy*; the verbal noun darb may not be defined twice as in a hypothetical *darbu-lwalad.

Other important facts concerning " definition " are given subsequently, notably with reference to the phrase-marker ſílli (see below, pp. 101–5).

---

[1] ya does not, however, exclude other " definers ", cf. ya-mḥámmad y-axúuya ! *(O) my brother Mohamed !*

THE CONSTRUCT AND THE NOMINAL SENTENCE

The sequence of nouns illustrated in the preceding section by
báab ilbéet and ginént ilbéet is traditionally referred to in Arabic
grammar as *the construct.* The indefinite báab béet *a house door*
and ginéenit béet *a house garden*, in which the article is not
prefixed to the second noun and the first noun is therefore not
defined, are also examples of the construct. Sequences of constructs, in which the final noun only may be associated with the
article, are also possible, e.g. báab béet ilmudIir *the door of the
manager's house,* mawaᶜiid fáthï máktab taftiiʃ ilpaʃporṭáat *the
office hours of the passport department* (lit. *the hours of opening
the office of inspecting the passports*). *'s, of,* or a compound is
generally necessary in translation. Notice that, although most
constructs exhibit a singular/plural difference only in their first
component, e.g. ᶜáarib innagáah/ᶜawáarib innagáah *lifeboat/s,*
there are nevertheless some in which two components vary,
e.g. yáṭa-lᵣídda/yuṭyáan ilᵣídad *bonnet/s (car),* náaᵤir
ilmaháṭṭa/nuᵤᵤáar ilmaḥaṭṭáat *stationmaster/s.*

It may be noted that earlier examples such as ʃánṭa gíld
a leather bag are partly defined as noun-adjective phrases
because of final -a, not -(i)t, in the noun (cf. the construct
ginéenit béet). Moreover, as expected, and again in contrast
with the construct, both components of the noun-adjective
phrase are prefixed with the article when the context is
definite, e.g. ᶜiʃʃánṭa-ggíld *the leather bag*; cf., too, ᶜálam ḥíbr
fountain-pen and ᶜálamak ilḥíbr *your fountain-pen.*

Adjectives are not interposed between constituent nouns of
the construct but are placed at the end of the total phrase,
e.g. sáaḥil xaliig issuwées ilyárbi *the west shore of the Gulf of Suez,*
in which ilyárbi is associated with sáaḥil; mádnit gáamiᵣ ᵣálya
the tall minaret of a mosque is another example, cf. mádnit
gáamiᵣ ᵣáali *the minaret of a tall mosque.* Other examples are
rubáaṭ (masc. sing.) gázma ᶜásmar *black shoe-laces* and rubáaṭ
gázma súmra *black-shoe laces, i.e. laces of* or *for black shoes.*

An alternative form to, say, the sáaḥil xaliig issuwées
ilyárbi of the last paragraph involves the use of a particle (min
or li) between the nominal elements sáaḥil and xaliig issuwées
so that the construct relation no longer obtains between them;
any adjective associated with sáaḥil will then follow it
immediately and, moreover, the total noun-adjective phrase

will be defined by the prefixation of the article, i.e. ſissáaḥil ilɣárbi min xalíig issuwées. In the example ſissáaḥil ittáani m-ilbáḥr (or l-ilbáḥr) ilſáḥmar *the other shore of the Red Sea* the particle separates two noun-adjective phrases. These particle constructions, however, have a distinctly literary flavour about them.

Considering two-component examples of the noun-adjective phrase as well as the construct in terms of the association of components with the definite article, we have so far seen the following possibilities :

(i) Both components without the article, e.g. béet kiblír *a big house* ;

(ii) both components with the article, e.g. ſilbéet ikkiblír *the big house* ;

(iii) the first component without, the second with the article, e.g. báab ilbéet *the door of the house*.

The fourth possibility, i.e. the first component with and the second without the article, e.g. ſilbéet kiblír *the house is (a) big (one)*, is the pattern of the so-called nominal sentence. In translation, the appropriate form of the present tense of the verb *to be* is usually necessary. Constructs and noun-adjective phrases may, of course, constitute the first component of the nominal sentence, cf. ſibbáak ittazáakir maftúuḥ *the booking-office (ticket-window) is open*, ɣubúur ilkanáal lingilíizi ɣáɣbī giddan (giddan is adverbial) *the English Channel crossing is very unpleasant*.

bitáaɣ

ſilbáab bitaɣ ilbéet is a very common alternative to báab ilbéet *the door of the house*. When bitáaɣ is used, then the article must be prefixed to the first noun. In the great majority of contexts, the construct and the construction with bitáaɣ may be used indifferently, but there are circumstances in which one is regularly employed rather than the other ; thus, for example, if in response to a knock at the door an occupant of the house is mistakenly on his way to the front door, a second occupant may direct him to the back door whence the knock came by exclaiming báab ilbéet ilwarrúani ! *(it's at) the back door !* ; the construction with bitáaɣ, i.e. ſilbáab ilwarrúani-btaɣ ilbéet, would be quite inappropriate to this context but may be used freely elsewhere. Notice that a further effect of the inclusion of **bitáaɾ** is that an adjective relating to the first noun follows that noun and is thus interpolated between the two nouns of the construction; **ʕilbáab ilwarráani-btaɾ ilbéet** is thus parallel to the earlier **ʕissáaḥil ilyárbi min xaliig issuwées** and both of them different from **sáaḥil xaliig issuwées ilyárbi**.

bitáaɾ itself is always in construct with the following noun and thus " looks both ways " in the total construction, since at the same time it must agree with the preceding noun in terms of gender and number. **bitáaɾ** is the masculine form of the total series **bitáaɾ-bitáaɾit/bitúuɾ**; cf. **ʕigginéena-btaɾt ilbéet** *the garden of the house*, which varies more or less freely with **ginént ilbéet**, and **ʕilbiyúut bituɾ** (or **bitaɾt**) **iʃʃírka** *the company's houses*, to which the construct **biyúut iʃʃírka** provides an alternative.

By virtue of this threefold differentiation of form, **bitáaɾ** and its following noun are adjectival in function, parallel to, say, **ʕaliil ilʕádab-ʕalíit ilʕádab/ʕuláal ilʕádab** *ill-mannered, rude*; such adjectival constructs are, however, rare.

Since a noun cannot be defined twice, e.g. by construct relationship with a following defined noun and by a pronominal suffix, **bitáaɾ** is essential in, say, **ɾilbit ikkabríit bitáɾti (bitaaɾa + pronominal suffix -i)** *my box of matches*.

PARTICLES

In the nominal sentence **dá-btaɾ issítt** *that belongs to the lady*, **bitáaɾ** behaves in the manner of such prepositional particles as **fi** *in*, **li** *to, for*, **bi** *by, with*, **min** *from, of*, **ɾand** *at, with*, **zayy** *like*, **ɾála** *on, against*, **wáyya** *with, in company of*, etc., in, say, **ʕilʕamiiʃ f-iddúrg** *the shirt is in the drawer*, **húwwa min máʂr** *he's from Cairo*. Such particles have no independent status and occur only before a noun or a pronominal suffix (see below). The prepositional phrase illustrated in the examples functions very commonly as the final component of the nominal sentence.

Certain particles, as **fooʕ** *on, above*, **táḥt** *below, under*, **gúwwa** *inside*, **bárra** *outside*, **ʕuddáam** *facing, opposite, in front (of)*, behave similarly to those of the preceding paragraph in, say, **ʕilhudúum fóoʕ iddaláab** *the clothes are on top of the cupboard* or **ʕissandúuʕ táḥt issiriir** *the box is under the bed*, but may also occur independently. In reply to **ɾúmar féen ?** *where is Omar ?*

we may say fooʕ *above, upstairs,* taḥt *below, downstairs,* gúwwa *inside,* bárra *outside,* ʕuddáam *in front.* These forms are also distinguished by the fact that adjectives may be formed from them by the addition of a suffix -aani, e.g. taḥtáani *lower,* guwwáani *inner,* barráani *outer.*

The forms of the last paragraph may be termed *adverbial particles.* They differ from *adverbs* in that certain of the latter, e.g. gíddan *very,* xáaliṣ *thoroughly, completely,* are regularly associated with adjectives, while others, as the " time-words " dilwáʕti *now,* baʕdéen *afterwards, later,* ʕimbáariḥ *yesterday,* ʕinnahárda *to-day,* búkra *to-morrow,* etc., like gíddan and xáaliṣ, never appear with a following noun or pronominal suffix.[1]

Note the " reciprocal " baʕḍ, which frequently follows a particle as in fooʕ báʕḍ *on top of each other,* záyyi báʕḍ *like each other, the same,* gámbi báʕḍ *next to one another,* wáyya báʕḍ *in each other's company.*

A particle complex may sometimes occur, as, for example, min ʕala in háat idduséeh min ʕa-lmáktab *fetch the file from the desk !*

The particle bi occurs frequently in adverbial and adjectival phrases, e.g. bi súrʕa *fast, quickly* (lit. *with speed*), b-izẓábṭ *exactly, perfectly,* ʕissáfar b-issikka-lḥadíid *rail travel* (lit. *the travel by the iron way*), ṭayyáara-b muḥarrikéen *a two-engined aircraft.*

PRONOUNS

Two classes of pronominal forms have to be distinguished : (i) independent pronouns, (ii) pronominal suffixes. The independent pronouns are as follows :

	Sing.	Pl.
1st person	ʕána *I*	ʕiḥna *we*
2nd person masc.	ʕínta *you*	ʕíntu *you*
2nd person fem.	ʕínti *you*	
3rd person masc.	húwwa *he, it*	húmma *they*
3rd person fem.	híyya *she, it*	

As with the adjective, gender distinctions (2nd and 3rd persons) relate to the singular only. This is true in general of Egyptian Arabic and will be found again elsewhere, notably in the verb and the demonstratives.

[1] Unlike gíddan, xáaliṣ, etc., the " time-words " are frequently associated with a preceding particle.

Pronominal suffixes, for their part, are added to nouns, verbs, and particles. Added to a verb, the 1st person singular suffix is **-ni**, not **-i** or **-ya** as with nouns and particles, but otherwise the suffixes are the same irrespective of the grammatical category with which they are associated. Singular suffixes except **-ni** and **-ha** differ in form according to whether the noun, verb, or particle ends in a consonant or a vowel. The suffixes are as follows :

Singular

	Post-consonantal	Post-vocalic		Plural
1st person	. -i	-ya	*my, me*	-na *our, us*
	(-ni after verb)			
2nd pers. m. .	-ak	-k	*your, you*⎤	-ku or -kum
2nd pers. f. .	-ik	-ki	*your, you*⎦	*your, you*
3rd pers. m. .	-u(h) [1]	-h	*his, its/him, it*⎤	-hum *their,*
3rd pers. f. .	-ha	-ha	*her, its/her, it*⎦	*them*

Final vowels are lengthened in accordance with the general rule when suffixes are added, e.g. **wáyya** *with*, **wayyáaki** *with you* (fem.), **wayyáah** *with him*. In the speech of many, final **-h** is not pronounced but the vowel is still long and prominent in **wayyáa** *with him*.

The " extra " vowel required to obviate a sequence of three consonants, which elsewhere is invariably **ĭ**, is more frequently **ă** or **ŭ** with the pronominal suffixes. With the exception of **-na**, which requires **ĭ**, the vowel is the same as that of the suffix, e.g. **ʃuxtăha** *her sister*, **ʃuxtŭku(m)** *your* (pl.) *sister*, but **ʃuxtína** *our sister*.

The suffixed forms of certain common particles are somewhat irregular and need special attention. The alternative forms in the following paradigms are given in the order corresponding to the estimated frequency of their occurrence in educated speech :

fĭ	bi	li [2]	wáyya
fíyya	bíyya	líyya	wayyáaya
fĭik	biik	liik, lak, or lik	wayyáak

[1] Often pronounced with a weak final h before a pause. This has been shown by the use of brackets where appropriate.

[2] Suffixed to verbs, there is a different set of li-forms (see below).

COLLOQUIAL ARABIC

fi	bi	li	wáyya
fíiki	bíiki	líiki or líki	wayyáaki
fiih	biih or bu(h)	lu(h) or liih	wayyáah
fíiha	bíiha	láha, líha, or líiha	wayyáaha
fíina	bíina	lína or líina	wayyáana
fíiku(m)	bíiku(m)	lúku(m) or líiku(m)	wayyáaku(m)
fíihum	bíihum	lúhum or líihum	wayyáahum

ɣála	ɣand	min	
ɣaláyya	ɣándi	mínni	
ɣaléek	ɣándak	mínnak	
ɣaléeki	ɣándik	mínnik	
ɣaléeh	ɣándu(h)	mínnu(h)	
ɣaléeha	ɣandáha	mínha or minnáha	
ɣaléena	ɣandína	mínna or minnína	
ɣaléeku(m)	ɣandúku(m)	mínku(m) or minnúku(m)	
ɣaléehum	ɣandúhum	mínhum or minnúhum	

It should be remembered that whenever a noun in -a is defined, as for example by suffixation, then -t- appears, e.g. gineena + u(h) = ginéntu(h) *his garden*, ɣarabiyya + na = ɣarabiyyítna *our car*.

It should also be borne in mind that a noun cannot be defined twice and that, therefore, bitáɣti and not the pronominal suffix -i was associated with ɣilbit in the earlier example ɣilbit ikkabriit bitáɣti *my box of matches*, to which may be added the comparable example gawazáat issáfar bitaɣítku(m) *your* (pl.) *passports*. Duals also require the bitaaɣ-construction, e.g. ɣilbetéen bitúuɣi *my two houses*.

Independent and suffixed pronouns are sometimes used together for emphasis, as in da-btáaɣu húwwa, múʃ bitaɣak ínta *that's his, not yours*.

The use of the independent 3rd person pronominal forms at the head of certain interrogative sentences and in agreement with a following noun is also noteworthy, e.g. hiyya-lfilúus ilmasmúuḥ bíiha mawgúuda-ʃ gawáaz issáfar bitáaɣi ? *is the currency allowance* (lit. *the money the permitted with it*) *stated* (lit. *present*) *in my passport ?*

rigléen *legs*, ʃidéen *hands*, ɣenéen *eyes* merit special notice when pronominally suffixed, since -n of the dual suffix is dropped, e.g. ɣenéeh *his eyes*, ʃidéeki *your* (fem.) *hands*. Notice particularly the forms of the 1st person singular, e.g. rigláyya *my legs*, not *rigleeya.

The nouns ςaxx *brother* and ςabb *father* also require particular attention. They are of the forms ςaxu and ςabu (*a*) before a pronominal suffix, (*b*) in construct; e.g. ςaxúuh *his brother*, ςaxu-brahíim *Abraham's brother*. Contrast ςáxxï múslim *a Muslim brother*, ςaxxéen *two brothers*, and compare, too, ςaxúuh ibrahíim *his brother Abraham* and ςáxu ςabúuh *his father's brother*. In vocative constructions, the form abu followed by a proper noun is to be translated *son*, cf. y-abu ςáli yá-bni ! (*O*) *Son of Ali, my son !* In similarly " less sophisticated " Arabic, the form aba may also be heard in vocative contexts when a father, father-in-law, or an older male relative or close friend of the family is being addressed, e.g. y-aba ςáli ! *Uncle Ali !*

Not only adjectives but also pronouns, verbs, demonstratives, etc., of the 3rd person are commonly in the singular feminine form in agreement with a preceding plural noun, e.g. ςilbiyúut di [1] hiyya-lli [2] ςultílak [3] ςaléeha *these are the houses I told you about* (*them*) ; notice, too, the extremely common use of the pronominal suffix referring back to an earlier noun or pronoun (see pp. 104–5).

The adverbial particles often occur with the pronominal suffixes, e.g. waráah *behind him*, ςuςádha *opposite her*. In most cases they may optionally be compounded with min, so that, for example, we may say ςiddul-áab tahtu-tráab or ςiddul-áab tahtï mínnu-tráab *there's dust under the cupboard* (lit. *the cupboard under it dust*). In the case of bárra *outside*, min is essential ; one cannot say *barraaha but must use bárra mínha *outside it* (fem.).

The particle ςand + pronominal suffix is an especially common combination and is perhaps particularly noteworthy since it generally relates in translation to an appropriate form of the verb *to have*, e.g. ςándak sagáayir ? *have you any cigarettes ?* li, wáyya, and máςa are often used in a similar way to ςand, li generally being used with reference to property and translatable by *to own, possess*, and wáyya and máςa usually relating to small, portable objects carried on the person, e.g.

---

[1] Feminine singular demonstrative adjective.
[2] The relative particle ςilli *the one that.*
[3] = ςult *I said* + lak *to you.*

líyya ɣízba *I have, own a farm*, maɣáak filúus ? *have you any money on you* ?

Finally, notice the use of li and a following time-word in, say, híyya f-issúuʕ láha sáaɣa *she's been at the market for an hour*.

fiih

ʕilʕóoɖɑ fiiha náas kitlir *there are a lot of people in the room* is parallel to ʕiddulaáb taḥtu-tráab *there's dust under the cupboard above*, but both sentences have the alternative forms which introduce the special and extremely common use of fi + the 3rd person sing. masc. suffix -h, corresponding in translation either to *there is, there are*, or to the indefinite article *a, an*. The alternative forms are fiih náas kitlir f-ilʕóoɖɑ and fiih turáab taḥt iddulaáb.

The noun following fiih is always indefinite. ráagil bárra is incomplete and may be completed by fiih in fiih ráagil bárra *there's a man outside, a man is outside*, which may be fairly contrasted with ʕirráagil bárra *the man is outside*; cf., too, fiih ráagil biyṣálli gúwwa *there's a man* (or *a man is*) *praying inside* and ʕirráagil biyṣálli gúwwa *the man is praying inside*.

fiih may be used independently as, for example, in the answer (ʕáywa) fiih (*yes*) *there is* to the question fih ḥáddi mawgúud ? *is* (*there*) *anyone there* ?

DEMONSTRATIVES AND DEICTICS

Of two series of demonstratives, pronominal and adjectival— the latter when following the noun—da (m.s.)/di (f.s.)/dool (pl.) *this/that, these/those* is much commoner than dúkha/díkha/ dúkham. The use of the latter series is usually pronominal and largely confined to cases of specific contrast, as múʃ dá lakin dúkha *not this but that* or ʕiʃʃánɖa di ʕátʕal min díkha *this bag is heavier than that*.

As with bitáaɣ of the adjectival phrase, the ordinal numeral following the noun (see below), and other contexts, a noun preceding da must take the article; if another adjective is present, then da may follow either noun or adjective, e.g. ʕilḥáaga di-lkuwayyísa or ʕilḥáaga-lkuwayyísa di *this nice thing*. díyya and díyyat are alternative forms of adjectival di but are comparatively rare and may be ignored for practical purposes.

da and di are often suffixed to the noun with attendant difference of accentuation; thus, both ʕilʕálam dá and ʕilʕalámda *this/that pencil*, ʕissána dí and ʕissanáadi *this year*, are possible forms. As a rule the first alternative is more emphatic but the differènce may relate in some cases to the geographical origin of the speaker.

Remember that the feminine singular form of adjectives, demonstratives, pronouns, verbs, bitáaɠ, etc., will where appropriate accompany plural nouns of non-personal reference, e.g. ʕikkútub di (or dool) *these/those books*, ʕilhagátdi kulláha *all these/those things*; plural forms are, of course, necessary in association with the dual noun, e.g. ʕikkitabéen dóol *these/those two books*.

The deictic forms, translated usually *here/there is/are . . .*, are ʕaho (m.s.)/ʕahe (f.s.)/ʕahum (pl.) and the invariable ʕáadi. Before pause, ʕaho and ʕahe are generally pronounced with final h.

The deictics are used with either a noun or a vèrb and, in the case of ʕaho/ʕahe/ʕahum, independently. They may either precede or follow the noun they accompany, e.g. either ʕahúm (or ʕahé) ikkútub or ʕikkútub ahúm (or ahéh) *there are the books !* Following the noun and in isolation, a variety of related forms occur as alternatives, thus

Q. (i) ʕirrúagil féen ? *where is the man ?*   A. ʕahóh or ʕahúwwa (or, rarely, ʕahúwwat)

(ii) ʕilʕóoɖa féen ? *where is the room ?*   ʕahéh or ʕahíyya (or, rarely, ʕahíyyat)

(iii) ʕilwiláad féen ? *where are the boys ?*   ʕahúm or ʕahúmma (or, rarely, ʕahúmmat)

With verbal forms, we find as expected ʕaho géh ! *here he is !* (lit. *has come*), ʕahe gát ! *here she is !*, ʕahum gúm ! *here they are !* When verbal forms of other than the third person are involved, ʕahó is used as an invariable form in association with the appropriate independent pronoun, e.g. ʕahó-na (= ʕana) géet ! *here I am !*, ʕahó-nti géeti ! *here you* (fem.) *are !* ʕahúwwa is sometimes used for ʕaho in this context, e.g. ʕahuww-ána géet !, ʕahuwwá-nti géeti !

ʕáadi can be substituted for ʕaho/ʕahe/ʕahum but it must always precede the noun or verb, e.g. ʕáadi mahaṭṭítna ! *this is us !, this is our stop !* Ɛáadi is compounded with the suffixed, as opposed to the independent pronoun in, say, Ɛadíiku (= Ɛahó-ntu) géetu ! *there you* (pl.) *are !* Noteworthy, too, is the fact that the verbal -ni is used as the first person singular suffix with Ɛáadi, e.g. Ɛadíini géet ! (= Ɛahó-na géet !) *here I am !*

Ɛáadi and Ɛaho/Ɛahe/Ɛahum may combine, or Ɛaho/Ɛahe/ Ɛahum may be repeated, e.g. Ɛadi (or Ɛaho) -ʃʃéex ɣazíiz ahóh ! *there's Sheikh Aziz !*

COMPARISON OF ADJECTIVES

The comparative adjective is invariable in form, i.e. exhibits no distinctions of gender and number, and is generally of the pattern ƐáCCaƐ, e.g. kibíir *big-*Ɛákbar *bigger,* ɣuɣáyyar *small-* Ɛáɣɣar *smaller ;* when the second and third radicals are the same, the comparative pattern is ƐaCáCC, e.g. xafíif *light—* Ɛaxáff *lighter,* muhímm (with prefix mu-) *important—*Ɛahámm *more important ;* of adjectives ending in -w and -i, the comparative pattern is ƐáCCa, e.g. ḥilw *sweet, nice, pretty—*Ɛáḥla *sweeter, etc.,* ɣáali *dear—*Ɛáɣla *dearer.*

The so-called comparative form (e.g. Ɛákbar) is to be translated by the English comparative (*bigger*) or superlative (*biggest*) according to context. Ɛilwálad ilƐákbar may correspond to either *the bigger boy* or *the biggest boy* but, without the article, an Egyptian comparative-superlative distinction may be marked by position : wálad ákbar may be properly translated *a bigger boy* but Ɛákbar wálad can only be *the biggest boy ;* Ɛilwálad ilƐákbar f-ilwiláad dóol and Ɛákbar wálad f-ilwiláad dóol *the biggest of those boys* are for some speakers variant possibilities. Similar alternatives in which pre-nominal position is associated with omission of the article and post-nominal position with its inclusion are also found with the ordinal numerals and with the interrogative Ɛánhu/Ɛánhi/Ɛánhum *which ?* (see below).

The particle min precedes a second noun or pronoun with which comparison is made, e.g. Ɛilwálad ákbar m-ilbínt *the boy is bigger than the girl.* It is possible but less usual to use the positive form of the adjective followed by the particle ɣan, i.e. Ɛilwálad kibíir ɣan ilbínt. This latter construction is used regularly with adjectives of colour and physical defect, e.g. Ɛilḥaʃíiʃ da Ɛáxḍar ɣan dá *this grass is greener than that.*

Ṣáktar *more* and ṢaṢáll *less* are used with those forms, especially participles, which have no comparative, e.g. húwwa mitṛállim Ṣáktar mínha *he is more educated than her*.

Pronominal suffixes may be added to the comparative form, e.g. Ṣayláahum *the dearest of them*.

NUMERALS

CARDINALS

It will be seen from the following list than *1* and *3–10* have two forms ("masculine" and "feminine"), that "tens" are characterized by a suffix -iin and "teens" by -ṭaaṣar, that "hundreds" from *300* on have their own special pattern, and that míyya *100* and Ṣalf *1,000* are like nouns in that they have dual and plural forms :

wáaḥid, wáḥda *1*, Ṣitnéen *2*, tálat, taláata *3*, Ṣárbaṛ, Ṣarbáṛa *4*, xámas, xámsa *5*, sitt, sitta *6*, sábaṛ, sábṛa *7*, táman, tamánya *8*, tisaṛ, tísṛa *9*, ṛáṣar, ṛáṣara *10*, ḥiḍáaṣar *11*, Ṣiṭnáaṣar *12*, talaṭṭáaṣar *13*, Ṣarbaṛṭáaṣar *14*, xamasṭáaṣar *15*, siṭṭáaṣar *16*, sabaṛṭáaṣar *17*, tamanṭáaṣar *18*, tisaṛṭáaṣar *19*, ṛiṣriin *20*, wáaḥid wi ṛiṣriin *21*, Ṣitnéen wi ṛiṣriin *22*, taláata-w ṛiṣriin *23*, Ṣarbáṛa-w ṛiṣriin *24*, xámsa-w ṛiṣriin *25*, sitta-w ṛiṣriin *26*, sábṛa-w ṛiṣriin *27*, tamánya-w ṛiṣriin *28*, tísṛa-w ṛiṣriin *29*, talatiin *30*, wáaḥid wi talatiin *31*, Ṣitnéen wi talatiin *32*, taláata-w talatiin *33*, Ṣarbiṛiin *40*, xamsiin *50*, sittiin *60*, sabṛiin *70*, tamaniin *80*, tisṛiin *90*, míyya *100*, míyya w-itnéen *102*, míyya-w tisṛa *109*, míyya taláata-w sittiin *163*, mitéen arbáṛa-w talatiin *234*, tultumíyya *300*, rubṛumíyya *400*, xumsumíyya wáaḥid wi xamsiin *551*, tusṛumíyya-tnéen wi sittiin *962*, Ṣalf *1,000*, Ṣálfï-w míyya *1,100*, Ṣálfï tusṛumíyya tisṛa-w xamsiin *1,959*, Ṣalféen míyya-tnéen wi tisṛiin *2,192*, xámast aláaf xumsumíyya-w sabṛiin *5,570*, ḥiḍáaṣar álf *11,000*, milyóon *1,000,000*, Ṣitnéen milyóon *2,000,000*, xámsa milyóon *5,000,000*.

It will be seen that "tens" from *20* on may be formed by adding -iin to the appropriate "masculine" unit; with vowel-elision in ṛiṣriin (*20*), xamsiin (*50*), sabṛiin (*70*), and tisṛiin (*90*); notice the vowel i, not a, in ṛiṣriin and Ṣarbiṛiin (*40*). In the case of "teens", add -ṭaaṣar to the "masculine" unit form ;

note -ṭṭ- in talaṭṭáaſar (13) and siṭṭáaſar (16): ḥiḍáaſar (11) and ſiṭnáaſar (12) should be learned separately but are clearly related to wáaḥid and ſitnéen. From 300 to 900 there is a regular pattern; tultumíyya (300), rubɣumíyya (400), xumsumíyya (500), suttumíyya (600), subɣumíyya (700), tumnumíyya (800), tusɣumíyya (900). The relation between the two forms of 3–10 numerals is not always a simple one of the presence or absence of final -a, cf. tálat, taláata (3), xámas, xámsa (5), sábaɣ, sábɣa (7), táman, tamánya (8), tísaɣ, tísɣa (9). Like the 3–10 numerals, wáaḥid, wáḥda (1) has two forms but all other numerals including ſitnéen (2) have one form only. míyya (100) and ſalf (1,000) behave in some ways like nouns and exhibit dual forms mitéen 200 and ſalféen 2,000. milyóon 1,000,000 is also basically nominal but, as will be seen, behaves in the manner of a loan-word.

Syntactically, enumerations involving a numeral and a noun require the recognition of numeral categories " 1 ", " 2 ", " 3–10 ", " 11 and above ", as well as that of such nominal categories as noun of personal reference and noun of value and measurement as opposed to those nouns—the great majority—which belong to neither category. In addition, it is neçessary to consider the relative order of numeral and noun and the possibilities of association with the definite article.

wáaḥid, wáḥda is mostly used adjectivally, e.g. kitáab wáaḥid one book, sittī wáḥda one woman. The numeral does, however, occur preceding the noun, as in the fairy-tale formula káan ſiih wáaḥid ſulṭáan there was once a (certain) sultan. Note-worthy, too, is the use of wáaḥid with the article as in ſilwáaḥid ma-byiſdárſ one can't, it can't be done.

The use of the numeral ſitnéen is to be compared with that of the dual form of the noun. It has already been seen that nouns referring to human beings—other than kinship terms—do not occur in a dual form but are regularly associated with the numeral; e.g. ſitnéen muɣallimíin two teachers, ſitnéen ɣasáakir two soldiers. In this context, nouns of the category stated appear in their plural form but certain common loan-words of value and measurement, which do not usually occur in a dual form, appear in the singular, e.g. ſitnéen ginéeh £2, ſitnéen mítr (sometimes, but rarely, mitréen) two metres, ſitnéen kíilu (or kéelu) two kilograms or kilometres.

" 3–10 " numerals occur in two patterns of enumeration, the first of which is the commoner: (i) " masculine " numeral + plural noun, (ii) " feminine " numeral + singular noun of value or measurement. Examples: xámas riggáala/ʃurúuʃ/banáat/daʃáayiʃ 5 *men/piastres/girls/minutes* but xámsa ginéeh/taɣriifa/malliim/kiilu 5 *£/half-piastres* [1] */millemes/kilograms* or *kilometres*.

" 11 and above," in contrast with " 3–10 ", require the singular form of a following noun of whatever category; with xámas riggáala/etc. of the preceding paragraph, compare hidáaʃar/talatiin/ʃálf ráagil/ʃirʃ/bint/daʃiiʃa 11/30/1,000 *men/piastres/girls/minutes*.

With the exception of wáahid, wáhda, numerals may not follow the noun unless the article is present. Without the article, only tálat riggáala 3 *men* and xamastáaʃar ráagil 15 *men* are possible, but with the article, both ʃittálat riggáala and ʃirriggáala-ttaláata *the 3 men* and, again, both ʃilxamastáaʃar ráagil and ʃirriggáala-lxamastáaʃar *the 15 men*, are found. The " feminine " form of " 3–10 " numerals is regularly used when the numeral follows the noun and, moreover, given the order noun-numeral, the noun is always plural in form, whatever the category of numeral involved. It will be seen, therefore, that when the numeral follows the noun, it behaves in respect of definition in the manner of the adjective, e.g. ʃiddíini-lkitabéen litnéen *give me both* (or *the two*) *books* (lit. *the books the two*), banáatu-ttaláata *his three daughters* (lit. *his daughters the three*).

In contexts in which the numeral does not enumerate a following noun, for example in isolation, following the noun, and in compound numerals, the " masculine " form of " 1 " and the " feminine " form of " 3–10 " numerals are used, e.g. wáahid wi ɣiʃriin 21, míyya xámsa-w sittiin 165.

The order of compound numerals corresponds to the English order with the important exception that units precede tens; the particle wi *and* always precedes the final numeral, e.g. ʃalféen míyya sitta-w tisɣiin 2,196, ʃálfi-w míyya 1,100. Not only are " 3–10 " numerals in compounds always in the " feminine " form but a following noun is always in the singular, e.g. míyya-w ɣáʃara ʃirʃ 110 *piastres*.

---

[1] taɣriifa is only used with reference to the numbers 1, 3, and 5.

mïit ſírſĭ-w ɤáſɑɾɑ is a commoner alternative form of the last
example and illustrates in another way the nominal nature of
mïyya; -t in miit is the -t of the feminine noun in construct,
cf., too, tultumſiit sána *300 years*. The plural form of mïyya is
miyyáat, as in ɤándu miyyáat *he has hundreds*. milyóon
1,000,000 behaves as a loan-word of value and measurement,
cf. ſitnéen milyóon *2,000,000* (cf. ſitnéen ginéeh *£2* above),
xámsa milyóon *5,000,000* (not *xamas malayiin); cf., too,
ɤándu malayiin *he has millions*. ſalf *1,000* also behaves in the
manner of a noun, cf. the dual form ſalféen *2,000*, the singular
form in ḥiḍáaſɑɾ álf *11,000*, the plural form in tísaɤt aláaf *9,000*.
The last example illustrates the interesting occurrence of a
linking -t-, not to be identified with -t of the construct, between
" *3-10* " numerals and nouns which elsewhere begin with ſ.

It is not with every ſ-beginning noun that this linking -t-
appears. Contrast with tálat-t-aláaf *3,000*, for example, tálat
ſuzúun bariid *3 postal orders*, or tálat ſaráanib *3 rabbits*.
-t- commonly occurs with nouns of the pattern ſaCCaaC, e.g.
ſayyáam *days*, ſafrúan *ovens*; moreover, such nouns, though
often with a in the first syllable when initial or in isolation,
appear with i when in close grammatical relation with a preceding noun or particle; thus, ſayyáam ilſusbúuɤ *the days of
the week* but liyyáam *the days*. ſilſayyáam, however, is a
possible form in place of liyyáam and, indeed, is on the whole
commoner among educated speakers. As far as the forms with
-t- are concerned, comparison should be made between xámas-t-
iyyáam *5 days* and xámas ſurúuſ *5 piastres*, sábaɤ-t-iṣnáaſ
7 kinds and sábaɤ banáat *7 girls*, tálat-t-úſhur and tálat ſáſhur
(or, more commonly, tálat ſuhúur) *3 months*. Once more,
xámas ſayyáam or xámsit ſayyáam (possibly due to the
identification of -t- with -t of the construct) tend to be commoner among educated speakers; what a man says, however,
depends on the situation in which he says it—the educated
man may tend in general to use xámas ſasdáas or xámsit
ſasdáas *five-sixths* but he will use xámas-t-isdáas when talking
to a fitter, for example.

FRACTIONS

The linking -t- is common with fractions, of which ſasdáas in
the preceding paragraph was an example and which exhibit

their own special pattern for fractions from *one-half* to *one-tenth*; nuṣṣ/Ṣanṣáaṣ ¹/₂, tilt/Ṣatláat ¹/₃, rubɛ/Ṣarbáaɛ ¹/₄, xums/Ṣaxmáas ¹/₅, suds/Ṣasdáas ¹/₆, subɛ/Ṣasbáaɛ ¹/₇, tumn/Ṣatmáan ¹/₈, tusɛ/Ṣatsáaɛ ¹/₉, ɛuʃr/Ṣaɛʃáar ¹/₁₀. The vowel of the singular pattern is u with the exception of tilt. With the exceptions of nuṣṣ and suds, the fractions are directly relatable to the other numeral forms. The dual is used quite regularly, e.g. tiltéen ²/₃. In junctions of " 3–10 " numerals and fractions, the exceptional form irbaɛ is especially noteworthy, e.g. tálat-t-irbaɛ (not *irbaaɛ) ³/₄. For fractions in which the denominator exceeds *10*, the cardinal numeral is used preceded by ɛála, e.g. waahid ɛala-hḍáaʃar ¹/₁₁, taláata ɛala ɛiʃriin ³/₂₀ ,taláata-w xámsa ɛala-ṭnáaʃar 3 ⁵/₁₂.

Fractions are particularly relevant to telling the time, cf. Ṣissáaɛa taláata-w ɛáʃara/rúbɛ/tilt/núṣṣ/núṣṣ illa xámsa *it's ten/a quarter/twenty/half/twenty-five past three* and Ṣissáaɛa taláata-(Ṣi)lla rúbɛ/tilt *it's a quarter/twenty to three.* Notice particularly Ṣissáaɛa taláata-w núṣṣi-w xámsa *it's twenty-five to four* (lit. *a half and five past three*).

It may be observed in passing, and still on the subject of time-reference, that the names of the first five days of the week are clearly related to other numeral forms ; thus, yóom ilḥádd *Sunday*, yóom litnéen *Monday*, yóom ittaláat *Tuesday*, yóom lárbaɛ *Wednesday*, yóom ilxamíis *Thursday* (yóom iggúmɛa *Friday*, yóom issábt *Saturday*). The article is omitted after kull *every*, e.g. kúllī yóom gúmɛa *every Friday.* The manner of specifying dates is illustrated by yóom ilxamíis, xámsa-w ɛiʃriin Ṣayúṣṭuṣ, sanat Ṣálfī tusɛumíyya-w sittíin *Thursday, 25th August, 1960.*

ORDINALS

There is a special " 3–10 " ordinal pattern. The pattern is shared by wáahid, wáhda, among the cardinals above. The ordinal is essentially adjectival in function, with masculine and feminine forms but, of course, no plural form. " 3–10 " ordinals are as follows : táalit, tálta *third*, ráabiɛ, rábɛa *fourth*, xáamis, xámsa *fifth*, sáatit, sátta ¹ *sixth*, sáabiɛ, sábɛa *seventh*, táamin, támna *eighth*, táasiɛ, tásɛa *ninth*, ɛáaʃir, ɛáʃra *tenth*.

---

¹ sáadis occurs as a learned form for sáatit ; cf. the fraction suds.

A noun accompanying the ordinal is, of course, always singular, but the numeral may precede or follow. When it follows, then there is the customary agreement in respect of gender ánd definition ; e.g. ráagil táalit *a third man*, Sirráagil ittáalit *the third man*, Sissítt ittálta *the third woman*. When the ordinal precedes, it is invariable in the masculine form and the reference of the whole phrase is definite ; thus, táalit ráagil (or Sirráagil ittáalit) *the third man*, táalit sítt (or Sissítt ittálta) *the third woman*. It has already been stated that this relation between pre-nominal position and definite reference in the absence of the article is also found with the comparative form of the adjective and with the " particularizing " interrogative particle Sánhu/Sánhi/Sánhum *which ?* To take one example, however, té alit sítt and Sissítt ittálta are not freely inter-changeable in all contexts. Use of the definite article is generally more " particularizing " and would, in this instance, relate to contexts in which more than three women are directly concerned ; thus, cf. Sissítt ittálta túdxul [1] *let the third woman* (of a known queue of women) *come in* and Sáadi táalit sítti túdxul *that's the third woman to come in* (there may or may not be any more). Another example of the latter type is Sahó da táalit riyíif yáklu [1] (or wáklu [1]) dilwaSti *that's the third loaf he's eaten.*

Ordinals from *eleventh* on have the same shape as cardinals but are distinguished as ordinals by the facts that (*a*) they always follow the noun and (*b*) the noun is always in the singular. Contrast Sirráagil ilḥiḍáaſar *the eleventh man* with the cardinal in ḥiḍáaſar ráagil *eleven men* and Silḥiḍáaſar ráagil or Sirriggáala-lḥiḍáaſar *the eleven men.*

Like wáaḥiḍ, wáḥda, and Sitnéen among the cardinals, so *first* and *second* need special attention. Sáwwil *first* may precede or follow the noun ánd is invariable in the former case, e.g. Sáwwil fáṣl or Silfáṣl ilSáwwil *the first chapter.* More common, however, at least following the noun, are the adjectival forms Sawwaláani-Sawwalaníyya/Sawwalaniyyíin, for the first two of which Sáwwal and Súula are often heard from educated speakers, e.g. Siṣṣáfḥa-lSawwalaníyya or Siṣṣáfḥa-lSúula *the first page*, dáraga Súula *first class.* táani, tánya *second* are often used

---

[1] Verbal and participial forms are explained below.

together with the plural form **tanyíin,** in the sense of *other*, e.g. **wáaḥid táani** *another one, someone else,* **ʕittanyíin féen ?** *where are the others ?* As with **ʕáwwal** and **ʕúula,** so **ʕáaxar** (masc.) and **ʕúxra** (fem.) are sometimes heard from educated speakers for **táani** and **tánya** in the sense of *other*, e.g. **ʕikkitáab ilʕáaxar** *the other book* ; cf. **dáraga tánya** (or **sukúndu**) *second class.*

ʕáaxar should not be confused with **ʕáaxir** *last*, which is an ordinal behaving in a completely parallel manner to **ʕáwwil** above, cf. **ʕáaxir fáʂl** or **ʕilfáʂl ilʕáaxir** *the last chapter*. Again in parallel with **ʕáwwil,** there are adjectival forms which, following the noun, are commoner than **ʕáaxir,** viz. **ʕaxráani-ʕaxraníyya/ʕaxraniyyíin,** and yet again, there are " learned " forms, **ʕaxíir** (masc.) and **ʕaxíira** (fem.), which are heard from educated speakers for the commoner **ʕaxráani** and **ʕaxraníyya.**

VERBS

TYPES OR CONJUGATIONS

The Arabic verb is divisible into four types or conjugations corresponding to differences in the pattern of the radicals. Thus, **kátab** *he wrote* has the favourite three-radical pattern but **ʕaal** *he said* has **aa** in place of a second radical, **ráma** *he threw* has **a** and **míʃi** *he went* has **i** in place of a third radical, and **ḥabb** *he liked, wanted,* has the same consonant as second and third radicals and no vowel between them. These conjugational types are termed (i) regular (**kátab**), (ii) hollow (**ʕaal**), (iii) weak (**ráma, míʃi**), (iv) doubled (**ḥabb**). Differences between the conjugations will be formulated subsequently ; similarly, it will later become apparent why for the time being verbs are quoted in the form of the 3rd person singular masculine perfect tense.

"FORMS" OR ASPECTS

A number of " forms " or aspects are applicable to all conjugational types. These forms may be divided for convenience into one *simple* form (as **kátab, ʕaal, ráma, míʃi,** and **ḥabb** above) and a number of others variously *derived* from the simple form. Ignoring for the present differences in the pattern of short vowels between simple and derived forms, two processes of derivation may be distinguished: (i) internal modification (ii) prefixation. Some forms combine both.

Three internally derived forms are characterized by:

(1) The doubling or gemination of the second radical, e.g. **fáhhim** *he explained*, **sállim** *he delivered*; this is by far the commonest of the derived forms.
(2) A long open vowel infixed after the first radical, e.g. **Ɛáabil** *he met*.
(3) **t** infixed after the first radical, e.g. **Ɛiftákar** *he thought, believed*; **Ɛi-** is prefixed, as in the forms derived by prefix below, in order to obviate the inadmissible pattern of two initial consonants.

The prefixes of forms derived in the second manner are:

(4) **(Ɛi)t-**, e.g. **Ɛitwágad** *it was found*.
(5) **(Ɛi)n-**, e.g. **Ɛinbásat** *he was happy*.
(6) **(Ɛi)sta-**, e.g. **Ɛistáfham** *he inquired*; notice the lack of vowel between the second and third radicals.

In the above prefixed forms, the prefixes are associated with the pattern of the simple form, but the prefix **(Ɛi)t-** also appears in " doubly derived " forms in association with forms (1) and (2) above, thus:

(7) = (4) + (1), e.g. **Ɛitkállim** *he spoke*.
(8) = (4) + (2), e.g. **ƐitnáaƐiſ** *he discussed*.

The foregoing forms of the verb may be tabulated as follows; the simple form is considered in the table to exemplify both zero-infix and zero-prefix. Only the regular verb-type has so far been exemplified but in the table (p. 67) all verb-types, regular (R), hollow (H), weak (W), and doubled (D), are illustrated.

It cannot be assumed for a given verb that the simple form corresponding to a derived form necessarily occurs, or vice versa. The " simple form " is simply one of a total range of " forms ". Moreover, there is no foolproof correspondence of meaning between the simple and a derived form or between two derived forms. The geminate form is often causative, e.g. **fáhhim** *he explained, made to understand* (cf. **fíhim** *he understood*), **náḍḍaf** *he cleaned, made clean* (cf. **niḍíf** *clean*), or intensive, e.g. **kássar** *he smashed* (cf. **kásar** *he broke*), but these are by no means the only possibilities and, with other derived forms, such

	Zero	(ʃi)t-	(ʃi)n-	(ʃi)sta-
Zero	(R) kátab¹ (H) ʃaal (W) ráma, míʃi (D) ḥabb	(R) ʼitwágad (H) ʃitbáaʃ *it was sold* (W) ʃitnása *it was forgotten* (D) ʃitʃádd *it was counted*	(R) ʃinbáʃat (H) ʃinbáaʃ *it was sold* (W) ʃinḥáka *it was told* (D) ʃinball *it was wetted*	(R) ʃistáfham (H) ʃistaʃáal *he resigned* (W) ʃistákfa *he had enough* (D) ʃistaḥáʃʃ *he deserved*
Germination of C2	(R) fáhhim (H) ḥáwwil *he transferred,* ʃáyyin *he appointed* (W) fáḍḍa *he emptied* (D) ḥáddid *he fixed, limited*	(R) ʃitkállim (H) ʃitḥáwwil *he was transferred,* ʃitʃáyyin *he was appointed* (W) ʃitfáwwa *he improved* (D) ʃitḥáddid *it was fixed, limited*		
(C1)aa-	(R) ʃáabil (H) gáawib *he answered* (W) náada *he called* (D) no ex. available	(R) ʃitnáaʃiʃ (H) ʃitgáawib *it was answered* (W) ʃitráaʼa *he agreed* (D) no ex. available		
(ʃiC1)t-	(R) ʃiftákar (H) ʃixtáar *he chose* (W) ʃiftára *he bought* (D) no ex. available			

¹ Where no translation is given, the form has been quoted above.

Infix

relations are even more difficult to establish in a general way.
In making his own word-list the student should learn the meaning of each existing form separately ; this is best done, moreover,
by collecting words and forms in useful sentences rather than in
isolation.

The prefix (Si)t- is generally a passive, intransitive, or
reflexive sign.   (Si)n- and (Si)t- are theoretically inter-
changeable ; thus, both Sitwágad and Sinwágad, Sitbáaṛ and
Sinbáaṛ are possible. In practice, however, the prefixes tend to
become specialized, e.g. Sinkásar *it was broken* rather than
Sitkásar, Sitṛámal *it was done* rather than Sinṛámal ; in general,
it would seem that (Si)t- is commoner than (Si)n- in Cairo.
(Si)t- forms associated with gemination and especially with -aa-
frequently require an accompanying particle, e.g. huwwa-
tnáaSiʃ wayyáah f-ilmawḍúuṛ *he discussed the matter with him,
they had a discussion about it* ; there is little difference of
meaning between huwwa kallímu(h) and huwwa-tkállim
wayyáah *he spoke to him*. As with *l* of the article, so the junction
of certain consonants with preceding *t* of the derived prefix has
special implications as to pronunciation. These are as follows :

(Si)*t* + d = (Si)dd-, e.g. SiddálaS *it was spilt*
(Si)*t* + ṭ = (Si)ṭṭ-, e.g. Siṭṭállaṛ *he peered through* (e.g.
window)
(Si)*t* + ḍ = (Si)ḍḍ-, e.g. Siḍḍáffar *it was plaited*
(Si)*t* + ṣ = (Si)ṣṣ-, e.g. Siṣṣáwwar *he was photographed*
(Si)*t* + ẓ = (Si)ẓẓ-, e.g. Siẓẓábaṭ *he was caught out* (*in wrong-
doing*)

(Si)*t* + s = (Si)ts- or (Si)ss-, e.g. Sitsálax or Sissálax *it was
skinned*
(Si)*t* + k = (Si)tk- or (Si)kk-, e.g. Sitkállim or Sikkállim *he
spoke*
(Si)*t* + ʃ = (Si)tʃ- or (Si)ʃʃ-, e.g. Sitʃáṛlil or Siʃʃáṛlil *it flared
up* (*fire*) (a quadriliteral
verb—see below)

(Si)*t* + z = (Si)dz- or (Si)zz-, e.g. Sidzáyyit or Sizzáyyit *it was
oiled*
(Si)*t* + g = (Si)dg- or (Si)gg-, e.g. Sidgáraḥ or Siggáraḥ *he was
wounded*

(Si)*t* + ɣ = (Si)dɣ-, e.g. Sidɣálab *he was defeated*

Notice from the table of derived forms that in forms exhibiting gemination or the infixation of aa, with or without the prefix (ʃi)t-, hollow and doubled verbs, when they occur, are treated exactly as regular verbs. In the case of hollow verbs, w or y appears as the second radical. Etymologically, hollow and weak verbs are those with w or y as second and third radical respectively. Verbs with y as first radical do not occur and those with w are not irregular save that in the derived form containing the infixed t, ʃiwt- = ʃitt- in pronunciation, e.g. ʃittáfaʕ *he agreed*, ʃittákal (ʁala) *he relied (on)*.

The prefix (ʃi)sta- appears in a pattern exhibiting gemination elsewhere in the common (hollow) verb ʃistaráyyaḥ *he rested*, but the example is unique of its kind and the pattern has not, therefore, been included in the table above.

Also omitted from the table are a few " learned " derived forms characterized by a prefix ʃa-, e.g. ʃársal *he sent*, corresponding to the more usual and typically colloquial · báʁat. ʃafáad (hollow) *he informed, it was useful* and ʃárḍa (weak) *it pleased, satisfied* are other examples of this derived form which occur in the speech of the educated, but the form is nevertheless rare and need never be used.

Colour verbs

Also excluded so far is a form of the verb which, unlike the others, relates regularly and almost exclusively to adjectives of colour. This form is characterized by gemination of the third radical, e.g. ʃiḥmárr *he went red, blushed*, ʃibyáḍḍ *he turned white*, etc. ʃiḥláww *it became sweet* (cf. ḥilw *sweet*) also belongs to this class.

Quadriliteral verbs

A large number of verbs contain four radicals ; four different ones, e.g. xárbiʃ *he scratched*, láxbaṭ *he confused* ; the first and third, or third and fourth, the same, e.g. kárkib *he muddled*, záʕṭaṭ *he was overjoyed* ; the same two in the same order in both syllables, e.g. wáʃwiʃ *he whispered*, báʃbaʃ *he ogled*.

The only derived form of quadriliteral verbs is with the prefix (ʃi)t-, e.g. ʃitláxbaṭ *he was confused*, ʃitʃáʕlil *it flared up (fire)*.

TENSES

For each form, two tenses, perfect and imperfect, must be distinguished. Distinctions of person, gender, and number within each tense parallel those of the independent and suffixed pronouns. The perfect tense is characterized by suffixes, the imperfect by prefixes (in three persons, by a combination of prefix and suffix). The tense affixes are the same for all forms and basically the same for all conjugational types, though some qualification in respect of doubled and weak verbs, and also of verbs of colour, will be made subsequently. It is because it is possible in the case of the perfect tense to derive all other persons from the unaffixed shape of the 3rd person singular masculine that verbs have been quoted primarily in relation to this " basic " shape.

In the overwhelming majority of cases the affixes are:

		Perfect	Imperfect	
		Suffix	Prefix	Suffix
Sing.	3rd person masculine	-	y(i)-	
	3rd person feminine	-it	t(i)-	
	2nd person masculine	-t	t(i)-	
	2nd person feminine	-ti	t(i)-	-i
	1st person	-t	ʕa-	
Pl.	3rd person	-u	y(i)-	-u
	2nd person	-tu	t(i)-	-u
	1st person	-na	n(i)-	

Note

The bracketed vowel of the imperfect prefixes (variously **i** or **u**—see below) is required by the phonological pattern and is not really part of the prefix.

With reference at first to the simple form only, the bases to which the above affixes apply are as follows:

	Perfect	Imperfect	Examples [1]
Regular {	CaCaC	{-CCiC	kátab, yíktib *to write*
	CiCiC	{-CCuC	túlab, yúṭlub [2] *to ask*
		{-CCaC	fíhim, yífham *to understand*

[1] Verbs are quoted in the corresponding perfect and imperfect 3rd pers. masc. sing. forms and translated by the English infinitive.
[2] See Note (*a*) below.

	Perfect	Imperfect	*Examples*
Hollow	CaaC	-CiiC -CuuC -CaaC	ſaal, yiſſil *to carry* ſaal, yiſúul *to say* naam, yináam *to sleep*
Weak	CaCa CiCi	-CCi -CCa	ráma, yírmi *to throw* nisi, yínsa *to forget*
Doubled	CaCC	-CiCC -CuCC	ḥabb, yiḥibb *to like, want* ḥaṭṭ, yiḥúṭṭ *to put*

Notes

(a) If, in the imperfect tense, the vowel between the second and third radicals of the regular type is **i** or **a**, then the vowel of the first syllable is **i**; if the vowel is **u**, then the vowel of the first syllable is usually **u** also. It is, however, fairly common to hear **i** for **u** in the first syllable, i.e. **yidxul** for **yúdxul** *he enters*, **yíṭlub** for **yúṭlub** *he asks*.

(b) **a** in the above formulation does duty for both open vowels; there is no doubt that much of the difference between the close vowels **i** and **u** could also be accounted for by reference to the consonant context. In Arabic writing short vowels are rarely written and when they are differentiation is threefold, corresponding to **i/u/a**; if Egyptian ever comes to be written as a language in the Arabic script, some modification of present conventions will be desirable.

The vowel-sequences **a-a** and **i-i** in the perfect tense of the regular verb correspond to a rough division of transitive and intransitive verbs, but there are numerous exceptions, e.g. **símiҁ** *he heard*, **misik** *he grasped*. The sequence **u-u** occurs for **i-i** with some speakers, e.g. **xúruṣ** *he was struck dumb*; **i-i**, however, is much more frequent and may always be used. It will be remembered that the **i-i** pattern exhibits elision of the second **i** when the perfect suffix begins with a vowel, e.g. **fihim + it = fíhmit** *she understood*, **fihim + u = fíhmu** *they understood*.

As far as hollow verbs are concerned, when the *imperfect* vowel is **ii** or **uu**, the same vowel (**i** or **u**) appears in place of **a** in those five forms of the *perfect* in which the suffix begins with a consonant, e.g. **ſilt** *I carried* (cf. **yiſiil**), **ruḥt** *I went* (cf. **yirúuḥ**). When the imperfect vowel is **aa**, the perfect vowel in these five persons may be either **i** or **u** and there is no certain means of predicting which, e.g. **nimt** *I went to sleep* (cf. **yináam**), **xuft** *I was afraid* (cf. **yixáaf**).

Two sub-types of weak verb must be recognized in the perfect, those ending in -**i** and those ending in -**a**. Final -**i** is lengthened when the suffix begins with a consonant (**miʃi + t = miʃiit** *you* (m.s.) *went*) and **y** appears when the suffix is vowel-beginning (**miʃi + it = miʃyit** *she went*). It is feasible to regard **miʃi** as **miʃiy**, -**iy** being pronounced as -**i**, whence **miʃiy + t = miʃiyt**, **miʃiy + it = miʃyit**. Final -**a** of the perfect, e.g. **ráma** *he threw*, is dropped in the formation of other persons from the 3rd person sing. masc., e.g. **rama + it = rámit** *she threw*.

The perfect suffixes for the **ráma**-subtype of weak verb and for the doubled verb are special in that for those five persons in which elsewhere the suffix is consonant-beginning the vowel **ee** precedes the suffix consonant; this is also a characteristic of colour verbs. Examples: **laʕéet/laʕéeti/laʕéet/laʕéetu/laʕéena** *you* (m.s.)/*you* (f.s.)/*I*/*you* (pl.)/*we found* (cf. **láʕa** *he found*), **ḥabbéet/ḥabbéeti/ḥabbéet/ḥabbéetu/ḥabbéena** *you* (m.s.)/*you* (f.s.)/*I*/*you* (pl.)/ *we liked*, **ʕiḥmarréet/ʕiḥmarréeti/ ʕiḥmarréet/ʕiḥmarréetu/ʕiḥmarréena** *you* (m.s.)/*you* (f.s.)/ *I*/*you* (pl.)/*we blushed, went red*.

The complete paradigms of the simple form of the four conjugational types is as follows :

Regular verb : kátab, yiktib *to write*, **ṭálab, yúṭlub** *to ask*, **fihim, yifham** *to understand*

		Perfect		
Sing.	3rd pers. masc.	kátab	ṭálab	fihim
	3rd pers. fem.	kátabit	ṭálabit	fíhmit
	2nd pers. masc.	katábt	ṭalábt	fihímt
	2nd pers. fem.	katábti	ṭalábti	fihímti
	1st pers.	katábt	ṭalábt	fihímt
Pl.	3rd pers.	kátabu	ṭálabu	fíhmu
	2nd pers.	katábtu	ṭalábtu	fihímtu
	1st pers.	katábna	ṭalábna	fihímna

Imperfect

Sing.	3rd pers. masc.	yíktib	yúṭlub	yífham
	3rd pers. fem.	tíktib	túṭlub	tífham
	2nd pers. masc.	tíktib	túṭlub	tífham
	2nd pers. fem.	tiktíbi	tuṭlúbi	tifhámi
	1st pers.	ʃáktib	ʃáṭlub	ʃáfham

Pl.	3rd pers.	yiktíbu	yuṭlúbu	yifhámu
	2nd pers.	tiktíbu	tuṭlúbu	tifhámu
	1st pers.	níktib	núṭlub	nífham

Hollow verb : ʃaal, yiʃíil *to carry, take away,* raaḥ, yirúuḥ *to go*, naam, yináam *to sleep,* xaaf, yixáaf *to fear, be afraid*

Perfect

Sing.	3rd pers. masc.	ʃaal	raaḥ	naam	xaaf
	3rd pers. fem.	ʃáalit	ráaḥit	náamit	xáafit
	2nd pers. masc.	ʃilt	ruḥt	nimt	xuft
	2nd pers. fem.	ʃílti	rúḥti	nímti	xúfti
	1st pers.	ʃilt	ruḥt	nimt	xuft

Pl.	3rd pers.	ʃáalu	ráaḥu	náamu	xáafu
	2nd pers.	ʃíltu	rúḥtu	nímtu	xúftu
	1st pers.	ʃílna	rúḥna	nímna	xúfna

Imperfect

Sing.	3rd pers. masc.	yiʃíil	yirúuḥ	yináam	yixáaf
	3rd pers. fem.	tiʃíil	tirúuḥ	tináam	tixáaf
	2nd pers. masc.	tiʃíil	tirúuḥ	tináam	tixáaf
	2nd pers. fem.	tiʃíili	tirúuḥi	tináami	tixáafi
	1st pers.	ʃaʃíil	ʃarúuḥ	ʃanáam	ʃaxáaf

Pl.	3rd pers.	yiʃíilu	yirúuḥu	yináamu	yixáafu
	2nd pers.	tiʃíilu	tirúuḥu	tináamu	tixáafu
	1st pers.	niʃíil	nirúuḥ	nináam	nixáaf

Weak verb : miʃi, yimʃi *to walk, go,* ráma, yírmi *to throw,* nisi, yínsa *to forget,* láſa, yilſa *to find*

Perfect

Sing.	3rd pers. masc.	miʃi	ráma	nisi	láſa
	3rd pers. fem.	miʃyit	rámit	nisyit	láſit
	2nd pers. masc.	miʃiit	raméet	nisiit	laſéet
	2nd pers. fem.	miʃiiti	raméeti	nisiiti	laſéeti
	1st pers.	miʃiit	raméet	nisiit	laſéet
Pl.	3rd pers.	miʃyu	rámu	nisyu	láſu
	2nd pers.	miʃiitu	raméetu	nisiitu	laſéetu
	1st pers.	miʃiina	raméena	nisiina	laſéena

Imperfect

Sing.	3rd pers. masc.	yimʃi	yírmi	yínsa	yilſa
	3rd pers. fem.	timʃi	tirmi	tinsa	tilſa
	2nd pers. masc.	timʃi	tirmi	tinsa	tilſa
	2nd pers. fem.	timʃi	tirmi	tinsi	tilſi
	1st pers.	ſámʃi	ſármi	ſánsa	ſálſa
Pl.	3rd pers.	yimʃu	yírmu	yínsu	yilſu
	2nd pers.	timʃu	tirmu	tínsu	tilſu
	1st pers.	nímʃi	nírmi	nínsa	nilſa

Doubled verb : ḥabb, yiḥibb *to like, want,* ḥaṭṭ, yiḥúṭṭ *to put*

		Perfect		*Imperfect*	
Sing.	3rd pers. masc.	ḥabb	ḥaṭṭ	yiḥibb	yiḥúṭṭ
	3rd pers. fem.	ḥábbit	ḥáṭṭit	tiḥibb	tiḥúṭṭ
	2nd pers. masc.	ḥabbéet	ḥaṭṭéet	tiḥibb	tiḥúṭṭ
	2nd pers. fem.	ḥabbéeti	ḥaṭṭéeti	tiḥibbi	tiḥúṭṭi
	1st pers.	ḥabbóet	ḥaṭṭéet	ſaḥibb	ſaḥúṭṭ
Pl.	3rd pers.	ḥábbu	ḥáṭṭu	yiḥíbbu	yiḥúṭṭu
	2nd pers.	ḥabbéetu	ḥaṭṭéetu	tiḥibbu	tiḥúṭṭu
	1st pers.	ḥabbéena	ḥaṭṭéena	niḥíbb	niḥúṭṭ

The perfect and imperfect affixes are applied to all derived forms in the same way as to the simple form; in contrast with the simple form of the regular and weak verb, however, the structure of the " base ", i.e. the remainder of the form when the affixes have been subtracted, remains the same in both the perfect and imperfect tenses of the derived forms, cf. fáhhim, yifáhhim *to explain*, gáawib, yigáawib *to answer*, ʕiftákar, yiftíkir *to think*, ʕitwágad, yitwígid *to be found*, ʕinkásar, yinkísir *to be broken*, ʕistá*r*mil, yistá*r*mil *to use*, ʕit*r*áyyin, yit*r*áyyin *to be appointed*, ʕitnáaʕiʃ, yitnáaʕiʃ *to discuss*. The facts of vowelling in the tenses and of vowel-correspondences between the tenses remain to be stated and are set out in the following table :

(Table follows on pp. 76–80.)

Regular	Hollow	Weak	Doubled
Simple form The second vowel of the imperfect may be **a** (or **α**), **i**, or **u**. As a general rule, when the second vowel of the perfect is **a**, the corresponding imperfect vowel is **i** or **u**, while **i** in the perfect corresponds to **a** in the imperfect. Certain consonants, however, occurring as second or third radical, "prefer" **a** in the imperfect even when the corresponding perfect vowel is also **a**; these consonants are **x, γ, ħ, ɛ, ħ, ş, ţ, z, d, r,** and sometimes **ς** (cf. **fáɛaħ, yíftaħ** *to open*, **ḍárub, yíḍrub** *to hit*). These remarks should only be taken as a general guide and the imperfect of any verb should be learnt in conjunction with the perfect as it is met.	When the imperfect vowel is **ii** or **uu**, the same vowel (**i** or **u**) appears in those five persons of the perfect which contain a consonant-beginning suffix, e.g. **ſilt** (cf. **yiſiil**), **ruħt** (cf. **yirúuħ**). In the less frequent case of imperfect vowel **aa**, the perfect vowel in these five persons may be either **i** or **u** and there is no way of predicting which.	As a general rule, if the perfect ends in **-i**, the imperfect ends in **-a**, and vice versa, e.g. **nísi, yínsa**, but **ráma, yírmi**. There are exceptions, however, e.g. **míſi, yímſi**, and **láɛa, yílɛa**, so that once again it is necessary to learn the vowels associated with each verb as it is met.	The vowel of the perfect is always **a**, that of the imperfect variously **i** (**yiħíbb**) and **u** (**yiħúṭṭ**). If the imperfect vowel is **u**, one of the radicals is almost certain to belong to the list of consonants given opposite under the regular verb.
Form with C2 geminated There is no vowel-differentiation between the	Treated exactly as the regular verb, e.g.	The perfect always ends in **-a**, the imper-	Treated exactly as the regular verb, e.g.

tenses. The first vowel is always a, e.g. lábbis, yiláhbis *to dress, clothe.* The second vowel is either o or a, generally a if preceded or followed by one of the consonants listed under the simple form above, e.g. náḍḍaf, yináḍḍaf *to clean.*	háawil, yiháawil *to transfer,* ṣáwwar, yiṣáwwar *to photograph.*	fect in -i, e.g. wádda, yiwáddi *to move, take away.* The 3rd pers. sing. masc. perfect of *all* derived forms of weak verbs ends in -a. *N.B.*—In all derived forms of the weak verb, the 3rd pers. sing. fem. suffix is -at, not -it, e.g. wárrat *she showed,* ṣiftárat *she bought.*	háddid, yiháddid *to fix, limit.*
Form with aa infixed after C1 Again no vowel difference between perfect and imperfect. The second vowel is always i, e.g. ṣáabil, yiṣáabil *to meet.*	Again treated as the regular verb, e.g. gáawib, yigáawib *to answer.*	Again the perfect ends in -a, the imperfect in -i, e.g. náada, yináadi *to call.*	No example available.
Form with t infixed after C1 The vowel sequence a-a occurs without exception in the perfect and usually corresponds to i-i in the imperfect, e.g. ṣiftákur, yiftíkir *to think, believe;* ṣiftáyal, yiftáyal *to work* is exceptional.	There is no vowel difference between perfect and imperfect, e.g. ṣixtáar, yixtáar *to choose, elect.* In contrast with the simple form the vowel a remains throughout both tenses, e.g. ṣixtárna *we chose.*	a-a always occurs in the perfect, invariably corresponding to i-iin the imperfect, e.g. ṣiftára, yiftíri *to buy,* ṣibtáda, yibtádi *to begin.*	No example available.

Regular	Hollow	Weak	Doubled
Form with (ši)t prefixed to simple form The perfect vowel pattern is always a-a, and that of the imperfect i-i, e.g. šitšágan, yitšigin *to be imprisoned.*	The vowel a(a) remains throughout perfect and imperfect, e.g. šitḥáal, yitḥáal *to retire.*	As in the regular verb, perfect vowelling is invariably a-a, with imperfect i-i, e.g. šitnása, yitnísi *to be forgotten.*	As in the hollow verb, the vowel a remains throughout, e.g. šitṛádd, yitṛádd *to be counted.*
Form with (ši)t prefixed and C2 geminated Vowelling is as for the corresponding form without (ši)t, e.g. šitʕállim, yitʕállim *to learn,* šitkássar, yitkássar *to be smashed.*	As for the regular verb, e.g. šidgáwwiz, yidgáwwiz *to be, get married.*	In contrast with the corresponding form without (ši)t, and in agreement with the other conjugational types, there is no vowel difference between perfect and imperfect, e.g. šitʕáwwa, yitʕáwwa *to become strong* (contrast ʕáwwa, yiʕáwwi *to strengthen*).	As for the regular verb, e.g. šidgánnin, yidgánnin *to go mad.*

Form with (ʕi)t prefixed and aa infixed after C1			
Vowelling is again as for the form without (ʕi)t, e.g. ʕitnáaʕij, yitnáaʕij *to discuss.*	As for the regular verb, e.g. ʕiggáawib, yiggáawib *to be answered.*	Again in contrast with the corresponding form without (ʕi)t and in agreement with the other conjugational types, there is no vowel difference between perfect and imperfect, e.g. ʕiddáawa, yiddáawa *to be treated, cured* (contrast dáawa, yidáawi *to treat, cure*).	No example available.

Form with (ʕi)n prefixed to simple form			
As for (ʕi)t + simple form above, e.g. ʕinkásar, yinkísir *to be broken.*	As for (ʕi)t + simple form above, e.g. ʕinbáaʕ, yinbáaʕ *to be sold.*	As for (ʕi)t + simple form above, e.g. ʕinháka, yinhíki *to be told, narrated.*	As for (ʕi)t + simple form above, e.g. ʕinball, yinbáll *to be wetted, get wet.*

Regular	Hollow	Weak	Doubled
Form with (ˁi)sta prefixed to simple form (with elision of first vowel)	**aa** in the perfect corresponds to **ii** in the imperfect, e.g. ˁistaˁáal, yistaˁíil *to resign.* In contrast with the simple form, (a)a remains throughout the perfect, e.g. ˁistaˁált yóu (m.s.)/I *resigned.*	There is no vowel difference between perfect and imperfect, e.g. ˁistákfa, yistákfa *to have enough.*	**a** in the perfect usually corresponds to i in the imperfect, e.g. ˁistamárr, yistamírr *to continue,* but cf. ˁistaháˁˁ, yistaháˁˁ *to deserve.*
As in the case of forms with C2 geminated (with and without (ˁi)t-), the vowel between C2 and C3 is either **a** or i depending on the consonants of the syllable, e.g. ˁistaˁmil, yistáˁmil *to use,* but ˁistáˁrab, yistáˁrab *to be surprised.* There is no vowel difference between perfect and imperfect tenses.			
Note.—A distinction is commonly made in educated colloquial between yistáhlik *consumes* and yustáhlak *is consumed;* the latter form is borrowed from the written language.			

Addenda

(i) There is no vowel difference between perfect and imperfect tenses of verbs of colour, e.g. ʕiḥmárr, yiḥmárr *to redden, blush*.

(ii) Quadriliteral verbs behave in respect of vowelling in the manner of the forms in which C2 is geminated, cf. wáʃwiʃ, yiwáʃwiʃ *to whisper* but báɠbaɠ, yibáɠbaɠ *to ogle*.

THE IMPERATIVE

The imperative is derivable in all cases from the 2nd person forms (masc. sing., fem. sing., and plural) of the imperfect, with the prefix omitted but the suffixes (of the fem. sing. and plural forms) retained. Since no form may begin with two consonants, ʕi- is required in the imperative forms of

(i) the simple form of regular and weak conjugational types, e.g. ʕiktib/ʕiktíbi/ʕiktíbu *write !*, ʕirmi/ʕírmi/ʕírmu *throw !*, ʕilʕa/ʕilʕi/ʕilʕu *find !* ;

(ii) the (C1)t- form, all conjugations, e.g. ʕiʃtáɣal/ʕiʃtáɣali/ ʕiʃtáɣalu *work !*, ʕixtáar/ʕixtáari/ʕixtáaru *choose !*, ʕiʃtíri/ ʕiʃtíri/ʕiʃtíru *buy !* ;

(iii) all derived forms containing a prefix, all conjugations, e.g. ʕitháal/ʕitháali/ʕitháalu *retire !*, ʕitkállim/ʕitkallími/ ʕitkallímu *speak !*, ʕistáɣlim/ʕistaɣlími/ʕistaɣlímu *inquire !*

Conversely, ʕi- is not necessary in the imperative forms of

(i) the simple form, hollow and doubled conjugations, e.g. ʃiil/ʃíili/ʃíilu *carry, take away !*, ruuḥ/rúuḥi/rúuḥu *go !*, ḥuṭṭ/ḥúṭṭi/ḥúṭṭu *put !* ;

(ii) the derived form (unprefixed) in which C2 is geminated, e.g. fáhhim/fahhími/fahhímu *explain !* ;

(iii) the (C1)aa- derived form (unprefixed), e.g. ʕáabil/ʕábli/ ʕáblu *meet !*; notice the feature of elision, expected with vowel-beginning suffixes in such a context.

THE PREFIXES bi- AND ḥa-

Contrast must be made between the use of the imperfect tense (a) without prefix and (b) with one of two (aspectival) prefixes, bi- and ḥa-. Compare, for example,

huwwa yíktib iggawáab dilwáʕti	he shall (or he is to) write the letter now
huwwa-byíktib iggawáab dilwáʕti	he is writing the letter now
huwwa ḥayíktib iggawáab dilwáʕti	he is going to write the letter now

bi- is used when reference is to continuative or habitual action, e.g. bitíʕmil éeh ? *what are you doing ?*, biyúxrug min ſúɣlu bádri-f ramaḍáan *he leaves work early during Ramadan*, ſana baɣráfu min múdda ṭawíila ſáwi *I've known him for a very long time*, biyikkállim ɣárabi-kwáyyis *he speaks Arabic well*.

ḥa- is a future prefix and usually relates to impending action and to the firm intention of doing something; thus, ḥa- is used in, say, ḥaktíblak baɣdï yoméen taláata *I'll write to you in two or three days' time*, ḥatínzil fì lukánda ? *are you going to stay in a hotel ?* but not in questions which seek instructions as to future action, as ſaktíblu walla ſéeh ? *shall I write to him or what ?* or níḍrab lúhum tilifóon ? *shall we phone them ?* Other examples of ḥa- are ſazúnni múſ min ilmuḥtámal innu ḥayíigi hína ʕablì búkra *I think it's unlikely he'll be here before to-morrow*, fìh ṭayyáara ḥatſúum issáaɣa tamánya *there's a plane taking off at eight o'clock*. The use of the prefix is also to be compared with that of the auxiliary yibſa (see below under Other means of time reference).

In place of ḥa-, the invariable raḥ or the inflected ráayiḥ (m.s.)/ráyḥa (f.s.)/rayḥíin (pl.) may sometimes be used; ḥayilɣábu, raḥyilɣábu, rayḥíin yilɣábu *they are going to play* all occur but the reader is advised to adopt only ḥa- for his own use.

Notice the elision of ſ of the 1st person singular when bi- and ḥa- are prefixed, e.g. bálɣab (bi + ſalɣab) *I play, am playing*, ḥálɣab (ḥa + ſalɣab) *I shall play, am going to play*.

THE IMPERFECT WITHOUT PREFIX

The commonest contexts in which the imperfect tense is used without the particles bi- and ḥa- are the following :

(1) in association with a series of forms which are themselves largely specialized by use with a following imperfect tense and may be called " auxiliaries ". Auxiliaries may

   (i) be of the pattern of the active participle (q.v. *infra*) and regularly inflected for gender and number;

particularly common is ɽáawiz (or ɽáayiz)/ɽáwza/ ɽawzíin *wanting to*, and also noteworthy is náawi/ náwya/nawyíin *intending to*; cf. ɽáawiz táakul ? *do you want to eat ?*, hᵥmma nawyíin yirúuḥu l-issúuᶜ *they intend to go to the market*. Notice, too, ɽammáal/ ɽammáala/ɽammalíin as in ɽammáal aᶜúll-úskut⁻ *I'm forever telling him to be quiet*;

(ii) belong to one of three sets of related verbal (including participial) forms, láazim/malzúum, múmkin/yímkin, and gáayiz/yigúuz. All these forms are invariable with the exception of malzúum, which is inflected for gender and number.

To consider each set in turn, láazim may or may not be associated with pronominal suffixes, usually with some difference of meaning. Examples are : láazim arúuḥ *I must, ought to go*, lazímn-arúuḥ *it is necessary for me to go, I need to go*, ᶜana malzúum arúuḥ *I must, am bound to go*. ɽala + pronominal suffix is often used in the same way as láazim, i.e. ɽaléek tirúuḥ *you ought to go*, and labúdd is likewise used substantially in the manner of malzúum, e.g. labúddï-trúuḥ *you must go, are bound to go*. In passing may be noted the related impersonal form yílzam, invariable in the form of the 3rd pers. sing. masc. imperfect tense, which is used with and without a pronominal suffix before a following noun, as in yílzam káam ginéeh ? *how much* (lit. *how many pounds*) *is wanted ?*, yilzámni-flúus *I need money*.

múmkin and yímkin occur both with and without pronominal suffixes, e.g. múmkin tiddíini kitáabak ʃuwayya ? *could you let me have your book a minute ?*, yímkin tiʃúfhum hináak (*perhaps*) *you may see them there*, yimkínn-addíilak xámsa-gnéeh báss *I can only give you £5*.

gáayiz and yigúuz are both necessarily associated with the particle li + pronominal suffix, e.g. gayízl-arúuḥ *I can* (*am allowed to*) *go*, yigúzlak tirúuḥ ? *are you able* (sc. *allowed*) *to go ?* The use of one form rather than the other seems to involve little or no difference of meaning.

(iii) be one of a set of specialized nominal forms which are
always used with a pronominal suffix agreeing with
the following verbal form ; these forms are **nifs, bidd,
ʕaṣd**, and **ɣúraḍ**, the last two of which are frequently
interchangeable.   Examples are **ʕana nifs-arúuḥ**
(= **nifsi** + **ʕaruuḥ**) *I very much want to go*, **ġúmar
bíddu-yráwwaḥ** *Omar would like to go home*, **ʕaṣdúhum**
(or **ɣaráḍhum**) **yikkallímu-mġáaḥ** *they are determined
to talk to him*. **nifs** should not be confused with (**bi**) **nafs**
in, say, **ʕana-b náfsi ḥarúuḥ** *I'll go myself*.

(2) as an independent form with an imperative sense, e.g. **ma
ḥáddiʃ yistáġmil maktábi w-ana ɣáayib** *nobody is to use my
office while I'm away*, **níxlaṣ m-ilkaláam ilfáariy** *let's stop
talking nonsense* ; similar use is observable in conjunction
with **ʕáḥsan** or **ʕilʕáḥsan** *better*, as in **núʕġud hín-áḥsan**
we had better stay here (lit. *let us stay here, it is better*), **ʕáʃrab
máyy-áḥsan** *I would rather drink water*, **ʕilʕáḥsan tirúuḥ
f-ilmáɣrib** *you'd better go in the evening*; the 1st pers. pl.
form is used with a similar sense following **yálla** and **yálla
bíina** as in **yalla-nrúuḥ nitɣádda** *let's go and have lunch*,
yalla bíina nitmáʃʃa *let's go for a walk*. It may be noted in
passing that elsewhere **yálla** is particularly common with a
following imperative, as **yálla ráwwaḥ** *go home!*, **yáll-
áʃrab** *drink up!*

(3) as one, other than the first, of a series of imperfect forms
linked by the particle **wi** *and*, **wálla** *or*, or **wála** *nor*,
e.g. **la ḥatʃúuf wala tísmaġ** *you're neither going to see nor
hear*, **la-byiʕra wala yíktib** *he neither reads nor writes*; the
omission of the prefixes is, however, optional.

(4) in association with and following a number of common
verbs including **ʕidir, yíʕdar** *to be able to*, **ġirif, yíġraf** *to
know how to*, **ḥabb, yiḥíbb** *to like to*, **xálla, yixálli** *to let,
allow to*, **fiḍil, yifḍal**, or **ʕáġad, yúʕġud** *to continue to*,
fáḍḍal, yifáḍḍal *to prefer to*, **ʕibtáda, yibtídi** *to start, begin to*,
ḥáawil, yiḥáawil *to try to*, **nisi, yínsa** *to forget to*. Examples
are : **niʕdar nikkállim w-iḥna maʃyíin** *we can talk as we go
along*, **yíġraf yiġúum** *he can swim*, **nisíit agíibu(h)** *I forgot
to bring it*, **ʕan-afáḍḍal asáafir b-iṭṭayyáara** *I prefer going
by air*, **ḥaḥáawil abaṭṭálu(h)** *I'm going to try to give it
up*. As will have appeared, these verbs are themselves

frequently used without prefix; both **yíɣraf yiɣúum** and
biyíɣraf yiɣúum are possible. Also very commonly used
without prefix to introduce a sentence is **ʕiftákar, yiftíkir**
to think, e.g. **tiftíkir issáfar b-ilʕáṭr áḥsan ?** *do you think
it's better to go by train ?* The active participles (see below)
of the verbs in the above list are, of course, similarly used
where appropriate with a following unprefixed imperfect,
cf. **miʃ ʕáadir asmaɣ ḥáaga** *I can't hear a thing*, **miʃ ɣáariʃ
aɣmil éeh** *I don't know what to do*. Notice in passing the
invariable form **tann**, which, pronominally suffixed, is often
used for **fiḍil, yifḍal,** or **ʕáɣad, yúʕɣud**, e.g. **tannúhum (or
fiḍlu** or **ʕáɣadu) yiʃtáyalu liḥaddí núṣṣ illéel** *they went on
working till midnight*.

(5) following and in agreement with a noun or pronominal
suffix when both belong to an object clause as in **xallíihum
yistarayyáḥu** *let them rest*, **hiyya ɣawzáak tiɣmillih zayyí
kída** *she wants you to do it like this*. The clause may be
introduced by the particle **ʕinn** as in **ʕizzáay tintízir
innúhum yiʃtáyalu ?** *how do you expect them to work ?*
Conveniently included at this point is the context in which
the clause contains two objects, as is commonly the case
following **ʕidda, yíddi** *to give*, e.g. **ʕiddíini-taṣríiḥ amḍíih**
give me the permit to sign (lit. *I sign it*), **míin illi middíik
ʕizní timʃi ?** *who's given you permission to go ?*, in which
middíik = participle + pronominal suffix.

(6) with a purposive or continuative sense following verbs of
motion, as in **xáraġ yígri** *he came out running*, **ráaḥ yiʃúuf
ilmudíir** *he went to see the manager*, **rúuḥ índah innaggáar
yíigi-yṣállaḥ ilbáab** *go and tell* (lit. *call*) *the carpenter to
come and mend the door*.

(7) in many " greetings " formulae, e.g. **ʕalláah yibáarik fíik**
in reply to **mabrúuk** *congratulations !*, **ʕalláah yisallímak**
in response to **maɣa-ssaláama** *good-bye !*

(8) in the alternative **ya ... ya ...** *either ... or ...* construction, often with an imperative sense, e.g. **ya-trúuḥ ya
tistánna** *either go or stay*, **ya taxúdha, ya ɣáli yaxúdha
y-ána-axúdha** *one of us takes her, either you, Ali or me* (lit.
either you take her or . . .).

(9) after **báɣdí ma** *after*, **ʕáblí ma** *before*, **lámma** *when*, **wáʕtí
ma** *at the time that*, **ɣándí ma** *while*, **bádal ma** *instead of*,

min γéer ma *without*, γalaʃáan or γaʃáan *in order to, so that*, and similar particles introducing an adverbial clause, e.g. báγdĭ ma nitγáʃʃa, ḥanrúuḥ issínima *we're going to the cinema after dinner* (lit. *after we dine*), ʃáblĭ ma yĭwṣal, ḥayiddĭlhum xóbar *he'll let them know before he arrives*, bitrúuḥ ilmadrása γa(la)ʃáan titγállim *you go to school to learn*.

(10) in the 2nd pers. sing. and pl. only

    (i) in the negative imperative, e.g. ma tĭdxúlʃ (or tud-) *don't go in !* (ma -ʃ is the sign of negation) ;

    (ii) following the " exhortative " particles ʃiyyáak/-ki/ -ku(m), ʃíwγa/ʃíwγi/ʃíwγu (an imperative series) and ma (not to be confused with ma of the negative), e.g. ʃiyyáak tĭgi wáxri ! *mind you* (masc. sing.) *don't come late !*, ʃíwγi-trúuḥi-hnáak ! *mind you* (fem. sing.) *don't go there !*, ma-trúuḥu-hnáak ! *why don't you go there, then !* Beware of the translation pitfall : ·ʃíwγa ma-tgíiʃ ! = *mind you come*, not **mind you don't come*. ʃiyyáak is also used like ʃinʃálla in the sense of *I hope*, e.g. ʃiyyáak tilʃáah hináak *I hope you'll find him there*.

THE VERB kaan, yikúun

The hollow verb kaan, yikúun *to be*, as a means of ringing the changes on the time-reference of sentences, has both independent status and also that of an auxiliary verb used with a following tense (or participle).

Examples of kaan, yikúun used as a main verb are ʃissandúuʃ kan malγáan *the box was full* (cf. the so-called nominal sentence ʃissandúuʃ malγáan *the box is full*), kúntĭ (or kúttĭ) γayyáan imbáariḥ *I was ill yesterday*, ʃilʃáklĭ ḥaykun gáahiz baγdĭ-ʃwáyya *the meal will soon be ready*. In fíih-type sentences and other particle-sentences of a kind noted above (see p. 51 ff.), the verb kaan, yikúun is invariable in the 3rd pers. sing. masc. forms, e.g. kan fíih ḥádsa f-iʃʃáariγ ɖilwáʃti *there was an accident in the street just now*, ʃana ḥaʃsimha bénku γaʃan ma-ykúnʃí fíh dáwʃa *I'm going to divide it between you so that there won't be any quarrelling*, kan γandína waʃti-ktíir *we had plenty of time*, ḥaykúun γandína-ɖyúuf búkra l-ilγáda *we shall have guests for lunch to-morrow*. The imperative forms kuun/ -i/-u are rare ; cf. xallíik rúagil ! *be a man !*

The use of **kaan, yikúun** as an auxiliary in association with the two tenses gives the following range of possibilities : ɤamal *he did, has done*/kaan ɤamal *he had done*/yikuun ɤamal *he will have done* ; biyiɤmil *he does, is doing*/kaan biyiɤmil *he used to do, was doing*/yikuun biyiɤmil *he will be doing* ; ḥayiɤmil *he will do, is going to do*/kaan ḥayiɤmil *he was going to do*. Examples are : **kan ɤamal iʃʃúɣli lamma daxált** *he had done the job when I went in*, **kan biyiɤmil iʃʃúɣli lamma daxált** *he was doing the job when I went in*, **ṣ-ilwáʃtï dá-ykunu-byiɤmïlu-ʃʃúɣl** *they will be doing the job then*, **kuntï ḥáɤmil iʃʃúɣli-w baɤdéen nisiit** *I was going to do the job but then forgot*. Notice the fact that *yikuun ḥa- does not occur and compare the use of ʃárrab + imperfect in, say, **yikun** (or **ḥaykun**) **ʃárrab yúxrug ṣ-ilwaʃtída** *he'll be about to come out then*.

kaan, yikúun may precede any of the so-called " auxiliaries " (see above), e.g. **kuntï ɤáawiz arúuḥ** *I wanted to go*, **kan bídd-arúuḥ** *I would have liked to go*, **ʃana ʃáasif ma kanʃi mumkinn-agi-mbáariḥ liʃanni kan lazímn-aẓúur axúuya ṣ-ilmustáʃfa** *I'm sorry I couldn't come yesterday but I had to visit my brother in hospital*. In this context, notice the use of the perfect (**ruḥt**) as opposed to the imperfect in, say, **kan láazim rúḥt** *I ought to have gone*.

PARTICIPLES

The simple form of the verb has both an active and passive participle ; to memorize the active pattern, notice that it is also that of the masculine ordinal numeral, e.g. ɤáarif *knowing, having known*, ʃáayif *seeing, having seen* (hollow verb), máaʃi *walking* (weak verb), ḥáaṭiṭ *putting, having put* (doubled verb) : the passive participle is characterized by a prefix **ma-** and, except in the case of the weak verb, by the vowel -uu- infixed between the 2nd and 3rd consonants, e.g. **maṣtúuḥ** *open*, **maʃdúud** *pulled* (doubled verb). The pattern of the weak passive participle is illustrated by **mánsi** *forgotten*. There is no passive participle of the simple form of the hollow verb, cf. **minbáaɤ** or **mitbáaɤ** *sold*, which are the participles of the derived **ʃin-** or **ʃitbáaɤ/yin-** or **yitbáaɤ** *to be sold* (cf. **baaɤ/yibíiɤ** *to sell*). Both participles are inflected for gender and number, i.e. ɤáarif-ɤárfa/ɤarfíin, ʃáayif-ʃáyfa/ʃayfíin, máaʃi-máʃya/maʃyíin, ḥáaṭiṭ-ḥáṭṭa/ḥaṭṭíin, maṣtúuḥ-maṣtúuḥa/maṣtuḥíin, mánsi-mansíyya/mansiyyíin.

Derived forms have one participle only ; generally speaking, it may be formed by substituting **m-** for **y-** of the 3rd pers. sing. masc. imperfect, e.g. **mitrími** (*having been*) *thrown* (Ɛitráma/ yitrími), **mináḍḍaf** *cleaning, having cleaned* (náḍḍaf/yináḍḍaf), **mixálli** *allowing, having allowed* (xálla/yixálli), **mitnáḍḍaf** (*having been*) *cleaned* (Ɛitnáḍḍaf/yitnáḍḍaf), **migáawib** *answering, having answered* (gáawib/yigáawib), **mitgáawib** (*having been*) *answered* (Ɛitgáawib/yitgáawib), **mixtílif** *differing, different* (Ɛixtálaf/yixtílif), **mixtáar** *choosing,* (*having*) *chosen* (Ɛixtáar/ yixtáar), **minkább** or **mitkább** (*having been*) *poured* (Ɛin- or Ɛitkább/yin- or yitkább), **minbáaƐ** or **mitbáaƐ** (*having been*) *sold* (Ɛin- or ƐitbáaƐ/yin- or yitbáaƐ). Notice those forms of the weak verb in which the participle, in contrast with the imperfect tense, ends in **-i**, e.g. **mitxálli** (*having been*) *left, withdrawn* (Ɛitxálla/yitxálla), **mitráaḍi** (*having been*) *placated, having agreed* (Ɛitráaḍa/yitráaḍa), **mistákfi** (*having been*) *satisfied, having had enough* (Ɛistákfa/yistákfa).

The participle of verbs of colour is characterized by the vowel **-i-** in the second syllable, e.g. **miḥmírr** (*having*) *turned red, blushing* (Ɛiḥmárr/yiḥmárr).

The prefix **musta-** is often preferred to **mista-** by educated speakers ; thus, **musta-** or **mistáƐlim** *inquiring, having inquired* (Ɛistáɛlim/yistáɛlim), **musta-** or **mistábʃar** *having good news, being optimistic* (Ɛistábʃar/yistábʃar), **musta-** or **mistaƐídd** *ready* (Ɛistaɛádd/yistaɛídd). In Classical and Modern Literary Arabic, derived forms of the verb have both an active participle (**-i-** in the final syllable) and a passive participle (**-a-** in the final syllable). In the Egyptian colloquial, this distinction is maintained by educated speakers for certain **musta-** (not **mista-**) participles ; **mustáƐmir** *colonist* and **mustáƐmar** *colonized* are " learned " forms but both are in current use. Compare, too, **da-ktáab mustáƐmil** (or **mistáƐmil**) *this is a second-hand book* and **Ɛilkitáab dá mustáƐmal** (not **mista-**) **kitíir** *this book is used a lot*. Usage, however, is not always fixed and individual variation is encountered. The " Classical " form is used by educated speakers for some participles of other than the Ɛista- derived form, e.g. **muxtálif** *different* for **mixtílif**, **munfáƐil** *angry* for **minfíƐil**, **mutaʃákkir** *thank you* for **mitʃákkir**, **mutawássiṭ** *average* for **mitwássaṭ**. The use of " learned " participial forms is one of the most. characteristic signs of *educated* colloquial. Notice, too, in colloquial usage such contrasts as mi̱ɽállim *teaching, having taught* (ɽállim/yiɽállim) and mu̱ɽállim *teacher*, mifáttiʃ *inspecting, having inspected* (fáttiʃ/yifáttiʃ) and mufáttiʃ *inspector*.

The participles with suffixes

Final **-a** of feminine forms is lengthened in accordance with the general rule (q.v. *supra*) when a consonant-beginning suffix is added, e.g. hiyya maskáah *she is holding him/it*, dí mafʃuláali-b sitta-gnéeh *this was sold to me (after bargaining) for £6*.

Although the participle is nominal (adjectival) in form and, unlike the tenses, exhibits no distinction of person, its partly verbal character is revealed by a number of features including its association with the 1st pers. sing. pronominal suffix **-ni** (not **-i**), e.g. hiyya maskáani *she is holding me*.

Use of the participles

It has just been said that the participle is nominal in form with no distinction of person. It is, therefore, possible to consider, say, káatib iggawáab in the sentence húwwa káatib iggawáab as a sequence of two nouns in construct and to translate *he is the writer of the letter*. But the participle of many verbs, of which kátab/yíktib *to write* is one, may be said to refer to the state of having performed the verbal action, and in the appropriate context the translation of húwwa káatib iggawáab is *he has written the letter*. Other verbs, notably verbs of motion, behave differently and it is not surprising that translation in English will often take different forms. Here are some examples:

hiyya-mnaḍḍáfa-lʕóoḍa *she has cleaned the room* (contrast bitnáḍḍaf ilʕóoḍa *she is cleaning the room*); huwwa ráakib ilḥuṣáan *he is riding (i.e. has mounted) the horse* (contrast biyírkab ilḥuṣáan *he is mounting the horse*); ʕana wáakil I *have eaten, am full*; ʕana mistaɽmílha min zamáan I *have used (or been using) it for a long time*; ʕana-mráttib ilhudúum *I've arranged the clothes*; humma sakníin fi béet mitráttib kuwáyyis *they live (i.e. have settled) in a well-appointed house*; ʕana laʕéetu-mgáawib ɽaléeh I *found he'd answered it*; ʕana laʕéetu mitgáawib ɽaléeh I *found it had been answered*; ʕana mistanníik baʕáali saɽtéen I've *been waiting two hours for you*;

huwwa middíini kilma-nnu gáay *he's promised me he'll be coming*.

There is no past-time sense with verbs of motion in the following examples :

huwwa ţáali؛ ba؛dĭ-ʃwáyya *he'll be coming out soon* (ḥa-, i.e. ḥayíʃla؛, is possible here and in the following examples) ; ؛ana-msáafir búkra *I'm leaving to-morrow*; ḥásan misáafir máşr *Hasan is going to Cairo*; huwwa náazil dúyri *he'll be (coming) down right away*.

Past-time reference is similarly often absent when the participle is associated with negation, e.g. ؛ana miʃ wáakil *I'm not going to eat* (or *I have not eaten*) ; hiyya miʃ minaḍḍáfa-lʃóoḍa *she's not going to clean the room* (or *she hasn't cleaned the room*) ; mantaʃ ؛áamil zayyĭ ma ba؛úllak ! *aren't you going to do as I tell you !*

In the common sentence-pattern illustrated by la؛éetu káatib iggawáab *I found he had written the letter*, the perfect tense may be used as an alternative to the participle, i.e. la؛éetu kátab iggawáab ; in the case of verbs of motion, however, a difference of meaning is involved between the use of participle or perfect tense, e.g. ʃúftu xáarig m-ilbéet *I saw him coming out of the house* and ʃúftu xárag m-ilbéet *I saw him come out of the house*. More striking, however, is the difference of meaning between the two sentences containing the participles káatib and xáarig ; use of the participle xáarig in the case of the verb of motion corresponds to that of the imperfect tense with the prefix bi- in the case of the non-motive verb, thus compare ʃúftu xáarig m-ilbéet *I saw him coming out of the house* with la؛éetu-byíktib iggawáab *I found him writing the letter*. With the verb of motion, the imperfect with bi- has the sense of habitual action, e.g. ʃúftu-byúxrug m-ilbéet kúllĭ yóom *I saw him come (or coming) out of the house every day*. Another example of the similar function of the motive participle and the non-motive imperfect tense with bi- is provided by ؛abílna şáaliḥ f-issíkka w-iḥna-mrawwaḥíin *we met Ṣāliḥ in the street as* (= wi) *we were going home* and ؛abílna* (= ؛aabil + pronominal suffix -na) şáaliḥ f-issíkka w-iḥna-bnitkállim wayya bá؛ḍ *Ṣāliḥ met us in the street as we were talking together*. With the prefix ḥa-, there is little or no observable difference of use between motive and

non-motive verbs, thus ʃúʃtu hayúxrug m-ilbéet *I saw him
about to leave the house* and laʕéetu hayíktib iggawáab *I found
him about to write the letter.*

Like the tenses, the participle may be preceded by kaan/
yikúun with corresponding differences in the time-reference of
the whole; thus, lamma daxált kan káatib (or kan kátao)
iggawáab *he'd written the letter when I went in* and ʕissittí
kanit minaḍḍáfa (or kanit naḍḍáfit) ilbéet *the woman had
cleaned the house.* There is again difference of behaviour
between motive and non-motive verbs, compare kan káatib
iggawáab *he'd written the letter* with kan máaʃi f-iʃʃáariɛ *he was
walking in the street*; one says kan náazil dúyri lakin ma-nzíiʃ
he was coming down straight away but hasn't done so but one
cannot say *kan kaatib iggawaab lakin ma katabuuj, cf. kan
hayíktib iggawáab lakin ma katabúuʃ *he was going to write the
letter but hasn't done so.* Similarly with yikúun, compare and
contrast f-ilwáʃti dá-ykunu xargíin *they'll be leaving then* and
f-ilwáʃti dá-tkun minaḍḍáfa (or naḍḍáfit) ilʕóoḍa *she'll have
cleaned the room by then,* f-ilwáʃti dá-ykunu xárugu *they'll have
left by then,* with f-ilwáʃti da-tkun bitnaḍḍaf ilʕóoḍa *she'll be
cleaning the room then.* In the pattern exemplified by laʕéetu
ɣáamil ʃúylu(h) *I found he'd done his work,* kaan may be
included or not before ɣáamil with little or no difference in
meaning; frequently, however, when kaan is included, its
inclusion will relate to the presence of a perfect tense form
elsewhere in the context, thus káan ɣáamil relates to niiʃi in
such an exchange as A. ʕilwálad miʃi bádri léeh ? B. laʕeetu
kan ɣáamil ʃúylu-w ʕultilu ráwwuḥ. *A. Why has the ooy gone
early ? B. I found he'd done his work and told him to go home.*

It will be seen from the foregoing that *the greengrocer has
closed* is a more literal translation of ʕilbaʃʃáal ʃáafil than *the
greengrocer('s) is closed*; the corresponding passive participle
maʃfúul cannot be used with a noun of personal reference but
cf. ʕiddukkáan maʃfúul *the shop is closed.* As a rule the passive
participle of this pattern is purely adjectival in function. In
some contexts there is little or no difference between the use of
this passive participle and the perfect tense of the derived forms
in which the prefixes ʕit- and ʕin- are associated with the simple
form of the verb, thus ʕana ʕabilt innaggúar wi ʕálli maktábak
maɣmúul (or itɣámal) *I met the carpenter and he told me your*

desk is (or *has been*) *made*; contrast the case of difference between ʃúſt iʃʃibbáak maſtúuḩ *I saw the window (was) open* and ʃúſt iʃʃibbáak infátaḩ *I saw the window open* (sc. *of its own accord*). In the majority of contexts the passive participle of the simple form of the verb tends to be preferred to the participles of the derived forms with the passive and intransitive prefixes ſit- and ſin-, thus mármi *thrown* rather than mitrími, makbúuḩ *poured* (*out*) rather than mitkább or minkább; it should nevertheless be remembered that grammatical statements are generally statements of tendencies rather than watertight rules, and accordingly we cannot use, say, mábni for mitbíni in mitbíni gáahiz *ready-built*: in some contexts, moreover, and notably in association with líssa, the two participles are clearly differentiated, thus compare ſiddóoraſ líssa malyáan *the jug is still full* with ſiddóoraſ líssa mitmíli *the jug has just been filled*, ſiddukkáan líssa maſtúuḩ *the shop is still open* with ſiddukkáan líssa mitfítiḩ *the shop has just been opened*, and ſilfustáan líssa mablúul *the dress is still wet* with ſilfustáan líssa mitbáll *the dress has just been wetted* (or *got wet*). Since ſit- is usually a passive prefix, corresponding derived forms with and without the prefix may be considered passive and active respectively, i.e. mináḍḍaf (active)-mitnáḍḍaf (passive) *cleaned*, migáawib (active)-mitgáawib (passive) *answered*; this also applies to quadriliteral verbs, e.g. miláxbaṭ (active)-mitláxbaṭ (passive) *confused*.

The fact of two nouns following a participle or tense-form in a transitive construction, as in, say, ṛáli-mkáttib fáṭma-ggawáab *Ali has made Fatima write the letter*, is readily assimilated by native speakers of English; the similarly constructed ṛáli ḍáarib ilḩéeṭa búhya *Ali has painted the wall* (lit. *has struck the wall paint*) or huwwa ſáaṭiſ ilḩáblī nuṣṣéen *he's cut the rope in two* (lit. *has cut the rope two halves*) tend to offer rather more difficulty, but more difficulty still is encountered with corresponding passive forms: cf. ſilḩéeṭa maḍrúuba búhya *the wall is* (or *has been*) *painted*, ſiggázma maḍrúuba warníiʃ *the shoes are* (or *have been*) *polished*, ſilṛáṣa mitkassára ḩíṭat *the stick has been broken into pieces*, ſilxáṭṭī mitſássim iṭnáaʃar ſism *the line is divided into twelfths*. Cf., too, ſilſóoḍa malyáana náas *the room is full of people*.

The passive participle of what may be called " prepositional

verbs ", i.e. those compounded of verb and particle, is invariable
in such patterns as Ṣana laṢéetu mitgáawib ṛaléeh *I found it* (m.)
had been answered, maḥkúum ṛaléeha b-issígnì tálat ʃuhúur
she's been sentenced to three months' imprisonment, Ṣilfilúus
ilmasmúuḥ bìiha *the permitted currency*. Compare the similar
structure of maksúur li ṛáli ṛáṣa *one of Ali's sticks is broken*,
which is paralleled by the (active) participle of the intransitive
verb ḍaaṛ/yiḍíiṛ *to be lost* in ḍáayiṛ li ṛáli-ktabéen *Ali has lost a
couple of his books, two of Ali's books have been lost*.

OTHER MEANS OF TIME-REFERENCE

There are, of course, numerous means of time-reference outside and in association with the system of tenses and participles,
with and without kaan, yikúun. Particularly noteworthy are

(i) zamáan (unsuffixed) in, say, zaman kanu-byiḥráṢul-
lfáḥmì-f Ṣafránhum (*formerly*) *they used to burn charcoal in
their ovens*, and zamáan + pronominal suffix in, for
example, zamánhum mìʃyu *they came some time ago*, law
kúnna-mʃiina sáaṛit ma Ṣultílak, kan zamánna-hnáak
dilwaṢti (a conditional sentence, q.v. *infra*) *if we'd gone
when I said (to you), we'd have been there some time ago* (or
by now).

(ii) the verbal form báṢa and the prepositional particle li, both
pronominally suffixed, and the prepositional particle min,
all three preceding a specific time-word; e.g. Ṣana
mistanniik baṢáali núṣṣi sáaṛa *I've been waiting half an
hour for you*, baṢáali sitt úʃhur ma ʃuftúuʃ *I haven't seen
him for six months*, hiyya f-ilbéet laha saṛtéen *she's been
in the house (for) two hours*, Ṣáhlan, ma ʃuftákʃi min
zamáan hullo, *I haven't seen you for a long time*.

(iii) the auxiliary ṢibṢa/-i/-u (imperative) and yíbṢa, etc.
(imperfect), followed by the imperative and imperfect
tense respectively, are used to mark future time; e.g.
ṣaḥḥiini-ssaṛa sitta w-ibṢa hátli mayya súxna ṛaʃan
ilḥiláaṢa [1] *call me at 6 o'clock and bring me hot water for
shaving* (note that without ṢibṢa, the order would be for
the water to be brought at once), xúd, Ṣadi-gnéeh ! w-ibṢa

---

[1] ṢibṢa may be placed before the first imperative, i.e. ṢibṢa
ṣaḥḥiini-ssaṛa sitta-w hátli máyya, etc.

raggaɣúuli (or wi tibʕa-traggaɣúuli) baɣdéen *here's a pound ! you can return it to me later*, ʕilʕáhsan innak tibʕa tisʕal ikkumsáari lamma yiigi yúʃlub ittazáakir *you'd better ask the ticket-collector when he comes around asking for the tickets*. The use of the auxiliary is to be compared both with that of the prefix ḥa- and with that of the imperfect .tense alone : ʕádfaɣ káam ? and ʕabʕ-ádfaɣ káam ? *how much shall I pay ?* are both requests for instructions, e.g. from a business superior, as to action which, in the first case, is to be immediate and, in the second, not. Both contrast with ḥádfaɣ káam ? *how much am I going to (have to) pay ?*, the most likely context for which is a bargaining-match in the market. ḥa- may be used with yibʕa but, as might be expected, ḥabʕ-azúrku baɣdéen *I'll call on you later* is a less definite, more remote undertaking than ḥazúrkn baɣdéen.

CONDITIONAL SENTENCES

ʕiza (or ʕin or law) kúntí-trúuh búkra, ḥaddíilak ilfilúus

ʕiza (or ʕin or law) rúḥti búkra, ḥaddíilak ilfilúus

law tirúuh búkra, ḥaddíilak ilfilúus

All (seven) of the above possibilities relate to the translation *If you go to-morrow, I'll give you the money*. Of the three con-ditional particles ʕiza, ʕin, and law, ʕiza is the commonest. The main difference between the Arabic patterns above concerns the presence or absence of kaan (inflected for person, gender, and number) following the particle ; moreover, if kaan is included, the following verb is in the imperfect but if kaan is omitted, the verb is in the perfect except after law, in which case either perfect or imperfect is permissible. Notice that the imperfect yikúun is never used after the conditional particles.

The second type of conditional sentence, involving difference of time-reference from the above, exhibits 'less variety of possible form : ʕiza (or ʕin or law) kúntí rúḥt imbáarih, kúnt iddétlak ilfilúus *if you had gone yesterday, I would have given you the money*. Egyptians brought up in the schools of tradi-tional grammar may say that only law is possible in this context but in fact all three particles are currently used. In this type

kaan is best included after the particle and is invariably followed
by the perfect tense, but an even more marked difference from
the earlier type is the essential presence of kaan in the *second*
clause. In the example given, since the context relates to
money which was not actually handed over, ḥaddíilak is
possible for Siddétlak in the second clause, i.e. Sana kúntī
ḥaddíilak ilfilúus *I was going to give you the money*, but in the
great majority of cases the perfect tense is necessary after the
second kaan, as in Siza kúntī géet imbáariḥ, kuntī ʃúftī ṛáli *if
you'd come yesterday, you'd have seen Ali*. law, especially
followed by the particle Sinn, is sometimes used for greater
emphasis, e.g. law Sinnak kuntī géet imbáariḥ, kuntī ʃúftī ṛáli
if ONLY you'd come yesterday, etc. Other practice examples
are: law kunna-mʃíina sáaṛit ma Sultíʃak, kunna-wṣílna-
hnáak dilwáSti *if we'd left when I told you, we'd have been there
now*, law kúntī ṭulabtåha mínni, kunt iddethåalak *if you'd asked
me for it, I'd have given it to you* and, of the first type, Siza
nazzílt ittáman ʃuwáyya, yímkin aʃtíri *if you brought the price
down a bit, I might buy*.

A conditional particle may introduce a nominal clause in the
manner of English *if*, *whether*, e.g. SisSálu-za kan miggáwwiz
ask him if he's married; this, of course, is not an example of the
two types of conditional sentence that have been considered
above, and the occurrence of the participle (miggáwwiz) should
be noted and also the fact that kaan is essential. With a
following tense form, Siza as well as kaan may be omitted, cf.
ma-yhímmiʃ (iza) gúm walla ma gúuʃ *it doesn't matter whether
they come or not*.

The use of kaan following the " optative " particle yaréet in,
say, yaréet kunt úṛraf innúhum ḥayiigu walla láS *I wish I knew
whether they are coming or not* is reminiscent of that in the conditional sentences above.

VERB-SEQUENCES

Verbal forms often immediately succeed each other where in
English a linking " and " or a device of rhythm or intonation
corresponds; the total verbal complex in Arabic is frequently
unitary in the manner of, say, " try and do " or " go and tell "
in, for example, " he's gone and told him." Arabic imperative

examples are: **xúd íʃrab !** *take and drink !*, **taɣáalu-ʕɣúdu !** *come* (pl.) *and sit down !*, **rúuḥ ráwwaḥ !** *go on home !*, **rúuḥ ʃáblu dilwáʕti !** *go and see him now !*, **xúdu-ʃrábu(h) !** *take it and drink it !*, **xúd ikkitáab waddíih l-axúuk !** *take the book (and take it) to your brother !*, **rúuḥ índah innaggáar yíigi-yʃállaḥ ilbáab !** *go and tell* (lit. *call*) *the carpenter to come and mend the door !*

The maximum number of such forms is five, as in the imperfect example **tiḥíbbī tíigi tiʕúum nirúuḥ niẓúur ɣáli?** *do you want to come and* (lit. *come and get up and go*) *visit Ali ?*, in which it will be seen that a change of person is involved between the first and second parts of the sequence; a partial sequence without change of person is probably limited to a maximum of three forms as in the example. In long sequences of this kind a verb of motion is almost certain to appear. Examples involving the perfect tense are (**ʕiḥna ʕáwwil ma-btadéena niʃtáɣal) gum ɣattalúuna** *(as soon as we started working) they came and interrupted us*, **ɣáli ʕáam ṭíliɣ gáab ikkitáab** *Ali went off to fetch the book*.

The verb **ʕaam, yiʕúum** (elsewhere *to stand up*) frequently occurs in these sequences of verbal forms and has already been illustrated. **ʕáam ḍarábni** *he hit me* is reminiscent of the jocular English *he upped and hit me*, but that **ʕaam** forms one piece with the following verb and that the meaning of the verb elsewhere is irrelevant to the total piece is shown by the fact that, say, **ʕúmtī nímt** = not only *I went off to bed* but also in the appropriate context *I fell asleep*. **ʕaam** serves to punctuate or mark off incidents as they are related as in, say, **miʃíit ʕam ḥáʃni** *I started off but he stopped me* and is especially common in this narrative function in association with **ʕaal** *he said*, e.g. **géh wi ʕálli … ʕúmt ana ʕultílu(h) … ʕam irráagil ʕálli …** *he came up and said to me … whereupon I said to him … then the man said to me. …*

SOME IRREGULAR VERBS

The perfect and imperfect tenses and the imperative of four commonly occurring verbs which do not conform to the standard pattern are as follows:

kal, yáakul *to eat*   xad, yáaxud *to take*

	Perfect	*Imper- fect*	*Impera- tive*	*Perfect*	*Imper- fect*	*Impera- tive*
Sing.	kal (*he*)	yáakul		xad	yáaxud	
	kálit (*she*)	táakul		xadt	táaxud	
	kalt (*you* (m.s.))	táakul	kul	xadt	táaxud	xud
	kálti (*you* (f.s.))	tákli	kúli	xádti	táxdi	xúdi
	kalt (*I*)	ʃáakul		xadt	ʃáaxud	
Pl.	kálu (*they*)	yáklu		xádu	yáxdu	
	káltu (*you*)	táklu	kúlu	xádtu	táxdu	xúdu
	kálna (*we*)	náakul		xádna	náaxud	

Note

dt in **xadt, xádti,** and **xádtu** is pronounced **tt,** i.e. **xatt, xátti,** and **xáttu.** Initial *t* of the perfect suffixes often has special implications as to pronunciation ; cf. **ʃaɣádt** (pronounced **ʃaɣátt**) *I/you sat down,* **ʃinbaʃáṭt** (pronounced **ʃimbaʃáṭt**) *I was/you were pleased.*

ʃidda, yíddi *to give*   geh,[1] yíigi *to give*

	Perfect	*Imper- fect*	*Impera- tive*	*Perfect*	*Imper- fect*
Sing.	ʃidda (*he*)	yíddi		geh	yíigi
	ʃiddit (*she*)	tíddi		gat	tíigi
	ʃiddéet (*you* (m.s.))	tíddi	ʃíddi	geet	tíigi
	ʃiddéeti (*you* (f.s.))	tíddi	ʃíddi	géeti	tíigi
	ʃiddéet (*I*)	ʃáddi		geet	ʃáagi
Pl.	ʃiddu (*they*)	yíddu		gum	yíigu
	ʃiddéetu (*you*)	tíddu	ʃíddu	géetu	tíigu
	ʃiddéena (*we*)	níddi		géena	níigi

Note

There is no imperative of **geh, yíigi** ; cf. **taɣáala/ taɣáali/ taɣáalu** *come (here)* ! **gaa-** and **guu-,** not **geh** and **gum,** are used when a suffix follows, e.g. **gáani** (or **gáali**) *he came to me,* **ma gúuʃ** *they didn't come.*

[1] Or gih.

Etymologically, hollow and weak verbs are those with **y** or **w** as 2nd and 3rd radical respectively. Verbs with **y** as 1st radical do not occur and those with **w**, e.g. wíṣil, yíwṣal *to arrive*, are regular with two exceptions, viz. wíṣif, yúṣaf *to stop* and wíṣiɛ, yúṣaɛ *to fall*, in the imperfect tense of which **w** is dropped and the vowel of the first syllable is **u**; thus

	Imperfect	*Imperative*
Sing.	yúṣaf *(he)*	
	túṣaf *(she)*	
	túṣaf *(you* (m.s.))	ṣúṣaf
	túṣafi *(you* (f.s.))	ṣúṣafi
	ṣáṣaf *(I)*	
Pl.	yúṣafu *(they)*	
	túṣafu *(you)*	ṣúṣafu
	núṣaf	

Note

i is sometimes heard for **u** in the first syllable of these verbs.

VERB + PRONOMINAL SUFFIX

The addition of pronominal suffixes to verbs involves differences of pronunciation, especially in the matters of vowel-length and accentuation, between the suffixed and unsuffixed forms. As has already been remarked above, final vowels are lengthened when a suffix is added, e.g. fíhmu-fihmúuh *they understood it/him*, fihmúuha *they understood it/her*, fihímti-fihimtíina *you* (f.s.) *understood us*. Final -h of the 3rd pers. sing. masc. suffix is not always pronounced but the final accented long vowel is retained, i.e. fihmúu. Again as with nouns, the " extra " vowel will vary with the suffix, e.g. fihimtína *you* (m.s.) *understood us*, fihimtǎha *I/you* (m.s.) *understood her*, fihimtǔhum *I/you* (m.s.) *understood them*.

Do not confuse the verbal tense suffix -**u** (2nd and 3rd pers. pl.) and the pronominal suffix -**u(h)** (3rd pers. sing. masc.) ; cf. kátabu either *they wrote* or *he wrote it*, bitiɛrúfu either *you* (pl.) *know* or *you* (m.s.) *know him* or *she knows him*.

The particle **li** + pronominal suffix is often added to verbs and has similar implications as to the placing of the accent in comparison with corresponding unsuffixed forms ; cf. ṣísmaḥ *excuse, forgive !*, ṣismáḥli *excuse me !*, ṣismaḥíili *excuse* (f.s.) *me !*

The following series of li-forms suffixed to verbs will be seen to differ from that given above under **Particles** : **li, lak, lik, lu(h), lîha, lína, lúku(m), lúhum**. If the " l-piece " consists of two syllables, i.e. **lîha, lína, lúku(m), lúhum**, and if the verbal form ends in a consonant, then **lîha, lína**, etc., are treated as separate words from the point of view of accentuation, e.g. **Sísmah lína** *excuse us !* If, on the other hand, the verb ends in a vowel, then the vowel following l is elided and the whole complex of verb + l-piece treated as one word, e.g. **Sismahúlna** *excuse* (pl.) *us !,* **Sismahílha** *excuse* (f.s.) *her !*

Double suffixation

It is quite common for both a pronominal suffix and an l-piece to be added in that order to a verb, in which case the same rules of accentuation as those given in the preceding paragraph obtain. This feature is especially frequent with **Sidda, yiddi** *to give,* e.g. **Siddihásli** *give it* (f.) *to me !,* **Siddíhli** *give it* (m.) *to me !,* **Siddetúlha** either *I/you* (m.s.) *gave it* (m.) *to her* or *you* (pl.) *gave to her,* **Siddetháalu(h)** *I/you* (m.s.) *gave it* (f.) *to him,* **Siddéthum lúhum** *I/you* (m.s.) *gave them to them.* Other examples are **hathálha** *bring it* (f.) *to her !,* **Simlahúmlu(h)** *fill them for him !,* **Simlahálhum** *fill it* (f.) *for them !,* **Simláahum lúhum** *fill them for them !*

THE VERBAL NOUN

Verbal nouns of the simple form of the verb are of more than one pattern ; **darb** *striking,* **Surb** *drinking,* **ŗámal** *doing,* **duxúul** *entering,* are examples, among which **darb** illustrates the commonest pattern. Patterns of derived forms are fixed ; where plural forms of the verbal noun occur, these are regularly in **-aat**, e.g. **taŗlimáat** *instructions,* **miŗaksáat** *quarrels.* Derived patterns, illustrated by regular verbs, are as follows :

Verb (Perfect)	Verbal Noun
ŗállim (*he taught*)	**taŗlíim** (pl. **taŗlimáat**) *teaching, instruction*
ŗáakis (*he quarrelled*)	**miŗáksa** (pl. **miŗaksáat**) [1] *quarrelling, quarrel*

[1] There is a tendency among educated speakers to use **mu-** for **mi-** as the prefix in verbal nouns of this form, cf., too, **muʃáwru** *consultation.* The loan-word **munáwra** *manoeuvre* exhibits the same pattern.

Verb (Perfect)	Verbal Noun
Siɛtáraf (*he confessed*)	Siɛtiráaf (pl. Siɛtirafáat) *confessing, confession*
Sinfágar (*it exploded*)	Sinfigáar (pl. Sinfigaráat) *exploding, explosion*
Sistáɣlim (*he inquired*)	Sistiɣláam (pl. Sistiɣlamáat) *inquiring, inquiry*
Sikkábbar (*he was self-satisfied*)	takábbur *self-satisfaction*
Sitfáahim (*he came to an understanding (with)*)	tafáahum *understanding*

Note

There is no Sit- form corresponding to Sinfigáar.

In the derived forms characterized by gemination of the second radical, by the infixation of long aa, and by the infixation of t, the verbal nouns of weak verbs end in -iya, -ya, and -a respectively, e.g. tasníya *seconding, supporting* (sánna, yisánni *to second, support*), minádya *calling* (náada, yináadi to call), Sibtída (Sibtáda, yibtídi *to begin*). The verbal noun of weak verbs is only common in these forms. The consonant y appears in the verbal noun of hollow verbs when in the form derived by the infixation of t, e.g. Sixtiyáar *electing, election* (Sixtáar, yixtáar to elect).

The verbal nouns of the "colour" verbs and quadriliteral verbs are of the patterns illustrated by Siḥmiráar *turning red, blushing* (Siḥmárr, yiḥmárr *to redden, blush*) and laxbáṭa *muddling, muddle, confusion* (láxbaṭ, yiláxbaṭ *to muddle, confuse*).

In accordance with the rule that a noun may not be defined more than once, when the verbal noun governs either two nouns or a pronominal suffix and a noun then the particle li must be included between the two; e.g. ḍárbu l-ilɛiyáal b-iʃʃaklída muʃ kuwáyyis *his beating the children like that isn't right*, kitábt (< kitáaba) ilwálad l-iggawáab yámda giddan *the boy's writing of the letter is completely illegible*.

Certain verbal nouns of the simple form are similar to collective nouns in that they may be suffixed with -a and -aat when reference is to the number of times an action is performed, e.g. ḍarábtu ḍárba gámda Sáwi *I gave him a really terrific blow*, ḍarábtu tálat ḍarbáat ɛala wiʃʃu(h) *I hit him three*

times on his face. In this intensive use the verbal noun usually
follows a given tense-form of the same root.

Further examples of the verbal noun are as follows :

xad wáſtí ţawíil fi ſamálha laţíifa b-iſſaklída (verbal noun
ſámal) *he took a long time to make it* (f.) *as nice as that,* fíh máaniſ
min ſuſáadi hína ? (ſuſáad) *is there any objection to* (or *do you
mind*) *my sitting here ?,* ſana-smiſtí ſan muſablítku maſa
báſd (muſábla) *I heard of your meeting* (or *that you had met*) *each
other,* ma baḥíbbíſ migíyyu hína-ktíir (migíyy) *I don't like him*
(or *his*) *coming here a lot,* ſilmáſyí-f wúşţ iſſáariſ xáţar ſaléek
(maſy) *it's dangerous (for you) to walk in the middle of the road,*
huwwa miſtímid ſala-msaſdíthum lú(h) (musáſda) *he's
counting on them* (or *their*) *helping him,* ma fíſ fáyda m-ilgidáal
(gidáal) *it's no use arguing.*

THE PHRASE- AND CLAUSE-MARKERS ſilli AND ſinn

ſilli usually introduces an adjectival (relative) phrase, less
commonly a nominal one ; ſinn introduces a subordinate
nominal clause only.

ſilli

ſilli is to be seen within the total context of " definition " (see
above). By joining either of the sentences biyízſal bisúrſa *he
loses his temper quickly* or yistaḥáſſ ittarſíya *he deserves promotion* to huwwa ráagil *he is a man* we obtain the new sentences
huwwa ráagil biyízſal bisúrſa *he is a man who loses his temper
quickly* and huwwa ráagil yistaḥáſſ ittarſíya *he is a man who
deserves promotion,* in the English translation of which the relative *who* is required to introduce the qualifying phrase. Now,
if the same original sentences are joined to huwwa-rráagil *he is
THE man,* then ſilli is necessary in Arabic, i.e. huwwa-rráagil
illi-byízſal bisúrſa *he is the man who loses his temper quickly* and
huwwa-rráagil illi yistaḥáſſ ittarſíya *he is the man who deserves
promotion.* ſilli is necessary if the preceding noun is defined.
This is reminiscent of noun-adjective agreement with and without the article as in ráagil ţawíil *a tall man,* on the one hand, and
ſirráagil iţţawíil *the tall man,* on the other ; compare similarly
şaḥibna-lmáşri *our Egyptian friend* and şaḥibna-lli tiſrafúuh
our friend whom you know (*him*).

In fact, ſilli, the definite article ſil, and other such
" definers ", occur in different, that is mutually exclusive,

grammatical contexts. Ṣilli introduces an adjectival (relative) *phrase*, which, in the corresponding indefinite context, either (i) begins with a verb or (ii) consists variously of a prepositional phrase or an adverb. The verbal form biygálli, for example, behaves adjectivally in, say, ráagil biygálli *a man saying his prayers*, which should be compared with fíih ráagil biygálli *a man is saying his prayers* (or *there is a man saying his prayers*) and, more particularly for the present purpose, with the definite Ṣirráagil illi biygálli *the man* (*who is*) *saying his prayers*. Parallel to the difference between ráagil biygálli (indefinite) and Ṣirráagil illi biygálli (definite) is that between, say, ráagil ɛa-lbáab ɛáyzak (indefinite) *a man at the door wants you* and Ṣirráagil illi ɛa-lbáab ɛáyzak (definite) *the man at the door wants you*, in which ɛa-lbáab is a prepositional phrase qualifying ráagil.

In certain contexts not only the presence or absence of the article with the noun but also a difference of prepositional particle in the prepositional phrase relates to the indefinite-definite distinction. It is possible for Ṣirráagil illi min máṣr (definite) *the man from Cairo* to correspond to ráagil min máṣr (indefinite) *a man from Cairo* but the more usual definite form is Ṣirráagil bitaɛ máṣr, in which bitáaɛ marks the definite nature of the adjectival phrase in the same way as min characterizes the indefinite min máṣr. A similar distinction to that between min and bitáaɛ holds between bi and Ṣábu/Ṣumm in, say, wálad bi báltu (indefinite) *a boy in a coat* and Ṣilwálad abu báltu (definite) *the boy in a coat*; Ṣábu is used when the antecedent is masculine, as in the example given, while Ṣumm relates to a feminine context, e.g. Ṣissáaɛa-lfáḍḍa Ṣummi Ṣástik gild *the silver watch with a leather strap*.

The vocative context, marked by the vocative particle ya, should be specially noticed. It has been said that a noun may not be defined more than once and this is borne out in the vocative example ya wálad ya ṭawíil *I say, the tall young man there !*, wherein the occurrence of ya excludes the definite article, cf. Ṣilwálad iṭṭawíil *the tall young man*. In the case of noun + adjectival phrase, however, not only is ya repeated before each element in the manner required by the definite concord pattern but also Ṣilli, bitaɛ, or Ṣabu remain to mark the phrasal nature of the second element, e.g. ya ráagil ya-lli bitʃálli [1] *I say, the man there saying his prayers !*, ya wálad ya ʈawíil ya-lli-hnáak *I say, the tall young man over there !*, ya ráagil ya-btaɣ máʂr *I say, you from Cairo !*, ya wálad y-abu báltu *I say, the boy in the coat !*

To sum up, attention should be paid particularly to difference of grammatical types as follows :

Indefinite	*Definite*	*Definite-Vocative*
ráagil ʈawíil	ʕirráagil iʈʈawíil	ya ráagil ya ʈawíil
ráagil biyʂálli	ʕirráagil illi biyʂálli	ya ráagil ya-lli bitʂálli
ráagil min máʂr	ʕirráagil bitaɣ illi min }máʂr	ya ráagil ya-btaɣ ya-lli min }máʂr
ráagil bi báltu	ʕirráagil abu báltu	ya ráagil y-abu báltu

The above patterns are to be distinguished from that of the nominal sentence and of the sentence pattern comprising definite noun + verb :

ʕirráagil ʈawíil	*the man is tall*
ʕirráagil biyʂálli	*the man is saying his prayers*
ʕirráagil min máʂr	*the man is from Cairo*
ʕirráagil bi báltu	*the man is in a coat*

In fiih-type sentences it is the indefinite noun-adjective phrase which follows fiih :

fih ráagil ʈawíil gúwwa	*a tall man is inside*
fih ráagil biyʂálli gúwwa	*a man is saying his prayers inside*
fih ráagil min máʂrī gúwwa	*a man from Cairo is inside*
fih ráagil bi báltu gúwwa	*a man in a coat is inside*

ʕilli is also used without a preceding noun and in the manner of English *he who, those who, that which* to introduce a nominal phrase or clause, e.g. ʕilli ɣandúhum filúus ɣandúhum nufúuz *those with money have influence*, háat illi fiih, ma ɣaléhʃ *never mind* (= ma ɣaléhʃ), *fetch what there is*, háat wáaḥid m-illi (= min + ʕilli) fóoʔ iʈʈarabéeza *bring one of those (which are) on the table*, xúd ill-ínta ɣáyzu(h) *take what you want*. It is similarly used following the interrogative particles miin and ʕeeh, as in míin illi wáaʃif hináak ? *who is that standing over there ?*, ʕéeh illi ɣáawiz tiɣráfu(h) ? *what is it (that) you want to know ?* and, following the demonstrative pronoun, as in dá-ll-ana ɣáwzu(h) *that's what I want*.

With a definite antecedent, including demonstratives, the use of the 3rd person pronominal forms húwwa/híyya/húmma

---

[1] Notice the *2nd* person verbal form.

in association with following ξilli characterizes a type of nominal
sentence which is to be contrasted with the adjectival phrase.
Compare ξilξálam húwwa-lli ḍáaʒ *it's the pen which has been lost*
and ξilξálam illi ḍáaʒ *the lost pen*, also ʒiyáal ḥásan húmma-lli
bárra *it's Hasan's children (who are) outside* and ʒiyáal ḥásan
illi bárra *(those of) Hasan's children (who are) outside*. Contrast
should also be made between sentence types with and without (húwwa/etc. + ξilli), for example between the above
ξilξálam húwwa-lli ḍáaʒ and ξilξálam ḍáaʒ *the pen has been lost*.
The two patterns are used in somewhat different circumstances ;
ξilξálam ḍáaʒ would as a rule open a conversation, while its
counterpart containing huwwa-lli would tend to be contrastive
and to constitute a reply to another speaker. Other examples
illustrating (húwwa/etc. + ξilli) in association with a preceding
demonstrative, pronominal and adjectival, are da húwwa-lli
ḍarábni *he's* (or *that's*) *the one who hit me*, ξilbéet da húwwa-lli
kúnna sakníin fiih (or da-lbéet illi kúnna sakníin fiih) *that's the
house we used to live in*.

A number of examples in the preceding paragraphs have
contained an important feature already illustrated without
comment elsewhere but particularly common in association
with adjectival phrases, both definite and indefinite. A " conjoint " relationship between the noun and its qualifying phrase
is indicated by the presence in the phrase of a pronominal suffix
agreeing with the noun ; the same device may also serve to link
sentence-clauses. The presence or absence of the pronominal
suffix often corresponds to such an English difference as that
between, on the one hand, *whom* and *whose* and, on the other,
who. " Conjoint " relationship covers the case of, say, ʃahr and
ismu in biyḥíggu-f ʃáhr ismu-lḥúgga *they go on pilgrimage in a
month called* (lit. *its name is*) *Al-Hugga*, as well as those of
ʒarabíyya and ṭalabtáha in ξilʒarabíyya-lli ṭalabtáha maw-
gúuda ? *is the car I asked for ready?*, and of waξt and fiih in ξéeh
ξánsab wáξtī ξáξdar aʃúufu fiih ? *what's the best time (at which)
I could see him ?* Further examples are :

Indefinite

zuhriyyáat ʒaléeha náʃʃ *engraved flower-vases* (lit. *flower-
vases on them* or *on which engraving*), fiih wáaḥid bárra ʒándu
ʃákwa *there's someone outside with a complaint*, ξúlli ʒala táman

kúllī ḥáaga-ʃtarétha *tell me the price of everything you bought,*
ɛandína ʃúylī-ktiir lazim niɛmílu(h) *we've a lot of work to do,*
ḥaʃtíri-ʃwáyyit ḥagáat abɛátha hadáaya-l Ɛaṣḥáabi *I'm going to
buy a few things to send as presents to my friends,* fiih sanadliƐ
búṣṭa maxṣúuṣa maktúub ɛaléeha *"mustáɛgil"* *there are
special post-boxes marked "Express"* (or *with "Express"
written on them*).

Definite

ṣáḥbi-lli béetu f-ilḥáyy iggidíid *my friend whose house is in the
new quarter,* Ɛahó-rráagil illi Ɛultílak ɛaléeh *there goes the man
I told you about,* Ɛáadi-rragil ill-ínta ɛáwzu(h) *there's the man you
want,* ɛágabak ikkitáab illi warretúulak imbáariḥ ? *did you like
the book I showed you yesterday ?*

Ɛinn

The nominal clause introduced by Ɛinn *that* occurs most
frequently as a subordinate object-clause following one of a
series of verbs including simiɛ, yísmaɛ *to hear,* Ɛiftákar, yiftikir
or ẓann, yiẓúnn *to think, believe,* ʃaaf, yiʃúuf *to see,* ɛirif, yiɛraf
to know, Ɛaal, yiƐúul *to say,* xaaf, yixáaf *to fear,* e.g. simiɛt inni
ɛáli (ḥa)yíwṣal búkra *I hear(d)* (*that*) *Ali is arriving to-morrow,*
Ɛaftíkir inn ilwálad ráaḥ ilbéet *I think the boy went home,*
Ɛaẓúnn inni ɛandúhum filúus kitiir *I think they've got a lot of
money,* nífriḍ inni ma ɛátʃi fiih *let's suppose there isn't any more.*
Ɛinn is followed, where appropriate, by the pronominal
suffixes, not by the independent pronouns ; e.g. Ɛaftíkir innu
raḥ ilbéet *I think he went home,* Ɛaftíkir innak ɛáarif ill-ána
ḥaƐulúulak *I think you know what I am going to say to you,*
huwwa biyƐúul innu-tnáƐal lakin aftikir innu-tráfad *he says he's
been transferred but I think he's been dismissed,* huwwa ɛayyáan
b-ilḥáṣba w-ana xáayif innu yiɛd-axúuh iṣṣuyáyyar *he's got
measles and I'm afraid he'll give it to* (lit. *infect*) *his young(er)
brother.* The demonstrative pronoun may be similarly suffixed
to Ɛinn as in Ɛana ma kúntiʃ ɛáarif innída kan ittartiib *I didn't
know that was the arrangement.*
Ɛinn also occurs after a few impersonal verbs such as yíẓhar
in, say, yíẓhar inni fih fáyda mínnu(h) *it seems there's some
point in it,* but, although post-verbal occurrence of Ɛinn is by
far the most frequent circumstance, it is nevertheless possible

for the particle to occur without a preceding verbal form [1]; e.g. ʕana mabṣúuṭ innak géet *I'm pleased you came*, ʕinta mutaʕákkid innak muʃ ɣáwzu(h) ? *are you sure you don't want it ?*, múʃ min ilmuħtámal innu ħayÍigi hína búkra *it's unlikely he'll come here to-morrow*, ʕilʕáħsan innína-nrúuħ bádri *it's best for us to go early*, ʕilʕimáan maɣnáah inn ilwáaħid yiʕáamin bi-lláah *the meaning of faith is that one believes in God*, muhímmi ʕáwi-nni kúlli wáaħid yítbaɣ niẓáum ilɲurúur *it is very important that everyone should (or for everyone to) follow the rule of the road*, ʕilɣaráaba-nni ma fíiʃ ʃákk innak bitʕúul ilħáʕʕ *the extraordinary thing is that there's no doubt you're telling the truth*.

NEGATION

The means of negation are:

(1) a negative particle variously pronounced muʃ or miʃ *not* which precedes the word, phrase, or clause negated;

(2) a "split" negative (of the French *ne ... pas* type) in which a particle ma precedes and ʃ is suffixed to the word negated;

(3) la ... wala ... *neither ... nor ...*

These particles are distributed as follows:

(1) is used

    (i) with nouns, adjectives, participles, adverbs, prepositional phrases, clauses, etc., and especially within the framework of the nominal sentence; e.g. múʃ ilwálad- *not the boy*, múʃ bi súɣɣa kída *not so fast*, múʃ min ixtiṣáaṣi *it's not (of) my responsibility*, ʕana miʃ fáahim da b-izẓábṭ *I haven't understood that properly*, ʕiħna fúʕara, miʃ aɣníya *we're poor, not rich*, múʃ bassi kída *that's not all* or *not only that*, ʕiggazmáadi miʃ ɣala ʕáddi *these shoes don't fit me*, ʕilħukúuma w-iggéeʃ múʃ ḍiddi báɣḍ *the government and the army are not opposed to one another*, ʕilʕúuṭa di lissa xáḍra-ʃwayya, miʃ mistiwiyya *this tomato is still a bit green, it's not ripe*, di muʃ ill-ana ɣáwzu b-izẓábṭ *this isn't exactly what I want*, di miʃ ʕáwwil márra-tʕúlli ɣaláada *this isn't the first time you've told me about it*.

    (ii) with the verbal auxiliaries of participial form, e.g. ɣáawiz, láazim, múmkin; e.g. muʃ ɣáawiz táakul ?

[1] *sc.* tense-form.

don't you want to eat ?, **muʃ láazim tiʃtiri** *you don't have to buy*, **muʃ múmkin óʈlaɛ ðúwaʃti** *I can't come out now.*

(iii) with a following imperfect prefixed with **ḥa-**, e.g. **miʃ ḥáʃdar aʃúufak búkra** *I'm not going to be able to see you to-morrow*, **ʃin ma-ʃríbtiʃ iddáwa, miʃ ḥatxiʃʃ** *if you don't take the medicine, you won't get better*, **ʃinnáas ilmadɛiyyiin miʃ ḥayáklu-w yiʃrábu-w húroma ʃaɛdʃin** *the guests aren't going to eat and drink standing up.*

(2) is used

(i) with verbal forms other than the imperfect prefixed with **ḥa-**, e.g. **ma-tɛúʃʃi ʃáktar min arbiɛíin kíilu f-issáaɛa** *don't drive at more than 40 kilometres an hour*, **ma-txáʃʃ ! ma yiʃdúrʃ yidḥak ɛaláyya** *don't worry, he can't get the better of me*, **ma-ʃtikirʃ innak ḥatilʃáaha ʃáɛba** *I don't think you'll find it difficult*, **ma-ʃdírtiʃ áagi f-ilmaɛáad** *I couldn't arrive on time*, **da suʃáal ana m-aʃdárʃ agáawib ɛaléeh** *that's a question I can't answer*, **ma gatlúuʃ ɛiláawa ɛaʃan ma-byiʃtayálʃi-kwáyyis** *he hasn't had a rise* (lit. *a rise has not come to him*) *because he doesn't work well*, **ʃúllu ma-ygíiʃ táani** *tell him not to come again.*

Notes

(a) There is no special imperative form in the negative context; the appropriate imperfect forms are used.

(b) **ʃ** is always last in a group of suffixes added to a verbal form. As in the case of other suffixes, the addition of **ʃ** implies the lengthening of a preceding vowel, e.g. **ma katabúuʃ** either *they didn't write* or *he didn't write it*; contrast **ma katabúuʃ** with **ma katabúhʃ** *they didn't write it.* The "extra" vowel will frequently appear before **ʃ** in order to obviate a sequence of three consonants, e.g. **ma rúhtiʃ** *I didn't go.*

(c) A maximum of three suffixes—excluding those of the tenses—may be added *en bloc* to a given form. Such a block consists of (pronominal suffix + (li + pron. suff.) + ʃ) and is illustrated by **ma baɛathaaliiʃ** *he didn't send it* (fem.) *to me*, of which **ma baɛatháaʃ liyya** is an alternative form. The second alternative containing the independent (li + suffix) form is essential in some contexts, probably for rhythmic reasons, e.g. **ma raggaɣháaʃ líyya** *he didn't return it to me* (not *ma raggaɣhaaliiʃ).

(*d*) ʃi is sometimes heard for ʃ before pause, e.g. **ma waʕʕaɣháaʃi** or **ma waʕʕaɣháaʃ** *he didn't drop it* (fem.). Further research may establish a connection between ʃi and feminine contexts but for practical purposes ʃ may always be used.

(*e*) The forms **gaa** and **guu** for geh and gum are used with ʃ as with other suffixes, e.g. **ma gáaʃ** *he didn't come, hasn't come*, **ma gúuʃ** *they didn't come, haven't come*.

(*f*) In the perfect tense of doubled and weak verbs, **-at-** not **-et-** appears in negative forms containing pronominal suffixes, e.g. **ʕana/ʕinta ma ḥabbatúuʃ** *I/you* (m.s.) *didn't like it*, **ʕinta ma kawatúuʃ** *you haven't ironed it*.

    (ii) with verbal auxiliaries other than those at (1) (ii), i.e. both those of verbal form, as **yímkin, yigúuz,** and also **bidd-, nifs-, ʕaṣd,** and **ɣáraḍ,** e.g. **ma yimkínʃi ḥáddi yúdxul min ɣéer tazkára** *no one can go in without a ticket,* **ma-yguzlákʃ** *you may not,* **ma biddúuʃ yiráwwaḥ** *he would rather not go home.*

    (iii) with the pronominally suffixed particles **ɣand, maɣa, li,** and **fi,** e.g. **ma ɣandínáaʃ wáʕti-ktiir** *we haven't much time,* **ma-mɣáhʃi-flúus yídfaɣ táman ilʕákl** *he hasn't any money to pay for (the price of) the meal,* **da ma lúuʃ máɣna xáaliṣ** *it doesn't make* (lit. *it hasn't any*) *sense at all,* **ʕilʕóoḍa ma fiháaʃ ʃababíik kifáaya ɣaʃan ittahwíya** *there aren't enough windows in the room for ventilation.*

Notes

(*a*) Of the particles which, pronominally suffixed, so frequently translate English *to have,* **ɣand, maɣa,** and **li** are associated with **ma -ʃ,** and so contrast with **wayya,** which is negated with **muʃ** (or **miʃ**), i.e. **míʃ wayyáaya** *I haven't (got it),* not *ma wayyayaaʃ.

(*b*) With **maɣa** and **li, ii** is used in the first pers. sing. negative, i.e. **ma-mɣíiʃ, ma líiʃ** (contrast **maɣáaya** and **líyya**); **maliyyáaʃ** occurs, but rarely.

(*c*) The vowel of the particle is elided in **ma l(a)háaʃ, ma l(i)kíiʃ, ma l(u)húmʃ, ma l(u)kúmʃ, ma l(i)náaʃ, ma m(a)ɣíiʃ, ma m(a)ɣákʃ, ma m(a)ɣakiiʃ,** etc.

(d) **ma ɣaléhʃ** *never mind, it doesn't matter* is an example of a
form which occurs only in the negative ; other examples
are the impersonal verbals **ma-yhímmiʃ** *it doesn't matter, it's
unimportant,* **ma-yṣúḥḥiʃ** *it's impossible.* Notice, too, the
use of ma **ɣadʃ** (pronounced ɣatʃ) and ma **ɣadítʃ** in, say,
ma **ɣátʃí ṭiih** *there isn't any more,* **ʕikkóora ma ɣadítʃí
bitnúṭṭi-kwáyyis** *the ball doesn't bounce properly any longer.*

(iv) as the negative form of **ṭiih** *there is/are,* e.g. **ma ṭiiʃ
máɣna-l lintiẓáar** *there's no point in waiting,* **ma ṭiiʃ
luzúum l-izzáɣal** *there's no need to be angry* (lit. *for
anger*), **ma ṭiiʃ** *there isn't any,* **ma ṭiiʃ ɣandína** (or **ma
ɣandínáaʃ**) **béeḍ l-ilṭuṭúur** *we haven't any eggs for
breakfast.*

Note

No **h** is pronounced in the negative form **ma ṭiiʃ** corresponding
to the affirmative **ṭiih.** **ma ṭiiʃ ḥáddí f-ilbéet** and **ʕilbéet ma
ṭihʃí ḥádd** *there's nobody in the house* mean the same but are not
equivalent grammatically ; in the second example **h** is necessary
in agreement with **beet** in the same way as **haa** was required in
the earlier example of **ʕilʕóoḍa ma ṭiháaʃ ʃababiik kifáaya
ɣaʃan ittahwiya** *there aren't enough windows in the room for
ventilation.*

(v) with examples of all the above four categories, when
compounded with **kaan, yikúun** ; it is **kaan, yikúun**
that takes ma **-ʃ,** e.g. **ma kánʃí-byiʃtáɣal ɣandína ?**
didn't he used to work for us ?, **ma kúntiʃ úɣraf
innúhum ʃuṭṭáar zayyï kída** *I didn't know they were as
clever as that,* **ma kúntiʃ ɣáawiz arúuḥ** *I didn't want to
go,* **ʕana ʕáasif ma kanʃí mumkínn-agi-mbáariḥ** *I'm
sorry I couldn't come yesterday,* **ma kánʃí-mɣaaya wála
wáḥda** *I didn't have a single one on me,* **ʕaḥyáanan ma
biykúnʃí ṭiih** *as a rule there isn't any.*

Note

In conditional sentences (see above), either **kaan** or the
following verb may take ma **-ʃ,** e.g. **ʕiza ma kúntiʃ tiigi búkra,
ḥaddíilu-lṭilúus,** or **ʕiza kúntï ma-tgíiʃ,** etc., *if you don't come
to-morrow, I'll give him the money.*

(vi) as an alternative to **muʃ** (or **miʃ**), with the independent
pronouns. These negative pronouns, written as single

forms, are as follows ; notice particularly the use of **ii**
in the 1st pers. sing. form and the existence of
alternative forms for the 3rd pers. sing. masc. and fem. :

	Singular		*Plural*
3rd pers. masc.	mahuwwáaʃ (or mahúuʃ)	3rd pers.	mahummáaʃ
3rd pers. fem.	mahıyyáaʃ (or mahíiʃ)		
2nd pers. masc.	mantáaʃ	2nd pers.	mantúuʃ
2nd pers. fem.	mantíiʃ		
1st pers.	maníiʃ	1st pers.	mahnáaʃ

Examples are **mantiiʃ gáyya-** (or **gáaya-**) **mṛáana ?**
aren't you (fem.) *coming with us ?*, **mántaʃ ṛáamil záyyi
ma baʃúllak ?** *aren't you going to do as I tell you ?*, but
alternative forms **muʃ ínti**, etc., and **muʃ ínta**, etc., are
possible and, indeed, **muʃ** + pronoun is far more
generally used than the " split " negative forms above.

(3) contains a negative particle **la** in the negative alternative
construction corresponding to English *neither . . . nor . . . .*
wa is prefixed to every **la** after the first and the number of
words, phrases, or clauses which may be preceded by the
particle is not limited to two. Examples are **láada** (= **la**
+ **da**) **waláada lakin dúkha** *neither this nor this but that*,
la-ɣáyyar wala-kbíir ʃáwi lakin mutawáɔɔit *neither too*
(lit. *very*) *small nor too big but average*, **la haṭʃúuf wala
tismaɣ** *you'll neither see nor hear*, **la binzáwwid wala
binnáɔɔaɣ, kaláınna wáahid** *we don't put our prices up or
down, we have fixed prices* (lit. *our speech is one*), **ma kánʃi
yíɣraf yíʃra wala yiktib** *he could neither read nor write*, **la
géh ɣandína f-ilmáktab wala ʃáabil ilmudíir wala háddi
ʃáaʃu xáaliɣ** *he's neither been to us* (here) *in the office nor met
the manager, nor has anyone seen him at all.*

It is possible for **ʃ** to be suffixed to a verbal form after the
first as in **la katábti f-iggaráayid wala ɣamáltiiʃ xúṭab** *I've
neither written for* (lit. *in*) *the press* (lit. *papers*) *nor made
speeches*; it is also possible for the first negative to be of
the **ma -ʃ** type, i.e. **ma katábtiʃ f-iggaráayid wala ɣamáltiʃ
xúṭab.**

Notes

(a) The particle **la** occurs sporadically elsewhere, as in **láa ʃéeʕ** *nothing*, **la ʃákk innak bitʕúul ilḥáʕʕ** *no doubt you're telling the truth*, and is conceivably identifiable (together with **ʃ**) as part of the unitary form **baláaʃ** as in **baláaʃ ḥíyal** *no tricks !*, **baláaʃ kaláam** *no* (or *stop*) *talking !*

(b) **la** may be compared with **laʕ** *no* ; cf. **ḥatiigi walla láʕ ?** *are you going to come or not ?*, **miʃ ɣáarif leh láʕ** *I don't know why not*. **laʕ**, when used for emphatic disagreement, often has the form **laa**, e.g. **láa, láa, ʕábadan** *no, no, never !*

(c) Do not confuse **wala** with **walla** *or* nor **la** with the comparatively rare emphatic particle **la** in **ʕúskut, l-aḍrábak !** *be quiet or I'll hit you !* Note the use of **wala** in, say, **ma-mɣiiʃ wala wáḥda** *I haven't a single one on me*.

Words commonly associated with negation

(i) **ḥadd** *anyone* and **ɣumr** *life* (+ pronominal suffix) occur in negative contexts either unaffixed or themselves affixed with **ma -ʃ**; unaffixed **ḥadd** is generally associated with **ma ʃiiʃ**: e.g. **ɣúmri ma ʃúftiʃ wáaḥid záyyu(h)** or **ma ɣumriiʃ ʃúfti wáaḥid záyyu(h)** *I've never seen anyone like him*, **ma ʃiiʃ ḥáddi yiɣraf yiɣmílu(h)** or **ma ḥáddiʃ yiɣraf yiɣmílu(h)** *nobody knows how to do it*.

(ii) **ʕilla** (less commonly **ɣeer**) *except* and **lissa** (*not*) *yet, still* are never themselves negated but frequently occur in negative contexts, e.g. **liḥáddi dilwáʕti ma-tkallimnáaʃ ʕilla ɣa-ssiyáasa** *up to now we haven't talked* (*about anything*) *except politics* (or *we've only talked about politics*), **ma ḥáddiʃ yiɣraf yiʕra xáṭṭi ɣéeri ʕána** *nobody can read my writing but me*, **lissa ma ɡáaʃ** *he hasn't come yet*, **géh walla lissa ?** *has he come yet or not ?*

(iii) Also common in negative contexts is **ḥáaga** (*any*)*thing* and its more emphatic counterparts **wála ḥáaga** and **ʕáyyi ḥáaga**, e.g. **ma-fhimʃi ḥáaga** *he didn't understand anything*, **ma-fhimʃi wála ḥáaga** *he didn't understand anything at all*, **ma gabliiʃ ʕáyyi** (or **wála**) **ḥáaga** *he didn't bring me a thing*. **wála ḥáaga** *nothing* may be used independently as in A. **zaɣláan léeh ?** B. **wála ḥáaga.** *A. What are you cross about ?* *B. Nothing.*

Emphatic negation

The term " emphatic negation " is reserved for the use of **ma** without **ʃ**. **ʃ** is omitted in emphatic exclamatory contexts such as **yaréetu ma ráaḩ** *I wish he hadn't gone*, **ɣúmri ma ʃúftī wáaḩid záyyu(h)**, which is a more emphatic form of the earlier **ɣúmri ma ʃúftīʃ wáaḩid záyyu(h)** *I've never seen anyone like him*, but omission occurs most frequently in association with' the " oaths " (**ḩulfáan**) ; the commonly occurring " oaths " are **wall&áahi** (lit. *and my God*), **w-innábi** (*and the Prophet*), **wi rabbína** (*and our Lord*), to which may be added for the present purpose **ʕinʃálla** (derived from **ʕin ʃáaʔ alláah** *if God wishes*) in the specialized use with a following perfect tense illustrated hereafter : thus, **láa wall&áahi m-áʕdar** or **láa w-innábi m-áʕdar** or **láa wi rabbína m-áʕdar** *no, by heaven, I can't*, **ʕinʃálla ma ḩáddī kál** *may nobody ever eat, then !*, **ʕinʃálla ma rúḩt** *go or not, as you please !*

Notes

(*a*) The " oaths " have greater variety, power, and binding force outside the towns and among less sophisticated townsmen. From sophisticated speakers, the above examples with **wall&áahi**, etc., mean little more than *I really can't*. The above use of **ʕinʃálla** is always associated with considerable displeasure and is more frequent in the speech of women.

(*b*) **la wálla** is a very common alternative to **láa wall&áahi**.

(*c*) Negative **ma** is not to be confused with a rather rare particle **ma** used with an imperative sense as in **ma titkállim** *speak up ! say something !*

INTERROGATION

It is often assumed that interrogation relates exclusively to the seeking of information but it should be remembered that the term is a grammatical one and that in general usage interrogative sentences may not only serve to elicit information but also be in the nature of suggestions (*what about having something to eat ?, wouldn't it be better if . . . ?*), exclamations (*really ?, what did I tell you ?, is it as late as all that !*), threats (*are you going to do as I tell you ?*), gestures of politeness (*can*

I help you ? (shop assistant), *may I give you some water ?*), requests for instructions (*shall I phone them or what ?*) or for advice and help (*do you think . . . ?, could you possibly . . . ?*), and so on. It may be that between Arabic and English such linguistic functions do not correspond; thus, ʕitfáḍḍal ʃáay may be reasonably translated *may I give you some tea ?* but is not interrogative in Arabic, and wálla *really ?* is much more of an exclamation (*you don't say so !*) than a question: in general, however, correspondence of function may be established between the two languages. Thus, for example, suggestions and requests for instructions tend to be associated not only with 1st person verbal forms in the imperfect without -ḥa (ʕarmiihum walla ʕéeh ? *shall I throw them away or what ?*) but also with introductory 2nd person forms tiḥibb and tiigi, as in tiḥibbí nitʕáabil yom lárbaʕ iṣṣúbḥ ? *shall we meet on Wednesday morning ?* (lit. *do you want . . .*), tiigi nistaḥámma ? *shall we go for a swim ?* (lit. *will you come . . .*). Similarly, an introductory tismaḥ/tismáḥi/tismáḥu meets the requirements of politeness in, say, tismaḥ tiwalláʕli *can I trouble you for a light ?*, tismaḥ áʕil ilbáab *do you mind if I close the door ?*, while tiftikir at the head of the sentence marks what follows as a question seeking advice or information, e.g. tiftikir aʕúllu ʕéeh ? *what ought I to say to him, do you think ?*, tiftikir fiih fárʕI ben láhgit máṣr w-iskindiriyya ? *is there any difference, do you think, between the speech of Cairo and Alexandria ?*

An Arabic sentence, affirmative or negative, may also be used as a question by varying the intonation. Compare the way in which the English sentences *he is the man I saw yesterday* and *is he the man I saw yesterday ?* differ. A questioning rise of the voice on *yesterday* corresponds to a similar feature at the end of Arabic interrogative sentences but in Arabic there is no difference of word-order as that between *he is* and *is he*. Get an Egyptian to say to you, both as statements and as questions, biyikkállim ɡárabi-kwáyyis *he speaks Arabic well* and *does he speak Arabic well ?* and the corresponding negatives ma-byikkallímʃi ɡárabi-kwáyyis *he doesn't*, etc., and *doesn't he*, etc., and notice particularly what happens intonationally to -kwáyyis; then, as always, mimic the informant. Get him, too, to utter the sentence on a tone of surprise or indignation, (*do you mean to tell me*) *he speaks/doesn't speak Arabic well ! ?* Here are some more examples to try out : ʃiʃtaréet irrádyu-btáaɣak b-ittaʕsíiṭ ? *did you buy your wireless on hire-purchase ?*, múmkin ḥágzǐ tazáakir muʕaddáman ? *can tickets be booked in advance ?*, tiɣraf ṭabíib ɣiyúun kuwáyyis ? *do you know a good oculist ?*, ɣandúku ṣabúun wiʃʃ ? *have you (got) any toilet soap ?*, ḥaykúun fih zawbáɣa ? *is there going to be a storm ?*, tiʕdar tifukkíli-gnéeh, min faḍlak ? *could you (please) change me a pound ?*, ma ɣandákʃ iggaríida-ṣṣabaḥíyya ? *haven't you got the morning paper ?*

We can put the earlier English question another way and say *he's the man I saw yesterday, isn't he ?*, in which the first part as far as *yesterday* is typically said as a statement, the rise of the voice taking place on *isn't he*. Egyptian Arabic does much the same thing with the very common muʃ kída (lit. *not so ?*) and says biyikkállim ɣárabi-kwáyyis, muʃ kída ? *he speaks Arabic well, doesn't he ?* The formula is reminiscent of others in European languages, cf. French " n'est-ce pas ", German " nicht wahr ", Spanish " (no es) verdad ". In English the device varies with the form of the verb in the first part of the sentence, e.g. *doesn't he, aren't you, haven't they, etc.* There is generally little difference of meaning between this use of muʃ kída and the less common device of prefixing muʃ to the sentence (cf. French " n'est-ce pas que . . ."), e.g. muʃ húwwa ragil ṭáyyib ? *isn't he a good man ?*, muʃ áḥsan inta tiɣmílu-b náfsak ? *wouldn't it be better if you did it yourself ?*

Another very common interrogative construction is with wálla *or* used to introduce an alternative and most frequently in the fixed formula walla láʕ *or not*. The sentence up to wálla has the interrogative (rising) intonation while from wálla on it has the typically declarative (falling) pattern. This is again paralleled in English. For example, húwwa-lli ʃúftu-mbáariḥ walla láʕ ? *is he the one you/I saw yesterday or not ?*, húwwa-lˡi ʃúftu-mbáariḥ walla káan fih wáaḥid táani ? *is he the one you/I saw yesterday or was it someone else ?*, ʕinta fáaḍi walla maʃyúul dilwaʕti ? *are you free or busy now ?*, ɣáayiz ʕáhwa sáada walla-b súkkar ? *do you want coffee with or without sugar* (lit. *unsweetened or with sugar*) ?, géh walla líssa ? *has he come yet or not ?*

The range of possibilities represented in English by (i) *he comes from Cairo, does he ?* (response on first being informed,

sc. so he comes from Cairo), (ii) *he comes from Cairo, doesn't he ?*
(seeking confirmation), and (iii) *he doesn't come from Cairo,
does he ?* (incredulous) corresponds to Arabic (i) baʕa húwwa
min mɑ́ṣr (non-interrogative), (ii) either miʃ húwwa min mɑ́ṣr ?
or húwwa min mɑ́ṣr, miʃ kída ?, and (iii) huwwa miʃ min
mɑ́ṣr, walla ʕéeh ? walla ʕéeh in (iii) is frequently pronounced
on a low level pitch of the voice.

The prefixation of sentences with the independent pronouns
of the third person is a common interrogative device, the pronoun being followed by a noun with which it agrees, e.g. huww-
axúuk gáyy innɑhɑ́rdɑ ? *is your brother coming to-day ?*, hiyya-
lʔilúus ilmasmúuḥ bliha mawgúuda-ʃ gawáaz issáʔar bitáaɡi ?
is the currency allowance stated in my passport ?, humma-
lʕagáanib biyiḥtáagu vîiza ɡaʃan yidxúlu mɑ́ṣr ? *do foreigners
need a visa to enter Egypt ?* Before a pronoun of persons
other than the third, húwwa is used as a neutral form, e.g.
matzaɡɡáʕʃi kida ! huww-an-ɑ́ṭraʃ ? *don't shout so ! I'm not deaf*
(lit. *am I deaf ?*).

Sometimes, but not often, an interrogative sentence is
characterized by the suffixation of ʃ (not to be confused with
negative ʃ) to verbs, fîih, ɡand + pronominal suffix and
similarly suffixed particles, e.g. ʃúftiʃ duséeh ɡa-lmáktab ? *did
you see a file on the desk ?*, ɡándakʃi sagáayir ? *have you any
cigarettes ?*, ɡúmrakʃi ʃúfti liɣbit kóorɑ ? *have you ever seen a
game of football ?*

In answer to negative questions, ʕáywa *yes* and laʕ *no* are
often used in a way misleading to English speakers, affirming
or denying the form of the question rather than the facts. For
example, in reply to ma rúḥtiʃ ? *didn't you go ?* may be heard
ʕáywa, ma rúḥtiʃ *no, I didn't* or láʕ, rúḥt *yes, I did*. laʕ for
ʕáywa and vice versa is, however, possible.

Specific interrogative particles

Interrogative sentences are also marked as such by the
presence of one of a series of specific interrogative particles
which are as follows : ʕeeh *what*, leeh *why*, feen *where*, minéen
whence, ʕimta *when*, ʕayy (also ʕánhu/ʕánhi/ʕánhum) [1] *which*,

---

[1] Elsewhere ʕayy and ʕánhu/etc. = *any*, but ʕánhu is comparatively rare ; cf. xúd ʕáyyi (or ʕánhu) -ktáab ɡáyzu(h) *take any
book you want.*

ʕizzáay how, kaam how much, many, ʕáddī ʕéeh (or ʕaddéeh) how far, how much, to what extent, miin who.

The typical unemphatic order of the following sentences containing these particles is an inverted one in relation to English : bitiʕmil éeh ? what are you doing ?, ʕikkilmáadi maʕnáaha ʕéeh ? what does that word mean ?, ʕinta ʕayyáan bi ʕéeh ? what's the matter with you ? (sc. what are you suffering from ?), ma-byiʃtayalúuʃ léeh ? why aren't they working ?, (ʕinta) ráayiħ féen ? where are you going ?, ʕagíib rúxga l-irrádyu-mnéen ? where do I get a wireless licence ?, ħatúxrug imta ? when are you going out ?, ʕiyátt (or ʕiyáadit) idduktúur bitiftaħ imta ? when does the doctor's surgery open ?, ʕinta ʕáwzu-b ʕáyyī lóon ? what colour do you want it ?, ħatiʕmil iʃʃúrba-zzáay min ʕéer láħma walla-xḍáar ? how are you going to make soup without meat or vegetables ?, ʕiʃtaréetu-b káam ? how much did you buy it for ?, ʕilʕárḍ ittáani ħayibtídi-ssáaʕa káam ? what time (lit. the hour how many) does the next performance start ?, ʕilħisáab ʕala miin ? who's going to pay (lit. the bill on whom) ?

Prepositional (adverbial) phrases, however, tend to follow the interrogative particle, e.g. naʕáltī ʕimta min ʃaʕʕitak ilʕadíima ? when did you move out of your old flat ?, fíkrak éeh f-innáas dóol ? what do you think of those people ?, ʕáalu ʕéeh f-innáʃra-ggawwiyya ? what was the weather forecast (lit. what did they say about, etc.) ?, ʕinnahárda káam f-iʃʃáhr ? what's the date to-day ?, ʕixtáaru káam wáaħid li mubaráat ilbuṭúula ? how many have they seeded for the (tennis) championship ? Dependent clauses similarly follow the interrogative particle in, say, garálku ʕéeh bitzaʕʕáʕu [1] wayya báʕḍ ? what's the matter with you shouting at one another (like that) ?, xáttī (> xadt) ʕaddī ʕéeh ʕaʃan titʕállim iʃʃuʕláadi ? how long did you take to learn the job ?

The placing of the interrogative particle at the head, e.g. féen huwwa ? where is he ?, léeh baṭṭáltu-ʃʃúʕl ? why have you (pl.) stopped work ?, often gives an emphatic turn to the sentence. This is not, however, the whole story. There would seem, for example, to be a tendency to place, say, feen before the definite phrase in féen ʃibbáak ittazáakir ? where is the booking-office ? or féen báab málʕab issábaʕ where is the entrance to the race-course ? or, again, féen litnáaʃar ginéeh salliftúhúmlak

[1] Pronounced bidz-.

min zamáan ? *where are the twelve pounds I lent you some time ago ?* ; none of these examples are more emphatic in tone than, say, **ſilſaʂanʂéer féen ?** *where is the lift ?* or **ſaláaſi fákka féen ?** *where can I get change ?* Contrariwise, the placing of **ſeeh** at the head of **ſééh illi-btiʒmílu(h) ?** *what are you doing ?* not only involves the necessary inclusion of **ſilli** but once again is more emphatic than its counterpart **bitiʒmil ééh ?** Any such emphatic flavour is absent, however, from the following examples, in which the particle is regularly placed at the head of the sentence, **ſeeh ſáħsan lukúnda f-ilbálad di ?** *what's the best hotel in this town ?*, **ſééh ſanwáaʒ illáħma-lli ʒandúkum ?** *what have you got in the way of meat* (lit. *what (are the) kinds of meat, etc.*) *?*, **ſééh iʈʈúʒm illi biʈʂíd bíih ?** *what bait do you use* (lit. *hunt,* sc. *fish, with*) *?*

Sentences with the specifically interrogative particles most frequently have the (falling) intonation of the declarative sentence. This is also so in English ; contrast *when did he come ?* and *did he come ?* The falling pattern is by no means the only possibility for the specifically interrogative sentence in either English or Arabic but, broadly, there is a similarity of intonational usage between the two languages. Commonly enough, however, one hears examples of a pattern sounding very foreign to English ears ; herein the final interrogative particle is pronounced on a monotone (no rise or fall) and on a higher pitch than the preceding syllable : **bitiʒmil ééh ?** uttered in this way may be represented graphically – ̅ –.

Those interrogative particles which are used pronominally are, of course, often preceded by prepositional particles, cf. **ʒamáltí kída ʒalaʃan ééh ?** *why* (lit. *for the purpose of what*) *did you do so ?*, **bitittíkil ʒala míin ?** *whom do you count on ?* Derivationally, it may be noted, **leeh = li + ſeeh, feen = fi + ſeen, minéen = min + ſeen.**

A few points of grammatical detail concerning individual members of the list of interrogative particles remain to be made. Word-order is sometimes relevant to the particle **miin** when associated with 3rd pers. sing. verbal forms. In colloquial Arabic word-order is fixed in noun-verb-noun sentences such as **ʒáli ʃáaf maħámmad** *Ali saw Mohamed,* **maħámmad ʃáaf ʒáli** *Mohamed saw Ali* ; similarly, **miin** in **míin ʃáaf ?** *who saw ?* is marked as the subject of the verb by the fact that it immediately precedes the verbal form : contrast ʃáaf míin ? *whom did he see ?*, in which míin is marked as the object by its occupation of immediate post-verbal position.   This position is generally reserved for the object ; thus, with the typical interrogative sentence order already noted above, we may find ʃáafu míin ? *who saw him ?*, in which míin follows the verb but not immediately and is thus in subjective relation to it.   There is an' alternative form to the earlier ʃáaf míin ? *whom did he see ?*, viz. míin illi ʃáafu(h) ?, which is, in fact, ambiguous and might also mean *who saw him ?* ; ʕilli may optionally be included after subjective míin, e.g. míin illi kátab ittaʕríir da ? *who wrote this report ?*, míin illi wáaʕif hináak ? *who's that standing over there ?*, míin illi middíik ʕiznī tímʃi ? *who gave you permission to go ?* The inclusion of ʕilli is the rule in participial (nominal) sentences of the kind illustrated in the last two examples but is not essential before verbal tense forms, cf. míin (illi) ʕállak inn-ána miʃ ráayiḥ ? *who told you I'm not going ?*

kaam requires a following noun in the singular, e.g. ḥatistánna kam yóom ? *how many days are you going to stay ?*, baʕáalak kam sána-f máṣr ? *how many years have you been in Egypt ?*, ʕiṭṭayyáara di-btáaxud káam ráakib ? *how many passengers does this plane take ?* In the sense of (pronominal) *how many* notice the association of kaam with wáaḥid as in ʕixtáaru káam wáaḥid ? *how many have they picked ?*

ʕánhu/ʕánhi/ʕánhum *which* behaves like the ordinal numerals in that it may precede or follow the noun it accompanies with similar implications as to the presence or absence of the definite article : if ʕánhu precedes, the noun does not take the article ; if it follows, the article is included.   Thus, ʕánhu-ktáab ? or ʕikkitáab ánhu ? *which book ?*, cf. táalit kitáab or ʕikkitáab ittáalit *the third book*.   If the sentence is extended, then the second pattern (with the article) requires ʕilli, the first does not, i.e. either ʕánhu-ktáab ɣáyzu(h) ? or ʕikkitáab anhú-ll-inta ɣáyzu(h) ? *which book do you want ?*, cf. táalit kitáab fi dóol or ʕikkitáab ittáalit illi-f dóol *the third one among those books*. ʕayy may not be used pronominally in the way of ʕánhu in, say, ʕanhú-ll-inta ɣáyzu(h) ? *which one do you want ?*, cf. ʕáyyi wáaḥid in, say, ʕáyyi wáaḥid ɣáyzu(h) ? *which one do you want ?*

The form ʕizzáyy, not ʕizzáay, is used in the common greetings formulae ʕizzáyyak, ʕizzáyy iɡɡíḥḥa, ʕizzáyy ilḥáal *how are you ?*, ʕizzáyy ilʕéela ? *how's the family ?*, etc.

EXCLAMATIONS AND "OATHS"

(a) The following exclamations (kilmáat ilʕistiɣráab) are common: ṣubḥáan alláah !, (ʃéeʕ) ɣaríib !, (ʃéeʕ) ɡaɡíib !, (ʃéeʕ) múdhiʃ !, yáa saláam !, ʕálla(h) !, ʕéhda or déhda !, fíih ʕéeh !, gára ʕéeh !, yígra ʕéeh ! The English equivalent of a given example will depend on the context and, to some extent, on individual taste. Selection may be made from *what !, well !, indeed !, well, I never !, fancy !, good heavens !, great Scott !, good lord !, bless my soul !,* etc.

Not only difference of intonation but also difference of association with other words will contribute to considerable difference of meaning for otherwise similar forms ; for example, **ya saláam** is associated with **ɡala dámmak** in the exclamation of disgust or disapproval **ya saláam ɡala dámmak, ya ʕaxi !** roughly *what an unpleasant fellow you are !* but with **ɡala kída** in the exclamation of approval **ya saláam ɡala kída !** *how delightful !* The introductory particle **ya** is found quite commonly in exclamations, cf. **ya ḥaláawa !** *how nice !,* **ya-xṣáara !** *what a pity !,* **ya ḥáwl l-illáah !** *what a loss !* (said on hearing of the death of a highly respected person).

Other common exclamations are : **ɡáal, ɡáal !** *excellent !,* **wálla(h)** or **láʕ, ya ʃéex !** *really !, you don't say !,* **ɡéeb ɡaléek !** *shame on you !,* **ḥaráam ɡaléek !** *shame on you !* (in religious matter), **ʕamma . . .** *what a . . . !,* as in **ʕamma ráagil !** *what a man !,* **ʕamma ḥárr !** *isn't it hot !, what heat !* **ʕaɡúuzu b-illáah,** roughly *oh dear !,* is used as an exclamation of disapproval or displeasure ; thus, for example, **ʕaɡúuzu b-illáah mínnak, ya ʕaxi !** *may God preserve us from you !* is an alternative to the earlier **ya saláam ɡala dámmak, ya ʕaxi.** **ʕiʃmíɡna** in, say, **ʕiʃmíɡna kída !** also relates to disapproval or surprise, i.e. *why do you do that ?* or *how can you say that ?* There seems to be little or no difference of meaning between **ʕiʃmíɡna kída !** and **léeh baʕa !** (notice in passing the very common colloquial form **báʕa,** which corresponds to the English parenthetic *then* at the end of sentences, e.g. *come on, then, let's see what you're made of, then*).

Finally, notice the exclamatory **yaréet** as in **yarétni rúḫt !** *if only I had gone !*

(b) The " oaths " (**ḥulfáan**) are often used for exclamation or emphasis, e.g. **walláahi-lṛaẓíim !** *good lord !*, **walláah-inta muʃ kuwáyyis !** *how very unpleasant you are !*, **walláah-ana ṛandi ḥáẓẓ !** *I'm indeed lucky !*

The " oaths " as such, i.e. to vouch for the truth of what is said, vary according to the educational standard and geographical origin of the speaker. Educated speakers use **walláahi-lṛaẓíim, walláahi,** and **w-innábi,** as in **walláahi-lṛaẓíim ma ʃúftu(h)** *I swear I didn't see him,* but the unsophisticated, especially in the countryside, use a greater range. They may, for example, swear to divorce or on the life of a member of the family as in **wi-ḥyáat íbni** *on my son's life* or **wi-ḥyáat abúuya** *on my father's life,* or local saints may be invoked as, for example, in the Cairene **wi-ḥyáat sayyídna-lḥuséen** or **wi-ḥyáat issayyída zéenab.** Such oaths are not, of course, used indiscriminately without reference to the personal background of the speaker. Only a married man with a son may swear by his son's life and swearing to divorce or on the good name of one's family are only used by married men as in the very strong oaths **ṛaláyya-ṭṭaláaʕ b-ittaláata !** or **ṛaláyya-lḥaráam min béeti !** For the single man, **walláahi-lṛaẓíim !** is the strongest oath.

The oaths as such have virtually no binding force among educated people to-day ; in contrast, however, if the Bedouin swears to divorce his wife unless his guest continues to eat, then he may well do so in the event of the guest's refusal. Embarrassment, not to mention discomfort, is generally avoided on such occasions by a nice interchange of " oaths ", but the rules of the game are only known to the initiated. The non-Arab is strongly advised not to use the oaths except in their exclamatory function and then to limit himself to educated usage ; he is otherwise almost certain to offend or, at best, to amuse the Arabic speaker.

IV. USEFUL SENTENCES AND VOCABULARY

PASSPORT FORMALITIES

Vocabulary [1]

passport	gawáaz issáfar, gawazáat issáfar ; pagpóor, pagsporṭáat [1]
passport office	ʕidáarit iggawazáat
embassy	sifáara, sifaráat
consulate	ʕunṣuliyya, ʕunṣuliyyáat
passport section	qism iggawazáat, ʕaqsáam iggawazáat
permit	taṣríiḥ, taṣriháat
visa	taʃʃíiro, taʃʃiráat ; vííza, vizáat
entry permit/visa	taṣríiḥ/taʃʃíira b-idduxúul
exit permit/visa	taṣríiḥ/taʃʃíira b-ilxurúug
transit permit	taṣríiḥ b-ilmurúur
residence permit	taṣríiḥ b-ilʕiqáama
stay	ʕiqáama
length of stay	múddit ilʕiqáama
temporary residence	ʕiqáama muʕaqqáta
permanent residence	ʕiqáama daaʕíma
the reason for the visit	ʕilyáraḍ min izziyáara
business trip	ríḥla l-ittigáara
holiday trip	ríḥla l-ilfúsḥa/l-issiyáaḥa
personal matters	masáaʕil ʃaxṣíyya
family matters	masáaʕil ɛaʕilíyya
stamp	ṭáabiɛ, ṭawáabiɛ
fiscal stamp	wáraʕit dámya
consular (fiscal) fees	rásm iddámya
date of the passport's expiry	taríix intiháaʕ ilpagpóor
(an) official	muwázzaf, muwazzaḟíin
abroad	f-ilxáarig
to get a passport	ṭállag, yiṭállag [1] pagpóor ; ʕistáxrag, yistáxrag gawáaz issáfar

[1] Both singular and plural forms of nouns are given where appropriate, and in that order. Verbs are given in the 3rd person singular masculine forms, first in the perfect tense, then in the imperfect.

to take out a new passport	xád, yáaxud paspóor gidlíd
to surrender the old passport	sállim, yisállim ilpaspóor ilʕadlím
to examine passports	ʃáaf, yiʃúuf gawazáat issáʕar
to grant an entry visa	ʕídda, yíddi taʃʃíirit idduxúul

Sentences

Do foreigners need a visa to enter Egypt / Syria / Iraq / Lebanon / Morocco ?	(ʕúlli min fáḍlak) humma-lʕagáanib biyiḥtáagu víiza ʒaʃan yidxúlu máṣr/súrya/ilʒiráaq/ libnáan/murráakiʃ ?
When can I collect my passport ?	ʕímta ʕáaxud paspóori ?
Please fill in these two forms and sign them.	min fáḍlak ʕímla-ṭṭalabéen dóol w-imḍíihum.
You need two photographs for your visa.	yilzámlak/lazímlak/láazim tigíib [1] ṣurtéen ʒaʃan ilvíiza.
What is your purpose in visiting Egypt ?	ʕéeh ilɣáraḍ min ziyártak li máṣr ?/ɣáraḍak ʕéeh min ziyáarit máṣr ?
How long may I stay in the country ?	ʕáʕdar astánna ʕaddéeh (or ʕaddī ʕéeh) f-ilbiláad ?
Ninety days with a tourist visa.	tisʒíin yóom bi víizit issiyáaha.
I am only travelling through the country.	ʕana ɣáawiz amúrri f-ilbiláad báss.
I need a transit visa.	ʕana miḥtáag(a) li taʃʃíirit murúur.
You must have an entry and an exit permit.	labúddī lík min taʃʃíirit duxúul wi taʃʃíirit xurúug.
Must I get a permit to stay (to take up work) ?	yilzámli taʃʃíirit ʕiqáama (ʒa(la)ʃan aʃtáɣal hináak) ?
I want a tourist visa.	ʕana ɣáawiz taʃʃíirit siyáaha.
I would like to apply for a three months' extension of this visa.	min fáḍlak ɣawiz (áktib ṭálab ʒaʃan) amídd ittaʃʃíira díyya tálatt úʃhur.
You must have your passport renewed.	láazim tigáddid gawáaz issáʕar bitáaʒak.
Your visa is valid until 31st October.	ʕittaʃʃíira-lli-mʒáak ga(a)líḥa-l listiɡmáal liɣáayit wáaḥid wi talatíin uktóobar.
Can I get a residence visa ?	mumkin ʕáaxud, law samáḥt, taʃʃíirit ʕiqáama ?

[1] The oblique stroke is used between alternative possibilities.

I wish to live and work in Egypt for some time; would you please inform me of the steps to take.

ſana ʒáawiz aʒíiʃ w-aʃtáɣal fi máṣri múdda. tísmaḥ tiſúll(i ſ)aʒmil ſéeh.

Is the currency allowance stated in my passport?

ḥiyya-lſilúus ilmasmúuḥ bíiha mawgúuda-ſ gawáaz issáſar bitáaʒi P/huwwa-ttaṣríiḥ bi ſáxdi-flúus mawgúud fi gawáaz issáſar bitáaʒi P

The passport officials will board the train at the frontier (-post).

ſilmuſattiʃíin ḥayiṭláʒu ſ-ilſáṭri ʒandi núſṭit ilḥudúud.

Have your passports ready.

gahhízu gawazáat saſárkum.

Your passport is in order.

gawáaz sáſarak maʒbúuṭ.

There is a stamp missing in your passport.

fih ṭáabiʒ náaſiṣ fi paspóorak/ paspóorak náſṣu(h) ṭáabiʒ.

Please hand in your passports.

min ſadlúku sallímu gawazáat saſárku.

Where is the British/American Consulate?

ſéen ilſunṣuliyya-lſingiliziyya/ lſamrikiyya P

There is only a Vice-Consul in this town.

ma fiiʃ hína ſilla wakíil ſúnṣul báss.

What are the office hours of the passport department?

ſéeh mawaʒíid ſátḥi .máktab taſtíiʃ ilpasportáat P/máktab taſtíiʃ ilpasportáat biyíftaḥ min káam li káam P

How much does the visa cost?

taſʃíirit idduxúul/ilxurúug bit-kállif káam P

I wish to seek employment in Egypt. Could you help me?

ſana ʒáawiz aʃtáɣal fi máṣr. min ſádlak tiſdar tisaʒídni P

I would like to break the journey here for twenty-four hours.

ʒáawiz astánna hín-arbáʒa-w ʒiʃríin sáaʒa.

Do I need to report to the local police-station for a three days' stay?

lazim arúuḥ núſṭit ilbulíiṣ ilmaḥálli ʒalaʃan astánna tálatt iyyáam P

Full name of passport holder.

ſismi ḥáamil ilpaspóor b-ilkáamil.

Nationality at birth/at present.

ſalginsíyya[1] ʒand ilmiláad/ ſ-ilwáſt ilḥáaḍir.

Date and place of birth.

taríix wi maḥáll ilmiláad.

Profession.

ſalmíhna.

Condition (single/married/. widow(-er)).

ſalḥáala ligtimaʒíyya (ſáʒzab/ mutazáwwig/ſármal(a)).

---

[1] The form ſal for the definite article, rather than ſil, is felt to be more appropriate to the utterance of written language, especially when initial in the utterance.

Description :
  Face: colour of the eyes;
    nose; complexion.
  Hair.
  Distinctive marks.
  Height.
  Remarks.
  Signature in full.

ʕalʕawṣáaf ilgismíyya :
  ʕalwágh : lóon ilʒaynéen ; ʕal-
    ʕánf ; lóon ilbáʃra.
  ʕaʃʃáʒr.
  ʕalʒalamáat ilmumayyíza.
  ʕaṭṭúul.
  mulaḥaẓáat.
  ʕalʕimḍáaʕ b-ilkáamil.

CUSTOMS

Vocabulary

customs, custom-house	ʕiggúmruk
custom-bond	máxzan iggúmruk
customs regulations	ʕilqawaniin iggumrukíyya ; qanúun igga-máarik
customs officer	muwáẓẓaf iggúmruk, muwaẓẓaffin iggúmruk
customs inspector	mufáttiʃ iggúmruk, mufattiʃíin iggúmruk
customs duty	ʕiḍḍariiba-ggumrukíyya
dutiable articles	ʕilḥagáat ilmafrúuḍ ʒaléeha ḍariiba
luggage	ʒaʃʃ
tariff	ʕittaʒriifa-ggumrukíyya
clearance	tatmiim
luggage clearance	ʕittatmiim ʒa-lʒaʃʃ
goods clearance	ʕittatmiim ʒa-lbaḍáayiʒ
customs declaration	bayáan ilmuḥtawayáat [1]
tobacco	duxxáan
cigarettes	sagáayir
cigars	sagáayir zanúbya
perfume	ʒiṭr, ʒuṭúur
liquor, spirits	xumúur ; maʃrubáat ruḥíyya
camera	ʕáalit ittaṣwiir, ʕaláat ittaṣwiir ; kámira, kamiráat
watch	sáaʒa, saʒáat
smuggling	tahriib
smuggler	muhárrib, muharribíin
fine	ɣaráama
export/import licence	taṣriiḥ ittaṣdiir/listiráad
consular declaration	ʕiqráar ilqunṣulíyya

[1] Lit. " description of the contents ".

customs-free	xáali (xálya, xaiyíin) iḍḍariiba
to conceal	xábba, yixábbi
to levy duty	ḥáddid, yiḥáddid ḍariibit iggúmruk
to clear	(goods) xállaṣ, yixállaṣ (ḡala) ; (passport) támmim, yitámmim (ḡala)
to smuggle	hárrab, yihárrab

Sentences

Where is the custom-house ?	(Súlli min fáḍlak) Siggúmruk féen ?
Please place your luggage on the counter.	min fáḍlak ḥúṭṭi ḡáffak ḡala-lbánk.
Here is my suitcase.	ʃanṭit(i S)ahéh !
Will you examine my trunk, please.	tismaḥ tifáttiʃ ʃanṭiti (min fáḍlak).
Your turn next, have the keys ready please.	Siddóora ḡaléek, ḥáddar mafatiiḥak min fáḍlak.
Have you anything to declare ?	ḡándak ḥáaga min ilmamnuḡáat ?
Are you carrying any of the articles on this list ?	maḡáak ḥáaga m-illi f-ilSáyma di ?
The new customs tariff comes into force on the 1st July.	qanúun iggamáarik iggidíid ḥayitṭábbaS [1] min Sáwwil yúlya.
Have you any spirits, tobacco, new watches, or perfumes ?	maḡáak Sáyyi maʃrubáat ruḥiyya, walla (or Saw) duxxáan, walla saḡáat gidíida, walla ḡuṭúur ?
I have this small bottle of perfume.	maḡáaya-Sḍáaxit ilḡiṭr iṣṣuḡayyáru di.
This is free of duty.	di ma ḡalehá͟ʃ ḍariiba/di xálya-ḍḍariiba.
Is that all ?	xuláaṣ ?/fiih ḥaga tánya ?
You can close your suitcase.	táyyib, SiSál ʃanṭitak.
Is my luggage passed ?	ḡáfʃi xúluṣ ?
I have an import licence for these goods.	maḡáaya [2] taṣriiḥ istiráad b-ilbaḍáayiḡ di.
You can take delivery of the case of liqueurs ; it has been cleared.	tiSdar táaxud ʃánṭit ilxumúur ; xúluṣ taftiʃha.
Please get me a taxi and take the luggage to it.	hátli táksi min fáḍlak wi wáddil-ḡáfʃi da fiih.
You are fined for not having declared these articles.	laazim tidfaḡ varáama ḡaʃan ma Saḡlántiʃ ilḥagáat di.

---

[1] Pronounce ḥayiṭṭ-.
[2] If carried on the person, otherwise ḡándi.

TRAVELLING

TRAVELLING BY ROAD

Vocabulary

road travel	ſissáfar b-ilɀarabiyyáat
highway, road	ṭarſíſ, ṭúruſ ; síkka, síkak
motor-car	ɀarabíyya, ɀarabiyyáat ; sayyáara, sayyaráat ; ſuṭumbíil, ſuṭumbiláat [1]
private car	ɀarabíyya malláaki, ɀarabiyyáat malláaki
hired car	ɀarabíyyit ilſúgra
taxi	táksi, taksiyyáat
coach, motor-bus	ſutublíis, ſutubisáat
overland coach	sayyáarit irriḥláat
lorry	lúuri, luriyyáat
truck	ɀarabíyyit náſl, ɀarabiyyáat náſl
van	ɀarabíyya muyláqa ; ɀarabíyya maſfúula ; ɀarabíyya búks
motor-cycle	mutusíkl, mutusikláat
gharry	ḥanṭúur,[2] ḥanaṭíir
two-wheeled trap	karétta, karettáat
bicycle ; wheel	ɀágala, ɀagaláat, ɀagal [3]
racing bicycle	ɀágalit sábaſ (or sibáaſ)
tandem	ɀágala mígwiz
moped	ɀágala buxxaríyya
cart	ɀarabíyya kárru, ɀarabiyyáat kárru
tram	ṭurmáay, ṭurmayáat
driver	sawwáaſ, sawwaſíin
conductor	kumsáari, kumsaríyya
cyclist	ráakib ɀágala
three cyclists	taláata rakbíin ɀágal
body	háykal (pl. hayáakil) ilɀarabíyya
chassis	ſasée(h), ſaseháat ; gísm issayyáara
bonnet	yáṭa-lɀídda, yuṭyáan ilɀídad
hood	kabbúud, kababíid
mudguard	ráfraf, rafáarif
wheel	ɀágala, ɀagaláat
hub	míḥwar, maḥáawir
tyre	kawítſ, kawitſáat

[1] In this and certain other sections below will be found a fairly large number of loan-words from European languages.
[2] Or ḥanṭúur.
[3] A collective form.

inner tube	kawítʃ guwwáani
rim	ṭáara, ṭaráat
brake	farmála, faráamil
gear-lever	vitíss
gear	tirs, turúus (or tirúus)
gear-box	ẓílbit ittirúus
gear-change (bicycle)	náaʕil itturúus
steering-wheel	diriksiyóon ; ẓágalit ilqiyáada ; ẓágalit issiwáaʕa
exhaust	ʕumbúubit ilẓáadim, ʕanablíib ilẓáadim ; ʃakmáan, ʃakmanáat
battery	baṭṭaríyya, baṭṭariyyáat
accelerator	baddáal ilbanẓíin
carburettor	karburitéer, karburiteráat
starting-handle	manafílla, manafilláat
windscreen wiper	masáaḥit ilʕizáaz
speedometer	ẓaddáad issúrẓa
self-starter	márʃi ʕutumatiik
bumper	ʕaksidáam, ʕaksidamáat
horn	nifíir, nifiráat
windscreen	ʕizáaz iʃʃibbáak
crankshaft	ẓamúud ikkiránk
ball-bearings	bily
ball-bearing race	kúrsi-lbíly
handlebars	gadóon, gadunáat
straight/dropped handlebars	ʕiggadóon ilẓídil/ilmaẓwúug
saddle	kúrsi, karáasi
pedal	bidáal, bidaláat
chain	ganzíir, ganazíir
fork	furʃ (ilẓágala)
frame	háykal ilẓágala ; mawasíir [1]
crossbar	ʕilmasúura-lʕuddamaníyya
spoke	silk, ʕisláak
bell	gúras, ʕigráas
carrier	kúrsi warráani, karáasi warraníyya
front lamp	lámba ʕuddamaníyya
rear lamp	lámba warraníyya
spare parts	qíṭaẓ ilyiyáar
spare wheel	ẓágala-stíbn
tools	ẓídad (sing. ẓídda)
tool-bag	ʃánṭit ilẓídad
jack	jaak, jakáat

---

[1] Lit. " tubes, pipes ".

pump	munfáax, manáaſix
screwdriver	mifákk ilſalúuwiʒ
hammer	ʃakúuʃ, ʃawakiiʃ
pincers	kammáaʃa, kammaʃáat
pliers	ʒarradíyya, ʒarradiyyáat
spanner	muftáah iʒʒawamíil
adjustable spanner	muftáah ingiliizi
repair	taʒlíih, taʒliháat
puncture	xurm ; xurſ, xurúuſ
patch	rúſʒa, rúſaʒ
solution	sirisyóon
fuel	waqúud
petrol	banʒiin
oil (lubricating-)	zeet (ittaʃhíin)
water	máyya
distilled water	máyya-mſaṭṭáru
petrol pump	ṭurúmbit ilbanʒiin, ṭurumbáat ilbanʒiin
petrol station	maháṭṭit ilbanʒiin, mahaṭṭáat ilbanʒiin
garage	garáaʒ, garaʃáat
lorry crane (or winch)	winʃ illúuri
speed limit	hádd issúrʒa
pot-hole	maṭább, maṭabbáat ; háfra, háfar (or hufráat)
collision	taʒáadum
accident	hádsa, hawáadis
level-crossing	muʒliſáan, muʒliſanáat
to drive	saas, yisúuʒ
to start up	dáas, yidúus ʒa-lmáʃi ſutumatiik
to overtake	ʒádda, yiʒáddi
to brake	ʃármil, yiʃármil
to slow down	hádda, yiháddi
to accelerate	dáas, yidúus banʒiin
to stop	wiſif, yúſaf (or yiſaf)
to park	rákan, yírkin
to repair	ʒállah, yiʒállah
to collide	ʒáadim, yiʒáadim
to run over	daas, yidúus
to somersault	ſitʃáʒlib (or ſiʃʃ-), yitʃáʒlib
to overturn	ſinſálab, yinſílib
to tow away	garr, yigúrr
to go uphill	ṭíliʒ, yíṭlaʒ ilʒilwáaya
to go downhill	nísil, yínʒil
to ride a bicycle	rikib, yírkab ʒágala
to cycle, go by bicycle	ráah, yirúuh b-ilʒágala

to pedal   báddil, yibáddil
to pump up a tyre   náfax, yínfux ilẓágala

Sentences

I have a tourer/saloon/sports car.
Ɛana ẓándi ẓarabíyyit makʃúufa/ ẓarabíyya ṣalúun/ẓarabíyyit sábaɛ (or sibáaɛ).

Do you own a car?
Ɛinta ṣáaḥib ilẓarabíyya?

My car is a two-seater.
ẓarabiyyíti-b kursiyyéen.

Who is going to drive to-day?
míin ḥaysúuɛ innahárda?

Have you got your driving-licence with you?
maẓáak rúxṣit issiwáaɛa?

Hadn't we better let the hood down? It is getting hot.
míʃ níftaḥ (or niʃíil) ikkabbúud áḥsan? Ɛiddínya ḥarrárit.

Look out for the bends, otherwise we shall skid.
xúd báalak min iddawaranáat, láḥsan nizzáḥlaɛ (or nidz-).

Did you see the traffic-lights?
ʃúfti ẓalamáat ilmurúur?

You have to pay a fine for speeding.
láazim tídfaẓ ɣaráama ẓalaʃáan súrẓit issiwáaɛa.

The traffic policeman has taken our number.
ẓaskári-lmurúur xád nímrit ẓarabiyyítna.

I had a breakdown on my last trip to Suez.
ẓarabiyyíti-tẓaṭṭálit w-ana ráayiḥ issuwées ilmárra-lli fáatit.

We've a puncture in one of the front wheels, but there's a spare.
fíih xúrmi-f wáḥda m-ilẓagaltéen ilɛuddamaniyyíin, lakin fíih ẓágala-stíbn.

The tool-box is under the seat.
sandúuɛ ilẓídad taḥt ikkúrsi.

If you are going to town I can give you a lift.
Ɛiza kútti ráayiḥ máṣr, Ɛáɛdar awaṣṣálak.

Switch on the headlights.
wállaẓ ikkaʃʃaʃáat.

You ought to change gear.
láazim tiɣáyyar issúrẓa.

Where can I park my car?
Ɛáɛdar árkin ẓarabiyyíti féen min fáḍlak?

The car park is over there.
máwɛaf ilẓarabiyyáat hináak aho(h)!

Where can I get this car repaired?
Ɛáɛdar aṣállaḥ ilẓarabíyya dí féen?

There is a garage around the corner.
fíih garáaʃ baẓd iddawaráan.

Where is the nearest petrol-station?
féen áɛrab maḥáṭṭiṭ banzíin?

I must fill up with petrol and check the tyre-pressures.
Ɛana láazim ámla-lẓarabíyya ban-zíin w-ákʃif ẓala-lẓágal.

How much are you going to charge for washing my car ?	táaxud (or ɣáawiz) káam fi ɣasíil ilɣarabíyya ?
Street signs :	ʕiʃaráat (or ɣalamáat) ilmuráur :
Slow.	háddi-ssúrɣa.
One-way street.	ṭariiq b-ittigáah wáaḥid.
Speed limit : 80 kilometres.	ḥádd issúrɣa : tamaníin kelumítr.
Slow. Major road ahead.	ḥáaðir.[1] ʕiṭṭaríiq ilmuqáabil húwa-rraʕíisi.
Halt.	qif !
Street repairs (roadworks).	tasˡíiḥ iṭṭaríiq.
Diversion.	taḥwíid.
Crossroads.	taqáaṭuɣ.
I'm fond of cycling.	ʕana baḥíbbi-rkáub ilɣágal.
Are your brakes in working order ?	ʕilfaráamil bitáɣtak bitiʃtáɣal kuwáyyis ?
Yes, but the chain is a bit loose.	ʕáywa, lakin igganzíir miráxrax ʃuwayya.
You were riding on the pavement, you'll have to pay a fine.	ʕinta kútti máaʃi b-ilɣagala ɣa-rraṣíif, láazim tídfaɣ ɣaráama.
I must pump the tyres up.	ʕana láazim ʕánfux ilɣágala.
I've a puncture in my back tyre and shall have to mend it.	ɣagálti-lwarraníyya maxrúuʕa, láazim aʕalláhha.
The front wheel is out of centre.	ʕilɣágala-lʕuddamaníyya maɣwúuga.
I have to renew my licence for another year.	lazim agáddid rúxṣit ɣagálti li múddit sána tánya.
I prefer the straight handlebar to the dropped one.	ʕan-afáḍḍal iggadóon ilɣídil ɣan iggadóon ilmaɣwúug.
The brakes are worn.	ʕilfaráamil xasráana.
You can cycle on the by-path.	tiʕdar tímʃi b-ilɣágala ʕ-iṭṭaríiʕ igganíbi.
The road to the farm is full of pot-holes.	ʕiṭṭaríiʕ illi ráayiḥ ilɣízba malyáan maṭabbáat.
You have to unfasten the bag from the carrier.	lazim tifúkk iʃʃánṭa min ɣala-kkúrsi.
No cycling !	mamnúuɣ rukáub iddarragáat húna ![2]

---

[1] These signs belong to the written language and contain many features peculiar to it. Pronounce ð as *th* in " the ".

[2] Written language.

TRAVELLING BY RAIL

Vocabulary

rail travel	ſissáſar b-issíkka-lḥadíid
railway	ſissíkka-lḥadíid
transport	naſl ; wasáaſil innáql
station	maḥátta, maḥattáat
train	ſatr, ſutúra (or ſuturáat)
freight train	ſátr ilbiḋáaga
express train	ſilſiksibrées ; ſissarííg
slow train	ſilſaſſáaſ
diesel train	ſiddíizil
inquiry office	máktab listiglamáat
booking office	ſibbáak ittazáakir [1]
fare	ſúgra
ticket	tazkára, tazáakir
platform ticket	tazkárit raglíf
ticket collector	kumsáari, kumsaríyya
waiting room	ḥúgrit lintiẓáar/ſistiráaḥa
buffet	buſée(h)
restaurant	mátgam, matáagim
cloak-room, left-luggage department	ſilſamanáat
lavatory	dóorit ilmáyya
platform	raglíf, ſargíſa
signal	ſiſáara, ſiſaráat
goods van	garabíyyit ilbiḋáaga
coach, carriage	garabíyyit irrukkáab, garabiyyáat irrukkáab
compartment	galóon, galonáat
seat	kúrsi, karáasi
corner corridor-seat	ſikkúrsi-lli-gámb ilmamárr
corner window-seat	ſikkúrsi-lli gámb iſſibbáak
sleeping-car	garabíyyit innóom
dining-car	garabíyyit ilſákl
engine	wabúur, waburáat
engine-driver	sawwáaſ ilſagr
stoker, fireman	gatáſgi, gataſgíyya
signalman	miḥwálgi, miḥwalgíyya
stationmaster	náazir ilmaḥátta, nuẓẓáar ilmaḥattáat
ticket inspector	muſáttiſ, muſattiſſin
guard's van	sibínsa [2]

[1] Lit. " ticket-window ".
[2] The last carriage in any train is called sibínsa.

porter	ʃayyáal, ʃayyallíin
soot	hibáab
smoke	duxxáan
rail	ʕadiib, ʕudbáan
railway-sleeper	falánka, falankáat
tunnel	náfaʕ
arrival	wuʂúul
departure	ʕiyáam
speed	súrʕa
the 9.40 express	ʕiksibrées issáaʕa ʕáʃra-lla tílt
to reserve seats	ḥágaz, yiḥgiz tazkára f-ilʕáṭr
to lean out of the window	ṭall, yiṭúll min iʃʃibbáak
to get into the train	ríkib, yírkab ilʕáṭr
to get out of the train	nízil, yínzil min ilʕáṭr
to get out while the train is going	nízil, ʾyínzil w-ilʕáṭrì máaʃi

Sentences

Where do I get a ticket ?	ʕaġiib tazkára-mnéen ?/féen ʃibbáak ittazáakir ?
Is the booking-office open ?	ʃibbáak ittazáakir maftúuḥ ?
Third return Cairo and a platform ticket, please.	tazkára ziháab wa ʕiyáab dáraga tálta li máʂr wi tazkárit raʂíif, min fáḍlak.
Are you travelling via al-Qanātir ?	ʕinta-msáafir ʕan ṭaríiʕ ilʕanáaṭir ?
Which is the shortest way from Cairo to Alexandria ?	ʕéeh ʕáʕʂar ṭaríiʕ min máʂrì l-iskindiríyya ?
What is the fare from Cairo to Suez ?	ʕilʕúgra káam min máʂrì l-issuwées ?/táman ittazkára káam min máʂrì l-issuwées ?/ʕittazkára-b káam min máʂrì l-issuwées ?
You have to pay a supplement on your ticket.	láazim tídfaʕ fárʕ [1] ʕala tazkártak.
Have your money ready.	ḥáḍḍar filúusak.
Can I break the journey ?	ʕáʕdar atxállif f-iṭṭaríiʕ ?
Where must I change ?	ʕaġáyyar féen ?
Where is the Station Hotel ?	féen lukándit ilmaḥáṭṭa ?
Where is the nearest hotel ?	féen áʕrab lukánda ?
Can you tell me if the train will be late ?	tíʕdar tiʕúlli min fáḍlak ʕiza káan ilʕáṭrì ḥayitʕáxxar walla láʕ ?

---

[1] Lit. " difference ".

Porter, please register this luggage to Shibin Al-Kawm.

ya ʃayyáal, min fáḍlak sággil ilɣaʃʃída li-ʃbiin ilkóom.

You will have to pay excess luggage on this trunk.

láazim tídfaɣ ʕúgra-zyáada ɣala-ssandúuʃ da.

Please bring the registration slip to me in the train.

min fáḍlak hátli wáṣl ittasgíil f-ilʕáṭr.

Please leave the suitcases in the left-luggage department.

min fáḍlak ḫúṭṭ iʃʃúnaṭ f-ilʕamanáat.

From which platform does the slow train start?

ʕilʕáṭr ilʕaʃʃáaʃ ḥayʕúum min ʕáyyï raṣíif?

Platform No. 4.

ʕirraṣíif nímra-rbáɣa.

I was lucky—I got a seat near the window with my back to the engine.

ʕana kútti maḥẓúuẓ —laʕéet kúrsi gámb iʃʃibbáak wi káan ḍáhri l-ilwabúur.

Did you reserve it?

kútti ḥágzu(h)?

All change!

kúll irrukkáab yiɣayyáru!

I have left my coat in the compartment.

ʕana síbt ilbálṭu-btáaɣi f-iṣṣalóon.

Where is the Lost Property Office?

féen máktab ilmafqudáat?/féen máktab ilḥagáat illi-tkun ḍáyɣa?

Where is the buffet?

féen ilbufée(h)?

Over there.

hináak aho(h)!

Is there a restaurant car on the train?

fíih ɣarabíyyit ʕákli f-ilʕáṭr?

The sleeping car is in the middle of the train.

ɣarabíyyit innóom fi wíṣṭ ilʕáṭr.

Arrival and departure times of trains are in the guide.

mawaɣíid ʕiyáam ilʕuṭuráat wi wuṣúlha f-iddalíil.

Here is the summer time-table.

dalíil ilʕuṭuráat f-iṣṣéef ahó(h).

I bought my ticket at a travel agency.

ḥagázt ittazkára min máktab issiyáaḥa.

Take your seats, please.

kúlli wáaḥid yúʕɣud fi makáanu(h), min faḍlúku(m).

Your suitcase is too large for the luggage-rack.

ʃanṭitak kibíira ʕáwi ɣala-rráff.

The big trunk goes in the luggage van.

ʕissandúuʃ ikkibíir láazim yirúuḥ ɣarabíyyit ilɣáṭʃ.

Don't lean out of the window.

ma-tṭúlliʃ min iʃʃibbáak.

How long do we stop here?

ʕilʕáṭri ḥayúʕaf hína ʕaddéeh?

You had better ask the ticket inspector when he comes to check the tickets.

ʕilʕáḥsan innak tíbʕa tísʕal ikkumsáari lamma yíigi yúṭlub ittazáakir.

TRAVELLING BY SEA

Vocabulary

sea travel	ʕissáfar b-ilbáḥr
port, harbour	míina, mawáani
steamship company	ʃírkit ilbawáaxir
passenger-boat	ba(a)xírat [1] irrukkáab
liner	ɣa(a)bírat [1] ilmuḥiṭáat
one-class liner	ba(a)xíra-b dáraga wáḥda
first class	dáraga ʕúula
second class	dáraga tánya ; sukáṇḍa
tourist class	dáraga siyaḥíyya
passage, crossing	ríḥla, riḥláat
bow	muqáddam ilba(a)xíra
stern	muʕáxxar ilba(a)xíra
hull	háykal ilba(a)xíra
fo'c'sle	ʕáɣla muqáddam ilba(a)xíra
mast	ṣáari, ṣawáari
anchor	mírsa, maráasi
cable	ḥábl ilmírsa
funnel	madxána, madáaxin
railings	suur ; darabzíin
deck	ḍáhr ilmárkib/ṣáṭḥ ilmárkib, ḍaháur/ṣuṭúḥ ilmárkib ; dekk
bridge	ʕódt [2] ilqiyáada
rudder	dáffa, daffáat
porthole	kúwwa, kuwwáat
gangway	síllim, saláalim
engine-room	ɣámbar ilɣídda
dining-saloon	máṭɣam
smoking-room	ḥúgrit ittadxíin
lounge, saloon	ṣalóon
1st class saloon	ṣalóon iddáraga-lʕúula
deck-chair	ʃizlíng (or ʃizlóon), ʃizlungáat
life-boat	ʕáarib innagáah, ʕawáarib innagáah
life-belt	ḥizáam innagáah, ʕiḥṃimit (or ḥizimit) innagáah
cabin	kablína, kabáayin
berth	siríir, saráayir
hammock	murgéeḥa, maragíiḥ
passenger	ráakib, rukkáab

[1] A somewhat literary form.
[2] Pronounced ʕoṭṭ.

captain	kábtin, kabáatin
sailor	baḩḩáar, baḩḩáara
stoker	ʒaṭáʃgi, ʒaṭaʃgiyya
steward	ʃarráaʃ, ʃarraʃíin ; xáaḏim, xádam
purser	ʒarráaf
harbour pilot	múrʃid ilmíina, murʃidíin ilmawáani
lighthouse	ʃanáar, fanaráat
tug-boat	raffáaʒ ʃirʃáad ilbawáaxir, raffaʒáat ʃirʃáaḏ ilbawáaxir
wake	mágra-lba(a)xíra
seasickness	duwáar ilbáḩr
to sail (depart)	ʃábḩar, yúbḩir [1]
to steer	wággih, yiwággih
to roll	ʃitmáayil, yitmáayil
to pitch	ʃitmárgaḩ, yitmárgaḩ
to book a passage	ḩágaz, yíḩgiz tazkára-ʃ márkib
to embark	ṭíliʒ, yíṭlaʒ ʒa-lmárkib/ríkib, yírkab ʒa-lmárkib
to disembark	nízil, yínzil min ʒa-lmárkib
to cast anchor	ráma, yírmi-lmírsa
to weigh anchor	ʃaal, yiʃíil ilmírsa

Sentences

Have you booked your passage ?	ḩagázt ittazkára ʒa-lba(a)xíra ?
Which route are you travelling by ?	misáafir bi ʃáyyi ṭoríiʃ ?
When are you sailing ?	ʃilba(a)xíra-lli ḩatsáafir ʒaléeha ḩatíṭlaʒ ʃímta ?
I'm travelling first class.	ʃana-msáafir b-iddáraga-lʃúula.
This cargo boat takes some passengers.	márkib ilbiḏáaʒa dí-btáaxud (báʒḍ ir)rukkáab.
How many knots does she do ?	bitsáafir bi súrʒit káam ʒúʃda ?
This steamer is not one of the fastest, but she is very comfortable.	ʃilba(a)xíra dí míʃ min ʃásraʒ ilbawáaxir, láakin issáʃar ʒaléeha muríiḩ giddan.
Where does this liner call ?	ʃilba(a)xíra di-btúʃaʒ ʃéen fi riḩlítha ?
Where is my cabin ?	kabínti ʃéen ?
I cannot stand the noise of the propellers.	ʃana miʃ ʃáadir astáḩmil dáwʃit ilmuḩarrikáat.
Where can I get a deck-chair ?	ʃaláaʃi kúrsi ʃéen, min fáḏlak ?
Is there a doctor on board ?	fíih duktóor ʒa-lba(a)xíra ?

[1] A " learned " form.

My wife has been seasick for some days.	ʕissítti-btáɛti ʕaɛábha duwáar ilbáḥr min káam yóom.
The English Channel crossing was very stormy.	ɛubúur ilkanáal lingilíizi kan ṣáɛbī giddan.
Are you a good sailor?	ʕínta ma-btitɛábʃi m-issáfar f-ilbáḥr?
We had a rough passage.	ʕirríḥla káanit mutɛíba ʕáwi.
The ship is rolling and pitching a lot.	ʕilba(a)xíra-btitmárgaḥ ʕáwi.
The sea is very rough.	ʕilbáḥrī háayig gíddan.
It's getting foggy.	ʕiḍḍabáab biyíktar.
Visibility is bad.	ʕirrúʕya ṣáɛba.
We are twenty miles off the coast.	bénna-w béen iʃʃátti ɛiʃríin mííl.
Where can I send a cable?	minéen aʕdar ábɛat tiliɣráaf, min faḍlak?
In the wireless operator's cabin.	min ʕóḍt [1] illasílki.
Get your passports and landing cards ready, the coast is in sight.	ḥaḍḍáru gawazáat issáfar bitaɛítkum wi-bṭaʕáat innuzúul, ʕarrábna ɛala-ʃʃáṭṭ.
The harbour pilot has already come on board.	múrʃid ilmíina wíṣil ɛa-lba(a)xíra.
We shall soon be alongside.	ʕíḥna ʕarrábna níwṣal ilbárr.
They are lowering the gangway.	ʕilbaḥḥáara biynazzílu-ssiʕʕála.
The crane is unloading a car on to the dock side.	ʕilwínʃi biynázzil ɛarabíyya ɛa-lmíina.

TRAVELLING BY AIR

Vocabulary

air travel	sáfar b-iṭṭayyáara
aeronautics	ɛílm iṭṭayaráan
air transport	ʕinnáql iggáwwi
aircraft, aeroplane	ṭayyáara, ṭayyaráat
seaplane	ṭayyáara-lmaʕíyya
jet aircraft	ṭayyáara naffáasa (or naffáaθa [2]), ṭayyaráat naffáasa
airship	munṭáad, manaṭíid
flight	ṭayaráan; sáfar b-iṭṭayyáara, ʕasfáar b-iṭṭayyáara
air-route	xáṭṭi gáwwi
air-lines	ʃarikáat iṭṭayaráan
Egyptian Airways	ʃírkit (or ʃárikat) máṣrī l-iṭṭayaráan

---

[1] Pronounced ʕoṭṭ.
[2] Pronounce θ as *th* in English " think ".

aerodrome, airport, airfield	mat̪áar, mat̪aráat
steward	mud̪íif, mud̪iffín
stewardess	mud̪íifa, mud̪ifáat
pilot	t̪ayyáar, t̪ayyariín
flight engineer	muhándis it̪t̪ayyáara, muhandisíin it̪t̪ayyaráat
wireless operator	muhándis illasílki
passenger	musáafir, musafríin
ground staff	muwazzafíin ilmat̪áar
engine	mákana, makanáat ; ɣídda, ɣídad
airscrew, propeller	marwáḥa, maráawiḥ
cockpit	máqɣad it̪t̪ayyáar
wing	gináaḥ (or ganáaḥ), ʕigníḥa
wingspan	t̪úul igginaḥéen
fuselage	gísm it̪t̪ayyáara
rudder	dáffa, daffáat
tail	deel, diyúul
fuel oil	mazáut (or mazútt)
wind direction	ʕittigáah irríiḥ
vibration	zabzába
safety belt	ḥizáam ilʕamáan
air pocket	mat̪ábbi hawáaʕi
air-conditioning system	giháaz takyíif ilḥáwa
tank	xazzáan, xazzanáat
parachute	paraʃútt, paraʃuttáat
parachutist	ʕinnáazil b-ilparaʃútt
rate of climb	súrɣit iṣ̱ṣuɣúud
rate of descent	súrɣit ilhubúut̪
forced landing	ʕinnuzúul lit̪t̪iráari
civil aviation	ʕit̪t̪ayaráan ilmádani
military aviation	ʕit̪t̪ayaráan ilḥárbi
to fly	t̪aar, yit̪íir
to take off	ʕaam, yiʕúum
to land	nízil, yínzil
to crash	wiʕiɣ, yúʕaɣ [1]
to climb	ɣíli, yíɣla [2]

Sentences

Which is the shortest way to the airport ?	ʕéeh ʕáʕrab t̪aríiʕ l-ilmat̪áar ?
When does the next plane leave for London ?	ʕit̪t̪ayyáara-lli gáyya ḥatʕúum li lándan waʕtéeh ?

[1] More often in the feminine forms, wiʕɣit, túʕaɣ.
[2] More often in the feminine forms, ɣílyit, tíɣla.

The time-table is in the waiting-room.

gádwal ilmawaɛíid í-ilɛistiráaḥa.

I should like to travel without breaking the journey.

ɛana ɛáawiz asáafir fi ṭayyáara miʃ ḥatúʃaf fi ɛáyyi ḥitta tanya/ ɛana ɛáawiz asáafir min ɣéer tawáqquf.

How many passengers does this aircraft take?

ɛiṭṭayyáara di-btáaxud káam ráakib?

This plane carries fifty passengers and a crew of five.

ɛiṭṭayyáara di-btáaxud xamsíin ráakib wi ʃíiḥa xámas ṭayyaríin.

Where will they put my luggage?

ḥayḥúṭṭu ɛáfʃi féen?

In the luggage hold.

fi máxzan ilɛáfʃ.

The plane is just taxi-ing out of the hangar.

ɛiṭṭayyáara ṭálɛa min iggaráaʃ.[1]

There's a two-engined plane just coming in.

ṭayyáara-b muḥarrikéen gáyya.

Jets have a limited range.

ɛiṭṭayyaráat innaffáaθa bitsáafir masafáat ɛuɛayyára bass.

The load-capacity of an aircraft is limited to a certain weight.

ḥumúulit iṭṭayyáara maḥdúuda-b wázni maxɛúuɛ.

Each passenger is allowed to carry twenty kilos of luggage free.

masmúuḥ li kúlli-msáafir innu yáaxud maɛáah ɛiʃríin kéelu maggáanan.

You have to pay on excess luggage.

láazim tídfaɛ ɛala-lɛáfʃ izziyáada.

Are you liable to be airsick?

ɛinta bitdúux[2] min rukúub iṭṭayyáara?

The stewardess is serving a meal.

ɛilmuḍíifa bitɛáddim ilɛákl.

The meteorological station has announced a storm warning.

maṣláḥit ilɛarɛáad ilgawwíyya ɛaɛlánit taḥδíir[3] min ɛa(a)ɛifa.

The take-off has been delayed (because of fog).

ɛiṭṭayyáara-tɛaxxárit ɛan máwɛid ɛiyámha (ɛaʃan iḍḍabáab).

We landed at Al-Maza[4] at the scheduled time.

nizílna-f maṭáar ɛalmáaza í-ilmaɛáad ilmuḥáddad.

---

[1] In educated speech this word is very often pronounced with the final sound of " rouge " in place of ʃ.

[2] Pronounced bidd-.

[3] Pronounce δ as *th* in English " the "; ɛaɛlánit, too, is essentially a written form.

[4] Cairo Airport.

THE TOWN
Vocabulary

town	bálad,[1] biláad ; madíina
city	madíina, múdun
village	bálad, biláad ; qárya, qúra
capital	ẓa(a)ṣíma, ẓawáaṣim
provincial town	mudiríyya, mudiriyyáat ; márkaz,[2] maráakiz
country(side)	riif (pl. ṣaryáaf)
in the country	f-ilṣaryáaf
in town and country	f-ilbándar wi f-irríif
country (nation)	barr, burúur [3]
land (as opposed to sea)	barr
on sea and land and in the air	f-ilbáḥri-w ẓa-lbárri-w f-iggáww
suburb	ḍa(a)ḥíya, ḍawáaḥi
slum	ḥáyyi faqíir, ṣaḥyáaṣ faqíira
market (square)	suuṣ, ṣaswáaṣ
main square	midáan raṣíisi
street	ʃáariẓ, ʃawáariẓ
quarter	ḥayy, ṣaḥyáaṣ
lane	ḥáara, ḥawáari
blind-alley	ʃáariẓ mazdúud
side-street	ʃáariẓ ga(a)níbi
street corner	nágya, nawáaṣi ; rúkni ʃáariẓ, ṣirkáan ʃawáariẓ
crossing	ẓubúur ilmuʃáah, ṣamáakin ẓubúur ilmuʃáah ; taqáaṭuẓ
road-junction	taqáaṭuẓ ʃáariẓ ... (e.g. fuṣáad) maẓa ʃáariẓ ... (e.g. ẓimáad iddíin)
private road	ʃáariẓ maxẓúuṣi
pavement	raṣíif, ṣarẓífa
kerb	ḥáffit irraṣíif
traffic lights	ṣanwáar ilmurúur
traffic signs	ṣiʃaráat ilmurúur
garden	ginéena, ganáayin
park	muntázah, muntazaháat
bridge	kúbri, kabáari ; ṣanṭára, ṣanáaṭir [4]
river	nahr, ṣanháar
railway station	maḥáṭṭit issíkka-lḥadíid
hospital	mustáʃfa, mustaʃfayáat
town hall	baladíyya
cemetery	gabbáana, gabbanáat

[1] A feminine form.

[2] An administrative division, strictly.

[3] Cf. bárri máṣr " Egypt ".

[4] Or ṣanáaṭir.

post office	máktab ilbariid ; ſilbúsṭa
police station	márkaz ilbulíiṣ ; núṢṭit ilbulíiṣ ; karakóona, karakonáat
public library	maktába ɤá(a)mma
school	madrása, madáaris
college	kullíyya, kulliyyáat
university	gámɛa, ga(a)miɤáat
museum	máthaf, matáahif
Museum of Antiquities	Ɛantikxáana ; dáar ilƐaθáar ilmaṣríyya
Cairo General Library	Ɛilkutubxáana
exhibition	máɤraḍ, maɤáariḍ
mosque	gáamiɤ, gawáamiɤ
church	kiníisa, kanáayis
cathedral	katidraƐíyya, katidraƐiyyáat
synagogue	kiníst ilyahúud
fire station	Ɛilmaṭáafi ; maháṭṭit ilharíiɁ
block of flats	ɤimáara, ɤimaráat
shop	dukkáan, dakakíin
restaurant	máṭɤam, maṭáaɤim
café	Ɛáhwa, Ɛaháawi
bar, wine-shop	baar, baráat ; xammáara, xammaráat
flat, apartment	ſáƐƐa, ſúƐaƐ
shop-window	batríina, batrináat
policeman	ɤaskári bulíiṣ, ɤasáakir bulíiṣ
traffic policeman	ɤaskári-lmurúur
night-watchman	ɣafíir, ɣúfara
pedestrian	máaſi, maſyíin
street cleaner	kannáas, kannasíin
bus	Ɛutubíis, Ɛutubisáat
tramcar	turmáay, turmayáat
lorry	lúuri, luriyyáat ; kámyun, kamyunáat
car	ɤarabíyya, ɤarabiyyáat ; Ɛutumbíil, Ɛutumbiláat ; sayyáara, sayyaráat
private car	ɤarabíyya malláaki
cart	ɤarabíyya kárru, ɤarabiyyáat kárru
gharry	hanṭúur, hanaṭíir
gharry-driver, cart-driver	ɤarbági, ɤarbagíyya
taxi	táksi, taksiyyáat ; ɤarabíyyit Ɛúgra
taxi-rank	máwƐaf taksiyyáat
stopping-place	máwƐaf, mawáaƐif ; maháṭṭit ilƐutubíis (or maháṭṭit itturmáay)
palace	Ɛaṣr, Ɛuṣúur ; saráaya, sarayáat
night-club	kázinu (or kazíinu), kazinuháat

houseboat	ɤawwáama, ɤawwamáat
Nile steamer	ba(a)xíra nilíyya
Tourist police	ʃilbulíiʃ issiyáaḥi
dragoman	turgumáan, tarágma
beggar	ʃaḥḥáat, ʃaḥḥatíin
terminus	ʕáaxir ilxáṭṭ, ʕawáaxir ilxuṭúuṭ
entrance	duxúul, ṭúruʕ idduxúul ; baab, ʕabwáab
exit	báab ilxurúug, ʕabwáab ilxurúug
standing	wáaʃif, wáʃʃa, waʃʃíin [1]
sitting	ʕáaɤid, ʕáɤda, ʕaɤdíin [1]
3 standing (places)	tálat maḥalláat l-ilwuʕúuf
on foot	ɤa-lʕádam
first class	dáraga ʕúula
second class	dáraga tánya
to ride, get in or on a vehicle	ríkib, yírkab (ilɤarabíyya, etc.)
to get on a horse	ríkib, yírkab ɤala-lḥuṣáan
to get off	nízil, yínzil (min)
to walk	míʃi, yímʃi
to take a walk	ʕitmáʃʃa, yitmáʃʃa ; ʕitfássaḥ, yitfássaḥ

Sentences

How far is it to the shopping centre ?	ʕilmasáafa ʕaddéeh min hína-l ʃáariɤ issúuʕ (or l-iddakakíin) ?
Which is the shortest way to the town centre ?	ʕéeh ʕáʕrab ṭaríiʕ li wíʂṭ ilbálad ?
Can you tell me the way to the theatre ?	tiʕdar tiʕúlli min fáḍlak ilmásraḥ féen ?
Where is the post office ?	féen ilbúʂṭa/máktab ilbaríid ?
The second turning on the right.	ʕittaḥwíida-ttánya ɤa-lyimíin.
Don't cross the street unless the green light is on.	ma-tɤaddíiʃ iʃʃáariɤ ílla lamma-ykúun innúur láxḍar mináwwar.
There are the traffic lights.	ʕanwáar ilmuráur ahé(h).
Don't step off the pavement.	ma tinzílʃi min ɤa-rraʂíif.
The traffic is very heavy.	ʕilmurúur záḥma ʕáwi.
Mind the lorry !	ḥáasib (ḥásba, ḥasbíin[1]) illúuri ; xud (xúdi, xúdu[1]) báalak (báalik, bálkum) m-illúuri.
There is a traffic jam at the corner of Suliman Pasha Street.	ḟíih ɤáṭala (ḟ-ilmuráur) fi ʕáwwil ʃáariɤ silimáan baaʃa.
The streets are narrow.	ʕiʃʃawáariɤ dayyáʕa.
I've lost my way.	ʕana táayih (ʕana táyha, ʕiḥna tayhíin[1]).

[1] Masculine singular, feminine singular, and plural forms, in that order.

Turn to the left.	ḥáwwid ɛa-ʃʃimáal.
Straight on.	ɛala ṭúul ; dúɣri.
Where is the main entrance to the hospital ?	féen ilmádxal irraʕíisi bitaɛ ilmustáʃta ?
Where does Mr. Ali Fathi live ?	ʕissáyyid ɛáli fátḥi saakin féen ?
On the top floor.	fi ʕáaxir dóor f-ilɛimáara.
They have a flat on the ground floor.	lúhum ʃáʕʕa f-iddóor ilʕárḍi.
Can I get to Liberation Square by bus ?	ʕáʕdar aráuḥ midáan ittaḥríir b-ilʕutubíis ?
Take the lift. Or do you prefer the stairs ?	ʕíṭlaɛ f-ilʕaɛanɛéer. walla-tḥíbbi tíṭlaɛ b-issíllim ?
You have to get a ticket.	láazim tíʕṭaɛ tazkára.
Get your ticket at the ticket-office.	háat tazkártak min ʃibbáak ittazáakir.
You can also take the bus.	tiʕdar táaxud ilʕutubíis bárḍu(h).
The buses are crowded.	ʕilʕutubisáat záḥma.
Let the passengers off first, please.	ʕinnáazil ilʕáwwal, min faḍlúku(m).
We are full up. Next bus, please.	ʕilʕutubíis malyáan. xúd illi báɛdu(h).
In Alexandria there are both single- and double-decker trams.	fiih turmayáat bi doréen wi turmayáat bi dóor wáaḥid f-iskindiríyya.
Standing room only.	fiih maḥalláat wuʕúuf báss.
Pass down inside.	ʕidxúlu gúwwa min faḍlúku.
Don't push.	ma-tzúʕʕiʃ.[1]
Is there no queue ?	ma fiiʃ ṭabúur ?
Keep a passage clear.	wassáɛu síkka min faḍlúkum.
Fares, please.	tazáakir min faḍlúkum.
I've lost my ticket.	tazkárti ḍáaɛit.
Don't get off while the train is going.	ma tinzílʃi w-ilʕáṭri máaʃi.
When does the last bus leave ?	ʕáaxir ʕutubíis biyʕúum issáaɛa káam ?
Sunday traffic is limited.	ma fiiʃ ɛarabiyyáat kitíir yóom ilḥádd.
Where do I have to get off ?	ʕánzil féen ?
No thoroughfare.	ṭaríiq masdúud.[2]
Closed to pedestrians.	mamnúuɛ murúur ilmuʃáah.[2]
No admittance (private).	mamnúuɛ idduxúul (xaaɛɛ).[2]

[1] Pronounced **ma-dz** . . .

[2] Written language.

Have you seen the illuminated advertisements in the centre of the city ?

ʃúft ilʕiɣlanáat ilminawwára-lli-f wiʃt ilbálad ?

They are hosing down the roadways.

biyiysílu-ʃʃawáariɣ b-ilxaraʈíim.[1]

HOTELS

Vocabulary

hotel	lukánda, lukandáat ; fúnduq, fanáadiq
single room	ʕóoḍa-l ʃáxʂi wáaḥid
double room	ʕóoḍa l-itnéen
private bathroom	ḥammáam xuʂúuʂi
reception desk	yúrfit listiqbáal ; listiqbáal
key	muftáaḥ, mafatíiḥ
lounge	ʕistiráaḥa, ʕistiraḥáat
dining-room	ʕóḍt [2] ilʕákl ; yúrfit iʈʈaɣáam
writing-room	ʕóḍt [2] ikkitáaba
lobby	hool
gentlemen's cloakroom	dáwrit miyáah irrijáal [3]
ladies' cloakroom	dáwrit miyáah issayyidáat [4]
corridor	mamárr, mamarráat
service stairs	síllim ilxádam
lift	ʕaʂanʂéer, ʕaʂanʂeráat
fan	marwáḥa, maráawiḥ
air conditioning	takyíif háwa
bell	gáras, ʕagráas
bell-boy	farráaʃ, farraʃíin
chambermaid	xaddáama, xaddamáat
boots	massáaḥ iggizam
waiter	garsóon, garsonáat
waitress	garsóona, garsonáat
hall-porter	farráaʃ, farraʃíin
doorman	bawwáab, bawwabíin
manager	mudíir, mudiríin
proprietor	ʂáaḥib ilmílk, ʕaʂḥáab ilmílk
cook	ʈabbáax, ʈabbaxíin
to book (a room/accommodation)	ḥágaz, yiḥgiz (ʕóoḍa/maḥáll)
to lodge	síkin (or sákan), yúskun

---

[1] Singular xarʈúum.
[2] Pronounced ʕoʈʈ.
[3] Written language. Pronounce j as in English " jeep ".
[4] Written language.

to stay at (a hotel)	nízil, yínzil (fi lukánda)
to cancel (a booking)	láγa, yílγi (ḥágz ilᶜóoḍa)
to settle (the bill)	dáfaɛ, yídfaɛ (ilḥisáab)

Sentences

Which hotel are you staying at ?	ᶜinta náazil fi ᶜáyyï lukánda ?
The service is good (bad).	ᶜilxídma ṭayyíba (wiḥ∫a).
Can I have a single room ?	ɛáawiz ᶜóoḍa-l wáaḥid.
Is there central heating and running hot and cold water in the rooms ?	fiih tadfíya-w máyya súxna-w sáᶜɛa f-ilᶜíwaḍ ?
Here is the key to your room.	ᶜitfáḍḍal muftáaḥ ᶜóḍtak.[1]
The lift boy will take your luggage up.	ɛáamil ilᶜaṣanṣéer ḥayṭállaɛ ∫únaṭak fóoᶜ.
Can I have breakfast in my room ?	múmkin tigíbli fuṭúuri-f ᶜoḍti ?[1]
Where is the bathroom, please ?	féen ilḥammáam, min faḍlak ?
Please give me another towel and some soap.	ᶜiddíini min fáḍlak fúuṭa tánya-w ṣabúuna.
I have ordered a room with bath.	ᶜana ṭalábtï ᶜóoḍa-b ḥammáam.
Please enter your name and address in the visitors' book.	min fáḍlak ᶜíktib ismak wi ɛunwáanak fi dáftar izzuwwáar.
Will you please fill in this form.	ᶜímla-lbayanáat di min fáḍlak.
How long do you intend to stay ?	ḥaḍrítak[2] ḥatistánna f-illukánda ᶜaddéeh ?
What are your terms ?	ḥádfaɛ káam, min faḍlak ?
How much is bed and breakfast ?	ᶜilmabíit w-ilfuṭúur bi káam ?
I should like another blanket.	ᶜana ɛáawiz baṭṭaníyya tánya min faḍlak.
Have you reserved a room for me ?	ᶜíntu ḥagzíin ᶜóoḍa líyya ?
Where is the bar ?	féen ilbáar ?
I want to lodge a complaint with the manager.	ᶜana ɛáawiz akállim ilmudíir.[3]
Any letters for me ?	fiih gawabáat ɛa∫áani ?
Can you call me to-morrow at six o'clock ?	ṣaḥḥíini búkra-ssáaɛa sítta, min faḍlak.
Ring twice for the chambermaid.	ᶜíḍrab iggáras marritéen li ṭálab ilxaddáama.
Where did you put my brush and comb ?	ḥaṭṭéet ilfúr∫a w-ilmí∫ṭï-btúuɛi féen ?

---

[1] Pronounced ᶜoṭṭ-.
[2] Term of polite address.
[3] Lit. " . . . to talk to the manager ".

When can you let me have my laundry back?	ḥatrággaɛ ilyasíil waʃtéeh ?
Here is my laundry list :	ʃáymit ilyasíil bitáaɛ(i)-ahé(h) :
4 white shirts.	ʃárbaɛ ʃumɛáan bíiḍ.
3 coloured shirts.	tálat ʃumɛáan milawwiniin.
6 collars (starched).	sittí yaʃáat (minaʃíyya).
5 soft collars.	xámas yaʃáat miʃ minaʃíyya.
5 detached collars.	xámas yaʃáat munfáṣila.
2 vests.	fanillitéen.[1]
2 pairs of underpants.	libaséen.
1 pair of pyjamas.	bijáama.
10 handkerchiefs.	ɛáʃar manadíil.
5 pairs of socks.	xámast igwáaz ʃarabáat.
2 blouses.	biloztéen.[2]
3 slips.	tálat ʃumɛáan ḥaríimi.
2 nightdresses.	ʃamiɛéen nóom.
3 pairs of stockings.	tálatt igwáaz ʃarabáat ḥariimi.
1 linen dress.	fustáan tíil wáaḥid.
1 dressing gown.	róob wáaḥid.

Is there a barber's shop in the hotel?	fíih dukkáan ḥalláaʃ f-illukánda ?
I've forgotten my razor.	ʃana-nsíit mákanit ilḥiláaʃabtáɛti.
Can I have this suit pressed?	múmkin tikwíili-lbadláadi, min faḍlak.
Let me have the bill, please.	ʃiddíini ʃáymit ilḥisáab, min faḍlak.
I stayed at the Misr for a week.	ʃana-nzíltí-f lukándit mággrí-l múddit ʃusbúuɛ.
Is there anywhere to stay there?	fíih lukandáat hináak ?
I'm looking for a hotel which is not too expensive.	ʃana ɛáawiz lukánda mutawaṣṣíṭa.[3]
Do you like your hotel?	ʃillukánda ɛagbáak ?
The food is good and plentiful.	ʃilʃáklí-ktíir wi-kwáyyis.
The cooking is excellent.	ʃiṭṭábxi mumtáaz.
Can I book rooms for August?	ʃáʃdar áḥgiz ʃóoḍa-l ʃayúgṭuɛ ?
Sorry, we are booked up till October.	ʃáasif, ʃilʃúwaḍ kulláha maḥgúuza-lyáayit ʃuktóobar.
You should have booked long in advance.	kan láazim tiḥgiz min bádri ʃáwi.

[1] Sing. fanílla.
[2] Sing. bilóoza.
[3] Lit. " average "

RESTAURANTS AND MEALS

Vocabulary

restaurant	mátʒam, matáaʒim
café	ʃáhwa, ʃaháawi
bar	baar, baráat
breakfast	futúur
lunch	ɣáda
dinner	ʒáʃa
meal	ʃákla, ʃakláat
plate, dish	ṭábaʃ, ʃiṭbáaʃ
knife	sikkíina, sakakíin
fork	ʃóoka, ʃíwak (or ʃúwak)
spoon	maʒláʃa, maʒáaliʃ
tea-spoon	maʒláʃit ʃáay
cup	fingáal, fanagíil
saucer	ṭábaʃ fingáal
glass	kubbáaya, kubbayáat
tea-pot, coffee-pot	barráad, bararíid
milk-jug	ʃabríiʃ lában, ʃabaríiʃ lában
sugar-basin	sukkaríyya, sukkariyyáat
water-jug	ʃabríiʃ máyya
tray	ṣiníyya, ṣiniyyáat (or ṣawáani)
saucepan	kasaróola, kasaroláat
menu, bill of fare	ʃilʃáyma ; ʃáymit ilʃasʒáar [1]
course	ṣanf, ʃaṣnáaf
vegetarian	nabáati, nabatiyyíin
meat dish	ʃáklit láḥma
wine	xamr
spirits	maʃrubáat ru(u)ḥíyya
hors d'œuvre	muʃahhiyáat
dessert	fákha
sweet	(course) ḥilw ; (sweetmeat) túufi, tuʃyyáat
sandwich	sándawitʃ (or sandi-), sandawitʃáat
salt	malḥ
pepper	filfl
chilli	ʃárni filfl, ʃurúun filfl
parsley	baʃdúunis
mustard	mustárda
vinegar	xall
oil	zeet, ziyúut
butter	zíbda

[1] Lit. " price-list ".

clarified butter, ghi	samn
lard	díhnĭ xanzíir
fat	ʃaḥm
bread	ɤeeʃ
French bread	ɤéeʃ afrángi
local bread	ɤéeʃ báladi
loaf	riɤíif, ʕiryífa
toast	tust
tinned meat	láḥma maḥʃúuẓa
ham (also pork and bacon)	xanzíir
sausage	sugúʕʕ (c.),[1] ṣubáaɤ sugúʕʕ, ṣawáabiɤ sugúʕʕ
egg	beeḍ (c.), béeḍa, beḍáat [2]
fried eggs	béeḍ máʃli
scrambled eggs	béeḍ maḍrúub
boiled egg	béeḍa maslúuʕa
omelette	ɤígga, ɤiggáat
soup	ʃúrba
vegetable soup	ʃúrbit xuḍáar
lentil soup	ʃúrbit ɤáts
chicken soup	ʃúrbit firáax
tomato soup	ʃúrbit ṭamáaṭim
joint	fáxda
veal	láḥma-btíllu ; ɤaggáali
beef	láḥma báʕari
beefsteak	filée
mutton	láḥma ḍáani
lamb	láḥma ʕúuzi
fish	sámak (c.), sámaka, samakáat
pond fish	búlṭi
mullet	búuri
sole	sámak múusa [3]
vegetables	xuḍáar
potatoes	baṭáaṭiṣ (c.), baṭaṭṣáaya, baṭaṭṣáat
potato crisps	baṭáaṭiṣ maʕlíyya ; baṭáaṭiṣ maḥammára
rice	ruzz
lettuce	xaṣṣ (c.), xaṣṣáaya, xaṣṣáat
salad	ṣálaṭa, ṣalaṭáat
cabbage	kurúmb (c.), kurúmba, kurumbáat
cauliflower	ʕarnabíiṭ (c.), ʕarnabíiṭa, ʕarnabiṭáat

[1] (c.) = collective noun.
[2] Cf. ṭúurit béeḍ or ʕárbaɤ beḍáat " 4 eggs ", dástit béeḍ or ʕitnáaʃar béeḍa " a dozen eggs ".
[3] The names of other fish are given on p. 202.

carrots	gázar (c.), gazaráaya, gazaráat
spinach	sabáanix (or si-)
beans	fuul (c.), ḥabbáayit fúul, ḥabbáat fúul
peanuts	fúul sudáani
green beans	faṣúlya (c.), ḥabbáayit faṣúlya, ḥabbáat faṣúlya
peas	bisílla (c.), ḥabbáayit bisílla, ḥabbáat bisílla
onions	báṣal (c.), baṣaláaya, baṣaláat
garlic	toom (c.), ráas tóom, ráus tóom
pumpkin	ʕarɛ (c.), ʕarɛáaya, ʕarɛáat
marrow (small)	kúusa (c.), kusáaya, kusáat
melon	ʃammáam (c.), ʃammáama, ʃammamáat
Jew's mallow	muluxíyya
ladies' fingers	bámya
fruit	fákha, fawáakih
stewed fruit	fákha maṭbúuxa
cheese	gíbna
minced meat	láḥma mafrúuma ; kúfta
beer	bíira
cider	sáydar
mineral waters	miyáah fawwáara [1]
lemonade	lamunáatu
lemon juice	ɛaṣíir lamúun
orange juice	ɛaṣíir burtuʕáan
coffee	ʕáhwa
tea	ʃaay
cocoa	kakáaw
milk	lában
cream	ʕíʃta
pigeon	ḥamáam
duck	baṭṭ
turkey	díik rúumi
chicken	fárxa ; firáax
breast of chicken	sídri fárxa
leg of chicken	wírki fárxa
pastry, pastries	gatóo, gatoháat
cake	kaḥk (c.), káḥka, kaḥkáat
biscuits	baskawíit (c.), baskawíita, baskawitáat
jam	mirúbba
table napkin	fúuṭit ṣúfra, fúwaṭ ṣúfra
tablecloth	máfraʃ, mafáariʃ
bill, check	ḥisáab
tip	baʕʃíiʃ

[1] A " learned " form.

A FEW EGYPTIAN DISHES

kiʃk	dish of which yoghourt and flour are important ingredients
túrli	fried meat and vegetables in layers
ṭaɛmíyya	fried bean purée
kíbad wi kaláawi	liver(s) and kidneys
láḥma kustaléeta	chops (usually lamb)
ʃiiʃ kabáab	meat grilled on a spit
kúfta	minced meat similarly grilled
kabáab ḥálla	braised, stewed meat
láḥma-mḥammára	fried meat, lemon, onions, salt and pepper
láḥma rústu b-ilbéet	roast meat and egg pie served in slices
ɛiníyyit baṭáaṭiɛ b-illáḥm	tray of roast meat and potatoes (often obtainable from butcher's)
láḥma buftéek	escalope [1]
ḥamáam máʃwi	roast pigeon
ḥamáam máḥʃi	pigeon stuffed with rice and/or minced meat and fried in ghi
láḥma-b tarbíya	meat with white sauce and mixed vegetables
láḥma-b jáli	jellied meat
láḥma maslúuɛa	boiled meat
fáttit láḥma	bread and meat soup
sámak máɛli	fried fish
sámak máʃwi	baked fish
kúftit sámak	minced fish
kúftit gambári	minced prawns
ɛiníyyit sámak	fish baked in tomato sauce
sámak ɛámama	fish, onions, raisins, salt, pepper, mustard, dipped in oil and baked
sámak ma(a)yunáyz	boiled fish with mayonnaise; ail-au-liṭ
ɛálaṭit ṭaḥiina	sesame oil, salt, pepper, vinegar, spices
ɛálaṭit ṭamáaṭim	tomato salad
ɛálaṭit zabáadi	yoghourt (zabáadi) with the addition of salt, garlic, and dry mint
ɛálaṭit bidingáan (or bitingáan)	aubergine salad
báaba ɣánnu	aubergine and "ṭaḥiina" salad together
máḥʃi-krúmb	stuffed cabbage
máḥʃi waraɛ ɛínab or ḍúlma	stuffed vine leaves

[1] buftéek relates to the method of frying in crumbs.

máhʃi bidingáan	stuffed brinjals
máhʃi ṭamáaṭim	stuffed tomatoes
máhʃi waraʕ xáṣṣ	stuffed lettuce leaves
máhʃi kúusa	stuffed marrows
máhʃi baṭáaṭiṣ	stuffed potatoes
misaʕáaʒa	aubergine cooked in tomato sauce
ʕilḥággi rúzz	rice, raisins, liver or kidney of poultry casseroled
fúul midámmis	baked beans
fúul náabit	boiled beans

Sentences

Have you booked a table in advance ?	ʕinta ḥáagiz ṭarabéeza ?
Waiter, a table for four, please.	ya garṣóon, ṭarabéeza l-arbáʒa, min faḍlak.
Here is the menu.	ʕitfáḍḍal ilʕáyma.
What would you like ?	tiḥíbbi ʕéeh ?
There are many courses to choose from.	fiih ʕaṣnáaf kitíira tíʕdar tixtáar mínha.
Does the menu appeal to you or would you prefer to eat à la carte ?	tiḥíbbi táaxud ʕáklī káamil walla tixtáar ilʕaṣnáaf illi tiʒgíbak ?
I can recommend our fish.	ʒandína sámak kuwáyyis xáaliṣ.
The special dish to-day is mutton and spinach.	ʕilʕáklī-lmaxṣúuṣa-nnaháarda sabáanix b-illáḥma-ḍḍáani.
What have you in the way of meat ?	ʕéeh ʕanwáaʒ illáḥma-lli ʒandúkum ?
Anything you like ; we have all kinds.	ʕilli yiʒgíbak ; ʒandína kúlli ḥáaga.
I would like a lettuce and tomato salad dressed with oil and vinegar.	ʕana ʒáawiz ʒálaṭa xáḍra min faḍlak wi ʒaléeha xálli-w zéet zetúun.
What can I order for you ?	ʕáṭlub li siyádtak [1] ʕéeh ?
Could I have some kidneys or liver with rice and onions ?	tíʕdar tigíbli min fáḍlak kaláawi walla kibda b-ilbáṣal w-irrúzz ?
What alternative is there ?	ʒandúku ʕéeh táani ?
What would you like to follow ?	tiḥíbbi táaxud ḥáaga tánya ?
Are there any sweets ?	ʒandúku ḥílw ?
Would you like me to bring you some fruit ?	tiḥíbb agíblak fákha ?

---

[1] siyáada + ak ; pronounced siyáttak.

There is no more fruit.	ma ɣátʃi fiih fákha or ma-fɖilʃi fákha.
Would you like something to drink?	tiḥíbbi tiʃrab ḥáaga ?
Would you like Turkish or French coffee?	tiḥíbbi tiʃrab ʕáhwa túrki walla ʕáhwa faransáawi ?
How would you like it? Very sweet, sweet, a little sugar, or unsweetened?	tiḥibbáha-zzáay ? ziyáada, maẓbúuṭa, ɣa-rríiḥa walla sáada ?
I prefer Turkish coffee.	ʕan-afáḍḍal ilʕáhwa-ttúrki.
Have a cigarette.	tifáḍḍal sigáara.
Thank you but may I smoke my pipe?	mutaʃákkir ʕáwi, ʕana ḥadáxxan ilbíiba-otáɣti, law samáḥt ?
Where have I put my matches?	ʕana ḥaṭṭéet ikkabríit féen ?
Here we are, I've a lighter.	ʕitfáḍḍal, ʕana-mɣáaya walláaɣahé(h) !
Pass the ashtray, please.	nawílni iṭṭaʕṭúuʕa, min faḍlak.
Let me have the bill, please.	ʕiddíini-lḥisáab, min faḍlak.
Would you like a drink at the bar?	tiḥíbbi tiʃrab ḥáaga ɣa-lbáar ?
I would like to sit at a table outside in the fresh air.	ʕana ɣáawiz áʕʕud ɣala ṭarabéeza bárra f-ilḥáwa.
Come and have supper with us.	ʕitfáḍḍal ilʕáʃa ɣandína.
Come and take pot-luck with us.	taɣáala náakul ilmawgúud.
Heavy meals do not agree with me.	ʕilʕáklī-ttiʕíil biyitɣábni.
Shall I get you something light?	ʕagíblak ḥáaga xafíifa ?
What would you like for breakfast?	tiḥíbbi tifṭar ʕéeh ?
Can I have a boiled egg, bread and butter, and honey?	ʕiddíini béeḍa maslúuʕa, wi ɣéeʃ wi zíbda wi ɣásal ábyaḍ ?
Something cold.	ḥáaga sáʕɣa.
Iced drinks.	maʃrubáat muθallága.[1]
No gratuities.	mamnúuɣ ʕiɣtáaʕ ʕáyyi nuqúud l-ilxádam.
I have no appetite.	ʕana ma líiʃ níyya/nífsi mazdúuda.
He has a hearty appetite.	huwwa ʕakúul.
Here's health !	fiṣiḥḥítak !
Would you like to share our meal?	ʕitfáḍḍal kúl maɣáana ?
No, thank you. I have already eaten. *Bon appétit.*	mutaʃákkir gíddan, ʕana kált ʕáblī kída. b-ilḥána w-iʃʃífa.

---

[1] Written language. Pronounce θ as *th* in " think ".

SHOPPING

Vocabulary

shop	dukkáan, dakakíin
wholesaler's	dukkáan ilgúmla
retailer's	dukkáan ilʕattáazi
stores	maháll ilʕumáaʃ, mahalláat ilʕumáaʃ
store, depot	máxzan, maxáazin
baker's shop	máxbaz, maxáabiz
pastrycook('s)	halawáani, halawaníyya
butcher('s)	gazzáar, gazzaríin
fishmonger('s)	zammáak, sammakíin
poulterer('s)	farárgi, farargíyya
grocer('s)	baʕʕáal, baʕʕalíin
greengrocer('s)	xúḍari, xuḍaríyya
fruiterer('s)	fakaháani, fakahaníyya
stationer's, bookseller's	maktába, maktabáat
men's outfitter('s)	xayyáaṭ, xayyaṭíin
haberdasher('s)	xirdawáati, xirdawatíyya
hardware dealer('s)	bayyáaʕ ʕadawáat ilhidáada, bayyaʕíin ʕadawáat ilhidáada
cleaner's and dyer's	mahálli tanzíif ilmaláabis ; tintirarii
tobacconist('s)	daxáxni, daxaxníyya
dispensing chemist('s)	ṣaydáli, ṣaydalíyya
chemist's shop	ṣaydalíyya ; ʕagzaxáana, ʕagzaxanáat
cigarette kiosk	kúʃki sagáayir, ʕikʃáak sagáayir
shop assistant	ṣábi (or ṣaby), ṣubyáan
customer	zibúun, zabáayin
to buy	ʕiʃtára, yiʃtíri
to sell	baaʕ, yibíiʕ
to choose	ʕixtáar, yixtáar
to order	ṭálab, yúṭlub
to cancel	láya, yílyi
to exchange	báddil, yibáddil ; yáyyar, yiyáyyar
to deliver	sállim, yisállim
to fetch	gaab, yigíib
to bargain	fáaṣil, yifáaṣil
to wrap up	laff, yilíff

Sentences

At the baker's :	ʒand ilxabbáaz :
What can I get for you ?/Are you being served ?	ʕáyyi xídma ?

I want two fresh loaves of European bread. | ʃana ɣáawiz riɣiféen ɣéeʃ afrángi ɣabḥĭin.[1]

6 rolls, please. | sitt iryĭfa-frángi-ɣyayyarĭin, min faḍlak.

At the fruiterer's : | ɣand ilfakaháani :

Have you any apples, please ? | ɣándak tiffáaḥ, min faḍlak ?

I should like three pounds of pears, please. | ʃana ɣáawiz tálatt irṭáal[2] kummĭtra, min faḍlak.

Could you send me a dozen tangerines, half a dozen lemons, two pounds of bananas, and a pound of grapes ? | ʃibɣátli min fáḍlak iṭnáaʃar yusafandíyya, wi sittĭ lamunáat, wi raṭléen móoz wi ráṭli ɣinab ?

The walnuts and almonds are too dear. I'll take some peanuts instead. | ʃiggóoz w-illóoz ɣalyĭin ʃáwi.[3] ḥáaxud ʃuwáyyit fúul sudáani badálhum.

Strawberries are out of season, madam/sir. | múusim ilfaráwla fáat, ya sitt/ ḥáḍrit (or sáyyid).

Have you any figs or plums ? | ɣándak tĭin walla barʃúuʃ ?

Will you be having any cherries in to-morrow ? | ḥaykúun ɣandúkum kiréez búkra, min faḍlak ?

Shall I keep some for you, madam ? | ʃahgízlik ʃuwáyya (or tiḥíbb(i) aḥgízlik ʃuwáyya), ya sitt.

At the grocer's : | ɣand ilbaʃʃáal :

I want a packet of raisins and a pound of almonds. | ɣáawiz báaku-zbĭib wi ráṭli lóoz.

Half a pound of ground coffee and a quarter of a pound of tea, please. | núṣṣi ráṭli búnni matḥúun wi rúbɣi ráṭli ʃáay, min faḍlak.

Will you have granulated or lump sugar ? | tiḥíbbi súkkar náaɣim walla súkkar mákana ?

Half a litre of vinegar, please. | núṣṣi lítri xáll, min faḍlak.

I want a litre of olive oil and three pounds of flour. | ʃiddúuni min fáḍlak lítri zéet zetúun wi tálatt irṭáal diʃĭiʃ.

Have you any tinned fruit ? | ɣándak (or ɣandúku(m)) fákha maḥfúuza (or fákha f-ilɣĭlab) ?

At the market : | f-issúuʃ :

I want five pounds of tomatoes, please. | ɣáawiz xámast irṭáal ṭamáaṭim, min faḍlak.

[1] Cf. also ṭáaɀa (invariable) = " fresh " (of fruit, vegetables, etc.).
[2] Strictly, 1 rotl = approx. ⅞ lb.
[3] Arabic has nothing corresponding to the distinction between *too dear* and *very dear*.

The tomatoes and radishes are cheap and fresh.
Ṣiṭṭamáaṭim w-ilfígli-rxáaṣ wi ṣabḥíin (or ṭáaẓa).

Could you please weigh this chicken for me?
Ṣiwzínli [1]-lfárxa dí, min faḍlak?

Have you a small cabbage or lettuce and carrots?
ẓándak kurúmba-ṣyayyáṛa walla xaṣṣáaya-w gáẓar?

At the stores:
f-iddakakíin ikkibíira:

There is a sale on at the stores.
fíih taxfíiḍ f-ilmaḥalláat.

What sort of woollen material have you in stock?
Ṣéeh Ṣanwáaẓ ilṢaṣwáaf illi ẓandúkum, min faḍlak?

Can you show me your designs in silks?
warríini min fáḍlak Ṣanwáaẓ ilḥaríir illi ẓandúku?

We have a large selection.
ẓandína magmúuẓa-kbíira.

Four metres of red velvet, please.
Ṣárbaẓt imtáar Ṣaṭṣífa ḥámra (or ḥumr), min faḍlak.

That will do.
dá-ll-ana ẓáwzu(h).

A reel of black cotton.
bákaṛa sóoda.

A reel of black silk (thread).
bákaṛit xéet ḥaríir ásmar.

Three metres of that white elastic.
tálatt imtáar min ilṢástik lábyaḍ dá.

I also want a zip-fastener.
Ṣana ẓáawiz sústa.

Do you stock scissors?
ẓandúku-mṢaṣṣáat?

I want a thimble and some tape.
Ṣana ẓáwza [2] kuſtubáan wi-ʃwáyyit ʃiríiṭ.

I want a plain blue tie and a coloured handkerchief to match.
Ṣana ẓáawiz karafíṭṭa [3] zárṢa wi mandíil miláwwin yiwa-fíṢha (or yímʃi-mẓáaha).

Does this material wash well?
ṢilṢumáʃ da-byíbhat? [4]/Ṣillónda sáabit walla-byíṭlaẓ f-ilyasíil?

It's fast, it does not fade in the wash.
sáabit, ma-byibhátʃi f-ilyasíil.

Our van calls in your neighbourhood to-morrow.
Ṣilẓaṛabíyya-btaẓítna ḥatwáṣṣal biḍáaẓa ligránkum búkra.

At the cleaner's:
f-ittintiraríi:

I want these flannel trousers dry cleaned.
Ṣana ẓáawiz ilbanṭalóon ilfaníila dá yitnáḍḍaf ẓa-nnáaʃif.

When can I fetch them?
Ṣag(i)-axúdhum waṢtéeh?

---

[1] Pronounced Ṣiwzílli.
[2] All other examples have assumed a man speaking.
[3] Or karafáṭṭa, karafítta, karaváṭṭa.
[4] báhat, yíbhat " to fade "

Can this coat be dyed brown ?	múmkin tuṣbúyu-lbáltu dá búnni ?
Do you do mending ?	ṣintu-bṭírṭu [1] ṣúuṭ ?

At the chemist's :   ṭ-ilṢagzaxáana (or ṭ-iṣṣayḍalíyya) :

Do you keep razors and blades ?	ẓandúku-mwáas wi makanáat ḥiláaṢa ?
I want a shaving-brush and some shaving-soap.	Ṣana ẓáawiz ṭúrṣit ḥiláaṢa-w ṣabúun ḥiláaṢa.
I also want a tube of tooth-paste and a tooth-brush.	Ṣana ẓáawiz kamáan Ṣumbúubit maẓgúun isnáan wi ṭúrṣit isnáan.
How much will that be altogether ?	káam táman ilḥagátdi kulláha ?
Have you anything for head-aches ?	ẓandúku ḥáaga l-iṣṣuḍáaẓ ?
Can you recommend a gargle ?	tiṢdar tiṢúlli ẓala yarɣára-kwayyisa ?
I want some adhesive plaster, please, and a box of cough lozenges.	Ṣana ẓáawiz biláastar, min faḍlak, wi ẓ̱ílbit bastílya min bitáaẓit ilkúḥḥa.
A big packet of cotton-wool, please.	wáraṢit Ṣútni-kbíira, min faḍlak.
Please have this prescription made up for me.	min fáḍlak ḥaḍḍárli-rruṣítta díyya.
I want a good tonic.	Ṣana ẓáawiz dáwa-mṢáwwi, min faḍlak.
Can you let me have some cream for sunburn ?	tiṢdar tiddíini-ṣwáyyit kirṣim ẓaṣan ḥuráuṢ iṣṣáms ?

At the tobacconist's :   ẓand iddaxáxni :

Can you recommend a mild cigar ?	tiṢdar tiṢúlli ẓala núuẓ sigáar xaṣíiṭ ?
What kind of cigarettes do you stock ?	Ṣéeh Ṣanwáaẓ issagáayir illi ẓandúkum ?
Have you any lighter-flints (wicks, petrol) ?	ẓandúku-ḥgáarit (ṣaráayiṭ, banzíin) wallaẓáat ?
Sorry, we've only boxes of matches left.	Ṣáasiṭ, ma ẓátṣi ẓandína-lla ẓṣlab kabrṣit.

At the confectioner's :   ẓand ilḥalawáani :

A large box of chocolates, please.	sandúuṢ ṣukuláaṭa-kbṣir, min faḍlak.

[1] ráṢa, yírṣi " to darn, mend ".

How much is this bar (or packet) of chocolate?	Siʃʃukulaṭáaya dí-b káam?
Please wrap up the cake and pastries for me.	min fáḍlak liffíli-ṭṭúrṭa w-ilḥalawiyyáat.
Do not touch goods displayed on the counter.	mamnúuʒ láms ilbaḍáaSiʒ ilmaʒruuḍa.[1]

In the Muski [2]:   fi xáan ilxalíili :

Do come in, is there anything I can do for you?	Sitfáḍḍal, láazim xidma?
I want a few small things.	lazimni ḥagáat baṣíiṭa.
You've come to the right place.	Sitfáḍḍal, da maḥállak (lit. this is your place).
I'm at your service.	Súṭlub w-ana táḥtI Sámrak (lit. ask and I am under your order).
But do sit down.	báss itfáḍḍal istaráyyaḥ ʒa-lkúrsi.
Thank you.	mutaʃákkir.
Do you like (your) coffee very sweet, half and half, or without sugar?	tiḥíbbI tíʃrab Sáḥwa súkkar ziyáada walla maʒ búuṭa walla sáada?
No coffee, thank you all the same.	láS, káttar xéerak, Saḥwitak maʃrúuba, ʒíʃt.
What are you looking for?	Séeh ṭalabáatak? (lit. what are your requests?).
How much are you selling it (fem.) at?	bi káam tibíʒha?
Do you want to bargain or do you want a fixed price?	ḥaḍritak ʒawiz tifáaṣil walla ʒáawiz kaláam wáaḥid?
Give me a fair price, there's no need for bargaining.	min fáḍlak Súlli ʒa-ttáman b-ilḥáSS, ma ʃíiʃ luzúum l-ilfiṣáal.
We don't put our prices either up or down.	láa binzáwwid wala binnáSSaṣ.
What's the price, then?	Sittáman káam baSa?
Well now, to be fair, four pounds.	Sittáman b-iṣṣála ʒa-nnábi (lit. by praying on the Prophet), Sarbáʒa-gnéeh.
You've put me off.	ya ʃéex inta xaḍḍétni.
What sort of a price is that?	Séeh ittáman dá?

---

[1] Written form. Cf. the spoken ma tilmísʃ ilbiḍáaʒa-lmaʒráuḍa.

[2] The eastern bazaar in Cairo where the customer should bargain for his purchases.

I'll give you two and a half pounds.	ʕan-adfáʒlak itnéen ginéeh wi núṣṣ.
No, no, you're a long way off my price (said by shop-keeper).	láa, láa, líssa bádri (lit. *it is still early*).
Let's split the difference.	níʕsim ilbálad nuṣṣéen (lit. *let's divide the town in two halves*).
Done !	mabrúuk ! (lit. *congratulations*).
All right. Here's the money.	ʕalláah yibarik ṭiik (answer to mabrúuk). ʕitṭáḍḍal ilfilúus.
Can you change me a £1 note ?	tíʕdar tifukkíli-gnéeh, min faḍlak ?
Could you change me 50 piastres ?	min fáḍlak, ṭukkíli xamsíin ʕirʃ ?
Good morning, may I just take a look round ?	ṣabáaḥ ilxéer, múmkin báss atṭárrag ?

THE POST OFFICE

Vocabulary

The General Post Office	ʕilbúṣṭa-lʒumumíyya
letter box	ṣandúuʕ ilbúṣṭa
letter	gawáab, gawabáat
answer	gawáab, ʕagwíba
postcard	kártī bustáal, kurúut bustáal
printed matter	maṭbuʒáat
registered letter	gawáab muṣággal
express letter	gawáab mustáʒgal
telegram	tiliyráaf, tiliyrafáat
sample having no commercial value	ʒayyína láysa l-ilbíiʒ [1]
airmail letter	gawáab b-ilbaríid ilgáwwi
envelope	ẓárīi gawáab, ẓurúuf gawabáat
address	ʒunwáan, ʒanawíin
addressee	ʕalmúrsal ʕiléeh
sender	múrsil, mursilíin ; ráasil, rásliin
counter	bank, bunúuk
post-office official	miẓáawin ilbúṣṭa
postman	buṣṭági, buṣṭagíyya ; sáaʒi, suʒáah ; ʒáamil ilbaríid, ʒummáal ilbaríid
stamp	wáraʕit baríid ; ṭáabiʒ búṣṭa
wrapper, wrapping paper	wáraʕ láff

[1] Written form.

sealing wax	ʃámɛ-áḥmar
postage	ʕúgrit ilbariid
string	dubáara
postal order	ʕíznī barííd, ʕuzúun barííd
telegraphic transfer	ḥiláawa tiliɣrafíyya
fees, charges	dámya ; táman
post-free	min ɣéer wáraʕ búʃṭa
by airmail	b-iṭṭayyáara ; b-ilbariid ilgáwwi
by seamail	b-ilmárkib
abroad	f-ilxáarig
country	ʕirríɛ ; ʕilʕaryáaʃ
poste restante	yantáðir b-iʃʃibbáak ilbarííd [1]
collection times	lámm ilbúʃṭa ; máwɛid, mawaɛíid
ordinary letter	gawáab ɣáadi
parcel	ṭard, ṭurúud
money order	ḥiwáala
receipt-slip	ḥáfẓa, ḥawáafiẓ
distribution window	ʃibbáak ittawzííɛ
to post	ráma, yírmi gawáab (fī sandúuʕ ilbúʃṭa)
to receive	ʕistálam, yistílim
to stamp a letter	ḥaṭṭ, yiḥúṭṭ wáraʕit búʃṭa ɛa-ggawáab
to frank a letter	xátam, yíxtim gawáab
to send	báɛat, yíbɛat
to register	ɣóogar, yiɣóogar ; sággil, yisággil

Sentences

Has the postman been ?	ʕilbuʃṭági fáat (or ɣádda or gíh) ?
He delivered two letters and a postcard this morning.	huwwa gáab gawabéen wi kártī bustáal innahárda-ṣṣúbḥ.
The postman has left this form.	ʕilbuʃṭági sáab ilwaṣlída.
Letters are delivered three times a day.	ʕiggawabáat bititwázzaɛ tálat marráat f-ilyóom.
Where can I collect this parcel ?	ʕáʕdar astílim iṭṭárdī da-mnéen ?
Take this letter to the post-box, please.	ʕísʕiṭ iggawábda-f sandúuʕ ilbúʃṭa, min faḍlak.
The next collection is at six.	ḥaylímmu-ggawabáat baɛdī kídassáaɛa sitta.
You must pay excess-postage.	lazim tídfaɛ fárʕī ɛa-ggawábda.
Return to sender, address not known.	yuráddu ʕila-lmúrsil, ʕalɛunwáan ɣéer maɛrúuf.

[1] Written form. Pronounce ð as *th* in " thus " but with
" emphasis "; ð is the emphatic counterpart of ð.

Please forward.	yuḥáwwal ʕiléeh.
What is the postage for an air-mail letter to England ?	ʕiggawáab b-iṭṭayyáara l-ingiltíra-b káam ?
Where can I inquire for poste restante letters ?	ʕaʕdar ásʕal féen min faḍlak ʕiza káan fíih gawabáat mahgúuza líyya ?
Where can I get postage stamps ?	ʕáʕdar aʃtíri ṭawáabiʕ barííd minéen, min faḍlak ?
Two one-piastre stamps.	waraʕtéen búṣṭa min ʕábu ʕírʃi sáay.
Could I have a cable form, please ?	ʕiddíini min fáḍlak fúrmit tiliyráaf ?
I want to send these things cash on delivery.	ʕana ɣáawiz ábʕat ilbaḍáayiʕ dí-b ṭarʕiʕit iddáfɣi ʕand ittaslíim.
Would you register this letter for me, please ?	saggílli-ggawábda, min faḍlak ?
Do you want to register this parcel ?	ɣawiz tibʕat iṭṭárdi dá b-ilbarííd ilmusággal ?
You must complete the special form that has to accompany the parcel.	láazim tímla ilfúrma-lmaxṣúuṣa-lli ḥatitbʕit maʕa-ṭṭárd.
Please give me an international form to send money to England.	ʕiddíini fúrma dawlíyya ʕábʕat bíiha-flúus l-ingiltíra.
You have to seal a registered parcel.	lazim tiʃámmaʕ iṭṭárd ʕaʃan asaggilhúulak.[1]
I want to send a telegram.	ʕana ɣáawiz ábʕat tiliyráaf, min faḍlak.
Don't forget to put the name and address of sender.	ma tinsáaʃ tíktib ism ilmúrsil wi ʕunwáanu(h).
If it cannot be delivered, it will be returned.	ʕíza ma waṣalítʃ (or wiṣlítʃ), ḥatitráddi l-ilmúrsil.
A telegram with prepaid reply.	tiliyráaf wi ráddi xáaliṣ.
What is the telegram rate to England ?	ʕittiliyrafáat bi káam l-ingiltíra ?
Greetings telegrams are dearer.	tiliyrafáat ittaháani ʕáyla.
This letter is dated the 12th, but the post-stamp shows it was sent off on the 14th.	ʕiggawábda maktúub bi tariix iṭnáaʃar, lakin xitmi wáraʕit ilbúṣṭa bi tariix ʕarbaʕtáaʃar.
How long does a surface-mail letter take from here to America ?	ʕiggawáab ilʕáadi yáaxud ʕaddéeh min hína-l ʕamríika.

[1] Lit. " so that I may register it for you ".

THE TELEPHONE

Vocabulary

public telephone	tilifóon ɣumúumi
receiver, instrument	sammáaɣa, sammaɣáat
exchange	sintiráal
automatic exchange	sintiráal utumatíiki
extension	nímra da(a)xilíyya, nímar da(a)xilíyya
operator	ɣáamil ittilifóon
subscriber	ɣáaḥib ittilifóon
telephone booth	kabíinit ittilifóon
telephone directory	dalíil ittilifonáat
call	mukálma, mukalmáat
local call	mukálma maḥallíyya
trunk call	mukálma xa(a)rigíyya
night call	mukálma laylíyya
connection	tawɣíil
engaged	maʃɣúul
button	zuráar, zaráayir
slot	tuʕb, ʕitʕáab
to phone, ring up	kállim, yikállim f-ittilifóon; ḍárab, yiḍrab tilifóon li …
to ring (intr.)	rann, yirínn
to dial	dáwwar, yidáwwar ittilifóon
to connect	wáɣɣal, yiwáɣɣal
to book a call	ḥágaz, yiḥgiz mukálma
to cancel a call	láɣa, yílɣi mukálma

Sentences

Hello!	ʕalóo!
Are you on the phone?	ɣándak tilifóon?
Please give me a ring to-morrow evening.	ʕiḍrábli-tlifóon búkra b-illéel, min faḍlak.
How do I use the phone?	ʕizzáay astáɣmil ittilifóon?
Lift the receiver.	ʕírfaɣ issammáaɣa.
Then dial the number required.	wi baɣdéen dáwwar innímra-llinta ɣawízha.
Have you any change for the telephone?	maɣáak fákka ɣaʃan ittilifóon?
Put the money in before dialling.	ʕiʕʕiʃ ilfilúus ʕábli ma titkállim.
Could I use your phone, please?	ʕáʕdar astáɣmil tilifóonak, min faḍlak?
Hello, could I speak to Mr. Mahmoud Ali?	ʕalóo, múmkin akállim issáyyid maḥmúud ɣáli, min faḍlak?

Speaking.	ſána maḥmúud.
Are you 1563 ?	ſíntu (nimrit) ſálfī xumsumíyya taláata-w sittíin ?
Number engaged.	ſinnímra maſyúula.
There's no answer.	ma ḥáddiſ biyrúdd.
Put the receiver down and call again.	ḥúṭṭ issammáaɛa w-íḍrab táani.
I can't get through.	miſ ɣáarif attíṣil b-innímra.
Inquiries, please.	ſiddíini listiɣlamáat, min faḍlak.
Can you give me the number of Mr. Muhammad Salim, of 10 Station Road ?	tiſdar tiddíini nímrit issáyyid muḥámmad sáalim illi sáakin fi nímra ɣáſara, ſáariɛ ilmaḥáṭṭa ?
I have tried several times to ring the hotel, but there is no reply.	ſana ḥawílt attíṣil b-illukánda-ktíir láakin ma ḥáddiſ biyrúdd.
Sorry, wrong number.	ſáasif, ſinnímra ɣálaṭ.
The telephone is out of order.	ſittilifóon ɛaṭláan.
Is that the Travel Agency ?	da máktab issiyáaḥa, min fáḍlak ?
Just a minute, hold the line, please.	daſíſa wáḥda, xallíik ɛa-lxáṭṭ, min faḍlak.
Isn't there a public call-box around here ?	ma fíiſ kabíinit tilifóon ɛumúumi f-ilḥítta di ?
Miss, I want to book a call to Alexandria, please.	ɣáawiz áḥgiz mukálma l-iskin-diríyya, min fáḍlik, ya ſa(a)nísa (or madmuwazáll).
Where can I wait until my trunk call comes through ?	ſáſdar astánna féen liyáayit ilmukálma ilxarigíyya-btáɛti tíigi ?
Alexandria, booth No. 7.	ſiskindiríyya, fi kabíinit nímrit sábɛa.
Sorry, we were cut off.	ſáasif, ſilxáṭṭ itſáṭaɛ.
Could you please give a message to Mr. Fareed Abdalla ?	tiſdar min faḍlak táaxud risáala ɛaſan issáyyid faríid ɛabdálla ?
You are wanted on the phone.	ſinta maṭlúub ɛa-ttilifóon.

CORRESPONDENCE

Vocabulary

letter	gawáab, gawabáat
business letter	gawáab maɣláḥi, gawabáat maɣlaḥíyya
letter of congratulation	gawáab tahníya
letter of condolence	gawáab taɛzíya
postcard	kártī bustáal, kurúut bustáal
handwriting	xaṭṭ ; kitáaba yadawíyya (manuscript)
pen	ríiſa, ríyaſ

fountain-pen	ſálam ḥíbr, ſiſláam ḥíbr; ſálam ſabanóoſ, ſiſláam ſabanóos
ball-pen	ſálam ḥíbrī gáaf, ſiſláam ḥíbrī gáaf
pencil	ſálam ruſáaſ, ſiſláam ruſáaſ
nib	sínn irríſa, ſasnáan irríſa
penholder	ſíid irríſa, ſayáad irríyaſ
copying-ink pencil	ſálam kúbya, ſiſláam kúbya
coloured pencil	ſálam miláwwin, ſiſláam milawwína
gum, glue	samy
letter-file	duséeh iggawabáat, duscháat; miláff, milaffáat
card-index	fíhris, faháaris
paper	wáraſ (c.), wáraſa, waraſáat, ſawráaſ
notepaper	karráasa, karrasáat (or kararíis)
cardboard	kartúun
envelope	ẓarf, ẓurúuf
writing-pad, writing-paper	wáraſ kitáaba
blotting-paper	naſſáaſa, naſſaſáat
ink	ḥíbr
inkstand, inkwell	dawáaya, dawayáat (or diwy)
sealing wax	ſámẓ áḥmar
stationer's	maktába, maktabáat
writing-desk	máktab, makáatib
stationery	ſadawáat ilkitáaba
shorthand	ſixtizáal
typewriter	ſáala kátba, ſaláat kátba
carbon-paper	wáraſit karbúun
string	dubáara
folder	duséeh, duscháat
sender	múrsil, mursilíin
addressee	ſalmúrsal ſiléeh, ſalmúrsal ſiláyhim
address	ẓunwáan, ẓanawíin
enclosures	ſilmurfaqáat
heading, reference	mawḍúuẓ
signature	ſimḍáaſ (or ſímḍa), ſimḍaſáat
commercial term	ſiſtiláaḥ tugáari
trade mark	márka musaggála
clerk	káatib, kátaba
typist	káatib (kaatíba) ẓala-lſáala-lkátba
secretary	(male) · sikirtéer, sikirteríyya; (female) sikirtéera, sikirteriyyáat
book-keeper	máasik iddafáatir, maskíin iddafáatir; muḥáasib, muḥasbíin

book-keeping	másk iddafáatir
partner	ʃarīik, ʃúraka
owner	ṣáaḥib, ʕaṣḥáab
staff	muwaẓẓafīin
to write	kátab, yíktib
to type	kátab, yíktib ɣala-lʕáala-lkátba
to copy	náʃal, yínʃil
to answer	gáawib, yigáawib ; radd, yirúdd (gawáab)
to stick	lázaʕ, yílzaʕ
to seal	xátam, yíxtim
to fold	ṭáwa, yíṭwi
to tie	rábaṭ, yúrbuṭ
to send	báɣat, yíbɣat

Sentences

Where is the writing-room ?	féen ʕóḍt [1] ikkitáaba ?
There are envelopes and note-paper on the writing-desk.	fīih zurúuf wi karráasa ɣala-lmáktab hináak.
I have to write an urgent letter.	láazim áktib gawáab mistáɣgil.
Shall I type it ?	ʕaktíbu ɣa-lʕáala-lkátba ?
I am expecting important news.	ʕana muntáẓir ʕaxbáar muhímma.
I have to answer some letters.	ʕana láazim arúddī ɣala báɣḍi gawabáat.
I owe my friend a letter.	ɣaláyya ʕáktib li ṣáḥbi gawáab.
Can you lend me your fountain-pen ?	tísmaḥ tisallífni ʕálamak ilḥíbr ?
My fountain-pen is broken. Where can I get it repaired ?	ʕálam ilḥíbrī-btáaɣi maksúur. ʕaṣallâḥu féen ?
He writes a very clear hand.	xáṭṭu-kwáyyis ʕáwi.
Take this letter down in short-hand.	ʕíktib iggawábda b-ilʕixtizáal.
He can neither read nor write. He is illiterate.	húwwa ma-byiʕdárʃi láa yíʕra wala yíktib. huwwa ʕúmmi.
Get this letter done quickly, it must catch the evening post.	xállaṣ iggawábda-b súrɣa, lazim yílḥaʕ búṣṭit ilmísa.
Make three carbon copies of this invoice.	ʕíɣmil tálat núsax min ilfatúura di.
Have you filed the letters ?	ḥaṭṭéet iggawabáat f-idduseháat ?
I told you all about it in my last letter.	ʕana ʕultílak kúllī ḥáaga ɣan il-ḥikáaya-f ʕáaxir gawáab líyya.[2]
I read your letter with great pleasure.	qaráʕtu xiṭaabáka bi báaliy issurúur.[3]

[1] Pronounced ʕoṭṭ.

[2] Notice the use of li, with gawáab already defined by the preposed ordinal numeral.   [3] Written language.

My sincere congratulations.	ʕáxlaṣ ittaháani.
Many happy returns of the day.	kúlli sána w-ínta ṭáyyib.
I was very pleased to hear of your engagement (marriage).	(spoken) ʕana-nbaṣáṭti [1] giddan lamma-wṣílni xábar xuṭbítak (gawáazak) ; (written) laḥad suriʔtu jíddan [2] ʒindáma waṣalánii nábaʕu xuṭbátik (zaẉáajik [2]).
My sincere condolences.	ʕáxlaṣ ittaʒáazi (or ʕáxlaṣ ittaʒ-zíya) ; (spoken) ʕilbaʕíyya-f ḥayáatak.
May I express my deep sympathy.	laqad taʕaθθártu jíddan bi muṣaabíkumu-lʕalíim.
In reply to your letter of the 16th June.	ʕijaabátan ʒalaa xiṭaabíkum bi ṭaaríix siṭṭáaʃar yúnya.
In receipt of your favour I am pleased to inform you that ...	ʕijaabátan ʒalaa xiṭaabíkum yasurrúnii ʕan ʕuxbírakum ʕanna ...
I herewith acknowledge receipt of your circular.	ʕistalámtu xiṭaabákum iddáwrii.
My dear father.	waalídi-lʒazíiz.
Dear Ahmad.	ʒazíizi ʕáḥmad.
Dearest Susan.	ḥabi(i)bátii sáwsan.
Dear Professor/Doctor/Captain Fikri (Abdurrahman).	ʒazíizi-lʕustáaz/-dduktóor/ -lyuzbáaʃi fíkri (friendly) ; (more formal) ʕassáyyid il-muḥtáram ilʕustáaz fíkri ʒabd irraḥmáan.
Dear Mr. Fahmy.	(friendly) ʒazíizi-ssáyyid fáhmi ; (more formal) ʕassáyyid il-muḥtáram ilʕustáaz fáhmi ʒabdálla.
Dear Mrs. Fathiya Hilmy.	ʕassayyída-lfaaḍíla-lʕustáaza fathíyya ḥílmi. [3]
Dear Miss Fawzia Ahmad.	ʕalʕaanísa (-lmuhaδδába) fawzíyya ʕáḥmad.
The Manager, Cotton Ginning Co.	ʕassáyyid mudíir ʃírkit ḥálg il-ʕaqṭáan.
Dear Sir.	ʕassáyyid mudíir ʃírkit ...
Yours sincerely.	ʕalmúxliṣ.

[1] Pronounced ʕimbaṣáṭṭi.
[2] Pronounce j as in English " jeep ".
[3] Or ʕassayyída-lmuḥtárama fathíyya háanim ḥílmi.

I remain, Yours faithfully.

With kind regards.
With all good wishes.
Your affectionate son.
Your affectionate brother.

A personal letter :

Alexandria, 4th May,
1953

Dear Mrs. Ahmad Hilmy,

Many thanks for your kind
invitation to dinner. I am
sorry to say I shall be away
this week-end, but I shall be
very pleased to spend one
evening next week with you if
convenient.

With kind regards,
Yours sincerely,
Mohamed Abu Al-Farag.

(The same message as it
might be communicated by
'phone.)

wa tafaḍḍálu bi qabúul fáaʕiq
liḥtiráam.
maʕa ʕátyab attaḥiyyáat.
maʕa ʕátyab ilʕamáani.
ʕibnúka-lbáar.
ʕaxúuka-lmúxliṣ.

gawáab ʃáxṣi :

ʕalʕiskandaríyya, fi
ʕarbáʕa máayu, sanat ʕálfi
tusʕumíyya tamánya-w
xamsiin [1]
ʕassayyída ḥárum ilʕustáaz
ʕáḥmad ḥílmi [2]

ʃúkrun jaziilan ʕala daʕwáti-
kum l-ilʕaʃáaʕ. ʕana ʕáasif
liʕanni saʕáqḍi ʕúʃlat niháayit
ilʕusbúuʕ xáarij ilmadíina,
wala(a)kinnáhu yasurrúnii jíd-
dan ʕan ʕaqḍíya ʕumsíyatan
máʕakum filʕusbúuʕ ilmúqbil
ʕiða(a) wa(a)fáqakum ðáalik.
maʕa ʕátyab attaḥiyyáat
ʕalmúxliṣ
muḥámmad abu-lfárag.

mutaʃákkir giddan ʕala daʕ-
witkum l-ilʕáʃa. láakin ʕana
ʕáasif ʕáwi liʕanni ḥaʕáḍḍi
niháayit ilʕusbúuʕ bárra-
skindiríyya. ʕiza káan yiwa-
fíʕkum ʕáyyi yóom f-ilʕusbúuʕ
illi gáyy ʕakúun mabṣúuṭ gíddan ʕinn-aʕáḍḍi ʕumsíya
ʕandúkum. [3]

[1] This is, of course, simply an indication of the way in which the
figures denoting the year would be uttered.
[2] The following few short letters have been included, together with
other material in this section, in order to illustrate the difference between written language and that which is elsewhere the concern of
this book. Vocabulary apart, the grammar is substantially that of
written Arabic and cannot be accounted for in a book dealing
exclusively with the very different colloquial language.
[3] Notice the polite use of the *plural* pronominal suffix.

A short business note :
      Cairo, 8th June, 1959.

The Manager,
Municipal Electricity Co.
Dear Sir,
   I beg to inform you that our
electric meter is not working.
Please send someone to attend
to it. With thanks in anticipa-
tion.
     Yours faithfully,
        So-and-so.
A business letter :
     Suez, 10th August, 1959.

Dear Sir,

   We have pleasure in sending
you herewith invoice for two
hundred pairs of best-quality
men's shoes bought for your
account and to be shipped to
you on the 22nd inst. We hope
you will be pleased with the
goods, as the make is strong
and serviceable and the manu-
facturers guarantee the goods
to stand any climate.
   You will gather from the
invoice that we have been able
to obtain a special cash dis-
count of five per cent.

   I am,
    With compliments,
    Yours faithfully,
      So-and-so.

xiṭáab maṣláḥi qaṣíir :
    Ꜥalqa(a)híra, fi tamánya
         yúnya, sanat Ꜥálfi
   tusꜤumíyya tísꜤa-w xamsíin.
Ꜥassáyyid ilmudíir
ʃírkat innúur
sayyídi
   Ꜥáktub háaða li Ꜥuxbírakum
Ꜥanna ɣaddáad ilkahrabáaꜤ ɣin-
dána taɣáʈʈal, wa Ꜥárgu Ꜥan
tursílu mán yuʃlíḥuh. wa fi(i)
lintiðáar [1] lákum jazíil iʃʃúkr.
     muqaddímu
        fuláan.

xiṭáab maṣláḥi :
   Ꜥissuwées, fi ɣáʃara Ꜥaɣúṣʈuṣ,
    sanat Ꜥálfi tusꜤumíyya
      tísꜤa-w xamsíin.
Ꜥassáyyid mudíir ʃírkit
(kaza . . .) [2]
   surrúna Ꜥan nursíla Ꜥiláykum
maɣa háaða qa(a)Ꜥímati-
lꜤasɣáar bi míꜤatay záwjin
min Ꜥaḥsáni-lꜤaḥðíya-lxáaṣṣa
b-irrijáal Ꜥiʃtúriyat li ḥisa(a)bí-
kum wa satuʃḥánu Ꜥiláykum
f-iθθáani wa-lɣiʃríin mina-ʃʃáhr
ilḥáali. naɣmúlu Ꜥan tanáala-
lbiḍa(a)ɣátu Ꜥiɣja(a)bákum
liꜤanna-ṣṣináaɣa matíina wa
tataḥammálu kaθíiran wa-
lmuntijúuna yaḍmanúuna
ṣala(a)ḥíyat albiḍáaɣa li Ꜥáyyi
jáww.
   wa sataɣlamúuna min
qa(a)Ꜥímati-lꜤasɣáar Ꜥannána
ḥaṣúulna ɣala xáɣmin xáaṣṣin
lákum qi(i)mátuhu xámsa(tun)
f-ilmíꜤah.
   wa tafaḍḍálu bi qabúuli
fáaꜤiq liḥtiráam.
         fuláan.

[1] ð is only associated with written Arabic and is the " emphatic "
counterpart of ð.
[2] Lit. " The Manager (of the so-and-so company) ".

Addresses on envelopes:
... , Esq./Professor ... ,
4 Station Road,
Port Said.

Miss ...
5 Mo'iz Street, Flat 9, Cairo.

ɣanawíin iggawabáat:
Ɣassáyyid ilmuḥtáram
            ilƔustáaz fuléan,
4 (Ɣarbáɣa) ʃáariɣ ilmaḥáṭṭa,
bur saɣlid.
ƔalƔaanísa (-lmuhabbába)
   fuláana,
5 (xámsa) ʃáariɣ ilmuɣízz,
ʃíƔƔa nimrit 9 (tísɣa),
Ɣalqa(a)híra.

NUMERATION

Vocabulary

Cardinals:	ƔilƔaɣdáad ilƔasasíyya :
nil, nought	ṣifr
one	wáaḥid, wáḥda
two	Ɣitnéen
three	tálat, taláata
four	Ɣárbaɣ, Ɣarbáɣa
five	xámas, xámsa
six	sitt, sítta
seven	sábaɣ, sábɣa
eight	táman, tamánya
nine	tísaɣ, tísɣa
ten	ɣáʃar, ɣáʃara
eleven	ḥidáaʃar
twelve	Ɣitnáaʃar
thirteen	talaṭṭáaʃar
fourteen	Ɣarbaɣṭáaʃar
fifteen	xamasṭáaʃar
sixteen	siṭṭáaʃar
seventeen	sabaɣṭáaʃar
eighteen	tamanṭáaʃar
nineteen	tisaɣṭáaʃar
twenty	ɣiʃríin
twenty-one	wáaḥid wi ɣiʃríin
twenty-two	Ɣitnéen wi ɣiʃríin
twenty-three	taláata-w ɣiʃríin
twenty-four	Ɣarbáɣa-w ɣiʃríin
thirty	talatíin
forty	Ɣarbiɣíin
fifty	xamsíin
sixty	sittíin

seventy	sabɛíin
eighty	tamaníin
ninety	tisɛíin
hundred	míyya, miyyáat
one hundred and one	míyya-w wáaḥid
two hundred	mitéen
three hundred	tultumíyya
four hundred	rubɛumíyya
five hundred	xumsumíyya
six hundred	suttumíyya
seven hundred	subɛumíyya
eight hundred	tumnumíyya
nine hundred	tusɛumíyya
thousand	ɛalf, ɛaláaf
eleven hundred	ɛálfi-w míyya
one hundred and sixty-three	míyya taláata-w sittíin
two thousand one hundred and ninety-two	ɛalféen míyya-tnéen wi tisɛíin
five thousand five hundred and seventy	xámast aláaf xumsumíyya-w sabɛíin
million	milyóon, malayíin
two million	ɛitnéen milyóon

Ordinals : ɛilɛaɛdáad ilwaṣfíyya :

first	ɛáwwil ; ɛawwaláani, ɛawwalaníyya, ɛawwalaniyyíin
second	táani, tánya
third	táalit, tálta
fourth	ráabiɛ, rúbɛa
fifth	xáamis, xámsa
sixth	sáatit, sátta ; sáadis, sádsa
seventh	sáabiɛ, sábɛa
eighth	táamin, támna
ninth	táasiɛ, tásɛa
tenth	ɛáaʃir, ɛáʃra
(the) fifteenth	ɛilxamasṭáaʃar
(the) twentieth	ɛilɛiʃríin
(the) hundredth	ɛilmíyyʌ
(the) twenty-fourth	ɛilɛarbɛɛa-w ɛiʃríin
last	ɛáaxir ; ɛaxráani, ɛaxraníyya, ɛaxraniyyíin

Fractions : ɛilkusúur :

vulgar fraction	kásr iɛtiyáadi
decimal fraction	kásri ɛúʃri

half	nuṣṣ, ʕanṣáaṣ/ʕinṣáaṣ
third	tilt, ʕatláat/ʕitláat
quarter	rubʕ, ʕarbáaʕ/ʕirbáaʕ
fifth	xums, ʕaxmáas/ʕixmáas
sixth	suds, ʕasdáas/ʕisdáas
seventh	subʕ, ʕasbáaʕ/ʕisbáaʕ
eighth	tumn, ʕatmáan/ʕitmáan
ninth	tusʕ, ʕatsáaʕ/ʕitsáaʕ
tenth	ʕuʃr, ʕaʕʃáar/ʕiʕʃáar
(a) twentieth	wáaḥid ẓala ẓiʃríin
three twentieths	taláata ẓala ẓiʃríin
hundredth	wáaḥid ẓala míyya
3·5 (three point five)	taláata-w xámsa min ẓáʃara
4·75	ʕarbáẓa-w xámsa-w sabẓíin min míyya
2·01	ʕitnéen wi wáaḥid min míyya
figure	raqm, ʕarqáam
number	ẓádad, ʕaẓdáad ; nímra,[1] nímar
mathematics	riyáaḍa
arithmetic	ḥisáab
algebra	(ʕil)gabr
geometry	handása
addition	gamʕ
subtraction	ṭarḥ
multiplication	ḍarb
division	qisma
sum	gúmla
multiplication table	gádwal iḍḍárb, gadáawil iḍḍárb
percentage	nísba miʕawíyya
once	márra
twice	marritéen
three times	tálat marráat
to add	gámaʕ, yígmaʕ
to subtract	ṭáraḥ, yíṭraḥ
to multiply	ḍárab, yíḍrab
to divide	ʕásam, yíʕsim
to calculate	ḥásab, yíḥsib
to estimate	ʕáddar, yiʕáddar
to deduct	xáṣam, yíxṣim

[1] Especially as a means of identifying an object or place, e.g a house or flat.

Sentences

Twice two are four.	ſitnéen f-itnéen b-arbáɛa.
Three (times) two(s) are six.	taláata f-itnéen bi sítta.
Two into six goes three.	sítta ɛala-tnéen yisáawi [1] taláata.
Two and three make five.	ſitnéen záaſid taláata yisáawi xámsa.
Three from five leaves two.	xámsa náaqiṣ .taláata yisáawi-tnéen.
How long have you been waiting?	ſinta mistánni baſáalak ſaddéeh?
Three-quarters of an hour.	tálatt írbaɛ [2] sáaɛa.
What are your office hours?	ſinta-btiſtáɣal min káam li káam?
From nine to five.	min tísɛa-l xámsa.
I had ten days' leave.	ſana kan ɣándi ɛáſurt iyyáam ſagáaza.
I spent a year and a half in Egypt.	ſana maḍḍéet fi máṣri sána-w núṣṣ.
How far is it to Cairo?	ſilmasáafa ſaddéeh min hína-l máṣr?
It is 26 kilometres from here.	sítta-w ɛiſríin kelumítri min hína.
How long does it take to get there?	táaxud ſaddéeh min hína li-hnáak?
About an hour and a half.	sáaɛa-w núṣṣi taſríiban.
The train will leave for Shibin el Qanatir in thirty minutes.	ſilſáṭr illi ráayiḥ ſibíin ilſanáaṭir ḥayſúum baɛdi núṣṣi sáaɛa.
My seat is row ten, number twelve.	ſikkúrsi-btáaɛi nimra-ṭnáaſar f-iṣṣáff ilɛáaſir.
This ring is worth more than a pound.	ſilxáatim da-ysáawi ſáktar min ginéeh.
There were hundreds of children in that school.	ſilmadrasáadi kan fíiha talámza b-ilmiyyáat.
It is the last day of my holidays.	ſinnahárda ſáaxir yóom fi ſagázti.
He inherited a hundred acres from his father.	wáras ɣan abúuh míit faddáan.
Two-thirds of the book are uninteresting.	tiltéen m-ikkitáab maláaſ máɛna.
He sold half of his property.	báaɛ núṣṣi ſamláaku(h).
A year and a half ago I was in hospital.	ſana kútti f-ilmustáſfa min sána-w núṣṣ.

[1] Lit. " equals ".
[2] Notice the unexpected stress and short vowel in the final syllable (cf. the isolated form ſirbáaɛ).

Their boy is six months old.	Ṣibnúhum ẓandu sítt úʃhur.
He stayed abroad over three months.	Ṣáḍḍa Ṣáktar min tálat ʃuhúur f-ilxáarig.
In nineteen hundred and fourteen.	fi sanat Ṣálfi tusẓumíyya w-arbaẓtáaʃar.
The percentage of pupils studying mathematics is larger than that studying languages.	Ṣinnísba-lmiṢawíyya l-ittalámza-lli-byidrísu-ryáaḍa Ṣáktar m-illi-byidrísu luyáat.

COINAGE, WEIGHTS, MEASURES

Vocabulary

(the) coinage	(Ṣal)ẓúmla [1]
weights and measures	ṢalṢawzáan w-almaqaayíis [1]
coin	ẓúmla, ẓumláat
money	filúus [2]
change	fákka
small change	ẓúmla ṣaɣíira
foreign currency	ẓúmla Ṣagnabíyya
£1 note	wáraṢa-b ginéeh
50-piastre note	wáraṢa-b xamsíin Ṣírʃ
25-piastre note	wáraṢa-b xámsa-w ẓiʃríin Ṣírʃ
10-piastre note	wáraṢa-b ẓáʃara sáay
5-piastre note	wáraṢa-b xámsa sáay
£10 note	wáraṢa-b ẓáʃara-gnéeh
£5 note	wáraṢa-b xámsa-gnéeh
20-piastre piece	riyáal (fáḍḍa [3]), riyaláat (fáḍḍa)
10-piastre piece	ẓáʃara sáay (fáḍḍa), ẓaʃaráat sáay (fáḍḍa)
5-piastre piece	xámsa sáay fáḍḍa, xamsáat sáay fáḍḍa
2-piastre piece	núṣṣi-fránk, núṣṣi-frankáat
1-piastre piece	Ṣírʃi sáay, Ṣuráuʃ sáay
½-piastre piece	Ṣírʃi taẓríifa
milleme (1/10 piastre)	mallíim, malallíim
1½ piastres (not a coin)	taláata taẓríifa ; taláat-ábyaḍ
2½ piastres (not a coin)	xámsa taẓríifa ; xáms-ábyaḍ
pound sterling	ginéeh istirlíini, gineháat istirliníyya

[1] The vowel a is commonly associated with the article in such borrowings from Modern (written) Arabic.
[2] A feminine form.
[3] fáḍḍa = " silver ".

Weights :   ſilſawzáan :
  ton   ţinn, ſaţnáan
  cantar (approx. 75 lb.),   ſintáar, ſanaţſir
    quintal
  oke (approx. 2¾ lb.)   wiſſa, wiſaſ
  kilogram (2½ lb.)   kéelu, keluwáat ; kilugráam, kilu-
                   gramáat
  pound, rotl (¾ lb.)   raţl, ſirtáal
  ounce   wiſiyya, wiſiyyáat
  dram (400 drams = 1 oke)   dárhim, daráahim
  gramme   giráam, giramáat

Liquid measures :   makayſil issawáaſil :
  litre (4½ litres = 1 gal.)   litr, litráat
  gallon   galúun, galunáat

Linear measures :   ſalmaqa(a)yſis :
  kilometre (⅝ mile)   kéelu, keluwáat ; kilumítr, kilu-
                   mitráat
  metre (approx. 39 in.)   mitr, ſimtáar
  centimetre   santimítr (or g-), santimitráat
  millimetre   millimítr, millimitráat
  league   fársax, faráasix
  mile   miil, ſamyáal
  yard   yárda, yardáat
  foot   ſádam, ſiſdáam
  inch   búuşa, buşáat [1]

Square measures :   ſilmaqa(a)yſis ilmirabbáſa :
  acre   faddáan, fadadſin
  square metre   mítrī-mrábbaſ
  square yard   yárda-mrabbáſa
  100 square metres   mſit mítrī-mrábbaſ
  qirat (₂₄¹ faddaan)   ſiráaţ, ſararſiţ [2]
  busa (₂₄¹ qirat, i.e. approx.   búuşa-mrabbáſa, buşáat mirabbáſa
    3 square metres)

Cubic measures :   ſilmaqa(a)yſis ilmukaſſába :
  cubic metre   mítrī mukáſſab
  cubic inch   búuşa mukaſſába

---

[1] In the agricultural context of the measurement of fields, búuşa
= approx. 3 metres.
[2] The context is again that of land measurement; elsewhere
ſiráaţ = " the width of a finger ".

Grain measurement :

  kéela, keláat (the standard measuring canister and the amount it
    contains)
  Ɛardább, Ɛaradíbb (12 kéelas = 1 Ɛardább)
  wéeba, webáat (used only in countryside) (2 kéelas = 1 wéeba)
  Ɛádah, ƐiƐdáah (¼ kéela)

armspan	baaɛ, Ɛibwáaɛ
handspan	ʃibr, Ɛiʃbáar
fingerspan (between thumb and index finger)	fitr, Ɛiftáar
high	ɣáali, ɣálya, ɣalyíin
wide	ɣaríiḍ, ɣaríiḍa, ɣuráaḍ
long	ṭawíil, ṭawíila, ṭuwáal
deep	ɣawíiṭ, ɣawíiṭa, ɣuwáaṭ
scales	mizáan, mawazíin
ruler	maṣṭára, maṣáaṭir
tape measure	mazúura, mazuráat
to measure	Ɛaas, yiɛíis
to weigh	wázan, yiwzin
to measure out	káyyil, yikáyyil

Sentences

Can you lend me 50 piastres ?	tiƐdar tisallífni xamsíin Ɛirʃ, min faḍlak ?
I have no change on me.	ma-mɛíiʃ fákka.
Can I borrow a pound till to-morrow ?	tismah tisallífni-gnéeh li búkra ?
I have only a little silver.	ma-mɛíiʃ illa-ʃwáyyit fákka-ɡyayyaríin.
Are there silver coins in Egypt ?	fíih ɣúmla fáḍḍa-f máɡr ?
Yes, but they are really an alloy.	Ɛáywa, lakinnáha f-ilhaƐíiƐa sabíika.
Put a one-piastre piece in the slot.	ḥúṭṭi Ɛirʃi ɡáay f-ittúƐb.
I've lost £5.	ráah mínni xámsa-gnéeh.
I have to pay £3.	lazim áḍfaɡ taláata-gnéeh.
You can repay me next week.	tiƐdar tídfaɡ illi ɡaléek ilƐusbúuɡ illi ɡáay.
He has run into debt.	huwwa madyúun.
What do I owe you ?	ɣaláyya káam lík ?
He's a black marketeer.	huwwa-byiʃtáɡal f-issúuƐ issóoda.
Have you paid your income tax ?	dafáɡti ḍaríbt iddáxl illi ɡaléek ?
It is deducted from my salary.	Ɛiḍḍaríiba-btitxíɡim min mahiyyíti (or **muratttábi**).

Did you weigh yourself on the scales?	ɕinta wazánti náfsak ɤa-lmizáan?
I weigh 65 kilos.	wázni xámsa-w sittíin kéelu.
How many okes of oranges do you want me to buy?	ɤawízn(i)-aʃtíri káam wiʃʃit burtuɕáan?
Two kilograms will be enough.	ɕitnéen kéelu bi-kfáaya.
How much is a ton of charcoal?	tínn ilfáɧmi-b káam?
We have bought 50 lb. of potatoes.	ɕiʃtaréena xamsíin rátli batáatis.
We want twelve "bushels" of wheat.	ɕíɧna ɤawzíin ɕardábbi ɕámɧ.
How far is Alexandria from Cairo?	ɕilmasáafa ben mágri w-iskindiríyya ɕaddéeh?
I was driving at 50 kilometres an hour.	ɕana kútti sáayiɕ bi súrɤit xamsíin kéelu f-issáaɤa.
Let me have three metres of this ribbon.	ɕiddíini tálatt imtáar min iʃʃiríit da, min fadlak.
The garden is 35 metres long and 20 metres wide.	ɕigginéena túlha xámsa-w talatíin mítr wi ɤardáha ɕiʃríin mítr.
Will you take my measurements for a suit?	tismaɧ táaxud maɕáasi ɤalaʃan bádla?
These shoes are made to measure.	ɕiggazmáadi tafɕíil.
Have you a measure to see how long this cloth is?	ɤándak mítri ɤalaʃáan tiɕɕíis ilɕumáaʃa di.
Does your ruler show inches and centimetres?	mastártak mitɤállim ɤaléehalbuɕáat w-iɕɕantimitráat?
How many miles is it from Suez to Port Said?	ɕilmasáafa min issuwées li bur saɕíid káam míil?
I don't know the figure in miles, only in kilometres, but I'll work it out presently for you.	ɕana miʃ ɤáarif ilɤádad b-ilɕamyáal, ɕana ɤárfu b-ilkelúwáat báss — ɕana ɧaɧsibɧáalak ɧáalan.
Half a litre of milk, please.	núɕɕi lítri lában, min fadlak.
I have ordered two cubic metres of wood.	ɕana talábt itnéen mítri xáʃab mukaɤɤablíin.

THE HUMAN BODY, HEALTH

Vocabulary

head	raas,[1] ruus
face	wiʃʃ, wiʃúuʃ
skull	gumgúma, gamáagim

[1] A feminine noun.

forehead	ʃúura, ʃúwar
eye	ҳeen,[1] ҳuyuun (or ҳi-)
eyelid	gifn, gufúun
eyebrow	ḥáagib, ḥawáagib
eyelash	rimʃ, rumúuʃ
ear	widn,[1] widáan
nose	manaxíir
mouth	buҳҳ ; ḥának
lip	ʃiffa, ʃafáayif
cheek	xadd, xudúud
chin	daʃn,[1] duʃúun
jaw	ḍábba, ḍubúub
tooth	sínna, ʃasnáaṇ
neck	ráʃaba, raʃabáat (or raʃáabi)
gum	láθa [2] (or lása)
tongue	lisáan, ʃilsína
throat	zoor, ʃizwáar
tonsil	lóoza, líwaz
gland	ɣúdda, ɣúdad
hair	ʃaҳr (c.), ʃáҳra, ʃaҳráat
skin	gild, gulúud
bone	ҳaḍm (c.), ҳáḍma, ҳaḍmáat
rib	ḍálҳ, ḍulúuҳ
spine	silsílit iḍḍáhr
chest	sidr, sudúur
stomach	baṭn,[1] buṭúun
lung	ríʃa, riʃáat
heart	ʃalb, ʃulúub
bowels	ʃamҳáaʃ
liver	kibd (or kábid)
kidney	kílwa, kaláawi
shoulder	kitf, ʃiktáaf
arm	diráaҳ, ʃidríҳa
elbow	kuuҳ, kiҳáan
hand	ʃiid,[1] ʃidéen
wrist	xúnʃit ilʃíid
finger	ҳubáaҳ, ҳawáabiҳ
thumb	ʃiҳҳubáaҳ ikkibíir
middle finger	ʃiҳҳubáaҳ ilwiҳṭáani
little finger	ʃiҳҳubáaҳ iҳҳuyáyyar
joint	máfҳal, mafáaҳil
nail	ḍufr, ḍawáafir

---

[1] A feminine noun.
[2] Pronounce θ as *th* in English " think ".

thigh	faxd, ʕifxáad ; wirk, ʕiwráak
leg	rigl,[1] rigléen
knee	rúkba, rúkab
ankle	bízz irrígl
foot	rigl,[1] rigléen
toe	ṣubáaʕ irrígl
sole	káff irrígl
blood	damm
vein	ʕirʕ, ʕurúuʕ
blood circulation	ʕiddáwra-ddamawíyya
blood pressure	ḍáyṭ iddámm
illness, disease	múraḍ, ʕamráaḍ
hygiene	qawáaʕid iṣṣíḥḥa
nutrition	tayzíya
food	ʕakl
malnutrition	súuʕ tayzíya
dirt	wasáaxa
refuse	wásax
flies	dibbáan (c.), dibbáana, dibbanáat
pain	wágaʕ, ʕawgáaʕ
headache	ṣuḍáaʕ
sore throat	ʕiltiháab f-ilḥangára
cold	bard
influenza	ʕinfilwánza
catarrh	zukáam
cough	kúḥḥa
inflammation	ʕiltiháab
pneumonia	ʕiltiháab riʕawi
gastric trouble	táʕab f-ilmíʕda
tuberculosis	sull
bruise	xadʃ, xudúuʃ
cut	ʕaṭʕ, ʕuṭúuʕ
fracture	kasr, kusúur
medical examination	fáḥṣi ṭíbbi
treatment	ʕiláaʕ
medicine	dáwa, ʕadwíya
prescription	ruʃítta, ruʃittáat
injection ; syringe	ḥúʕna, ḥúʕan
vaccination, inoculation	taṭʕíim ; taxtíin
smallpox	gúdari
cholera	kúlira
typhus	taayfúus
typhoid	taayfúud

---

[1] A feminine noun.

paratyphoid	taayfuʕíid
dysentery	dusintárya
trachoma	tiraxóoma
international certificate of vaccination against smallpox	ʃiháada dawlíyya bi tuṭɣíim ḍidd iggúdari
ambulance	ɣarabíyyit ʕisɣáaf, ɣarabiyyáat ʕisɣáaf
hospital	mustáʃfa, mustaʃfayáat
ward	ɣámbar, ɣanáabir
doctor	duktúur (or duktóor), dakátra
nurse	mumarríḍa, mumarriḍáat
microbe	gurθúuma (or gursúuma), garaθíim (or -s-) [1]
blood test	ʃáḥɣi dámm
analysis	taḥlíil
toothache	wágaɣ lisnáan
contagious	múɣdi, muɣdíya
healthy	salíim, salíima, suláam ; fi ṣíḥḥa gayyída (of person) ; ṣíḥḥi (of climate, country, food)
convalescent	fi dóor innaqáaha
to cure, heal	ɣáalig, yiɣáalig
to anaesthetize	xáddar, yixáddar ; bánnig, yibánnig
to clean	náḍḍaf, yináḍḍaf
to extract	ʕálaɣ, yiʕlaɣ
to fill	mála, yímla

Sentences

What are Dr. Rushdi's consulting hours ?	ɣiyátt [2] idduktúuɪ rúʃdi-btíftaḥ ʕímta ?
Send for a doctor.	ʕíṭlub duktúur.
Did you consult a surgeon for the operation ?	ʕinta-staʃárti garráaḥ ɣaʃan ilɣamalíyya ?
What is the matter with you ?	ʕínta ɣayyáan bi ʕéeh ?
I don't feel well.	ʕana taɣbáan/ɣayyáan.
I feel very ill.	ʕana ɣayyáan ʕáwi.
I feel sick.	ʕálbi biyyúmmi ɣaláyya.
I feel giddy.	ʕana dáayix.
I feel weak.	ʕana hamdáan.
You have a sore throat.	ɣándak iltiháab f-ilḥangára.

[1] Pronounce θ as *th* in English " think ".
[2] = ɣiyásdit.

Your tonsils are swollen.	líwazak wárma.
I'm hoarse.	ʕana maḍbúuḥ.
I've caught a cold.	ʕana xátti bárd.
I keep sneezing and coughing.	ʕana báɣtaṣ w-akúḥḥi dáyman.
You must gargle and take a cough mixture.	láazim tityárɣar (or titráyraɣ) wi táaxud dáwa l-ilkúḥḥa.
Stay in bed for a day or two and take your temperature regularly.	láazim tistánna f-issiríir yoméen taláata w-itʕiis ḥarártak b-intiẓáam.
You are feverish, put the thermometer under your tongue.	ʕinta ɣándak ʕirtifáaɣ fi dáragit ilḥaráara — ḥúṭṭ ittirmumítri táḥti-lsáanak.
The temperature is going up (down).	ʕilḥaráara murtáfiɣa (munxáfiḍa).
Your pulse is very irregular.	nábḍak muṭṭárib (or míṣ maẓbúuṭ).
His heart is very weak.	ʕálbu ḍaɣíif gíddan.
He has pneumonia.	ɣándu iltiháab riʕawi.
You must be taken to hospital.	láazim tiráuḥ ilmustáṣfa.
I prefer a private clinic.	ʕan-afáḍḍal ɣiyáada xáaṣṣa.
The patient must not be disturbed.	láazim ilɣayyáan yitánni mistaráyyaḥ.
What are the fees for a visit to an ear, nose, and throat specialist?	duktúur ilʕáni w-ilʕúzun biyáaxud káam f-ikkáṣf?
I shall have to give you a thorough examination.	ʕana láazim ákṣif ɣaléek káṣti káamil.
We shall have to take an X-ray.	láazim níɣmil káṣti ʕaṣíɣɣa.
Is your digestion all right?	hádmak kuwáyyis?
The medicine was no good.	ʕiddáwa ma natáɣ.ʃ
Take these pills and a teaspoonful of this powder after meals.	xúd ilḥugúbda wi maɣláɣit ʃáay min ilmasḥúʕda baɣd ilʕákl.
Shake the bottle.	rúgg ilʕizáaza.
For external use only.	li listiɣmáali-lxaarígi fáqaṭ.[1]
Poison.	summ.
You have broken your arm.	diráaɣak ikkásar.
We shall have to keep your leg in plaster.	láazim niḥúṭṭi ríglak f-iggíbs.
He has fractured his skull.	ráasu-tɣawwárit.
You have had a bad concussion.	kan ɣándak ʕirtigáaɣ f-ilmúxxiʃdíid.
I am injured.	ʕana-ggaráḥt.
I've sprained my ankle.	rígli-ltáwaḥit.
His illness got worse.	ʕilɣáya túʕul ɣaléeh.
He is better.	huwwa xáff.

[1] Written language.

The cut is healed but you can still see the scar.	ʕiggárḥi ṭáab láakin ʕásaru lissa mawgúud.
I must dress your wounds.	láazim arbúṭlak iggárḥ.
I cannot hear well.	ʕana ma baʕdárʃ ásmaʒ kuwáyyis.
He is deaf and dumb.	huwwa ʕáṭraʃ wi ʕáxraʒ.
Your inner ear is inflamed.	wídnak multáhiba min gúwwa.
I am short-sighted (long-sighted).	ʕana ʒándi ʕíʒar náẓar (ṭúul náẓar).
Do you know a good oculist?	tíʒraf ṭabíib ʒiyúun kuwáyyis?
He is blind.	huwwa ʕáʒma.
I need a pair of glasses.	ʕana ʒáawiz naḍḍáara.
He squints a little.	huwwa ʕáḥwal ʃuwayya.

At the dentist's:

Please come into the surgery.	min fáḍlak taʒáala-lʒiyáada.
This tooth hurts me.	ʕiddirsída-byiwgáʒni.
This front tooth hurts me.	ʕissínna-lʕuddamaníyya di-btiwgáʒni.
This tooth must be stopped.	ʕissinnáadi láazim tiṭḥáʃa.
The gums are bleeding.	ʕillása bitxúrri dámm.
I shall give you a local anaesthetic.	ʕana ḥaʒṭíik bínʒi maḥálli.
The root is decayed.	gídr issinnáadi-msáwwiʃ.
Can't you manage without drilling?	ma tiʕdárʃi tiʒmílha min ɣéer táʕb.
The tooth must be extracted.	ʕissínna láazim titxálaʒ.
I have a gumboil.	ʒándi xurráag.
What tooth-paste do you use?	bitistáʒmil ʕáyyi maʒgúun ʕasnáan?
I'm afraid you must have a denture.	láazim tiʒmíllak ṭáʕm isnáan.
You must have a gold crown on your tooth.	láazim niḥúṭṭi ṭarbáuʃ dáhab ʒala sinnítak.
I shall have to get a new tooth-brush.	ʕana láazim agíib fúrʃit isnáan gidíida.
Is the treatment finished?	ʕilʒiláag xúluʒ?

AT THE HAIRDRESSER'S

Vocabulary

gentlemen's hairdresser's	mizáyyin (or ḥalláaʕ) l-irrigáal
ladies' hairdresser's	mizáyyin (or ḥalláaʕ) l-issayyidáat
safety razor	mákanit ḥiláaʕa
razor blade	múus ḥiláaʕa, ʕamwáas ḥiláaʕa
shaving brush	fúrʃit ḥiláaʕa

shaving lotion	kulúnya l-ilḥiláaʕa
shaving soap/stick	ṣabúun ḥiláaʕa
shaving cream	maɣgúun ḥiláaʕa
hair-cream	diháan l-iʃʃáɣr
eau-de-cologne	kulúnya
haircut	ḥiláaʕa
beard	daʕn,[1] duʕúun
moustache	ʃánab, ʃanabáat
wave	tamwíiga, tamwigáat
parting	farʕ, furúuʕ
wash	ɣasl
shampoo	ʃampúu
hair-net	ʃábakit iʃʃáɣr
hairpin	dabbúus iʃʃáɣr
comb	miʃṭ, ʕimʃáaṭ
hairbrush	fúrʃit ʃáɣr
perfume	ʑiṭr, ʑuṭúur ; rúiḥa, rawáayiḥ
nail varnish	diháan ḍawáafir
talcum powder	búdrit tálk
face powder	búdrit wiʃʃ
lipstick	ʕáḥmar ʃafáayif
tweezers	mulʕáat
manicure	manikéer
manicurist	ʑa(a)mílit ilmanikéer
to shave	ḥálaʕ, yíḥlaʕ
to cut	ḥálaʕ, yíḥlaʕ (hair) ; ʕággar, yiʕággár
to trim	sáawa, yisáawi
to lather	ráɣɣa, yiráɣyi
to wave	máwwig, yimáwwig
to dry	náʃʃif, yináʃʃif
to dye	sábaɣ, yúsbuɣ
to massage	ʑámal, yiʑmil masáaj li . . .

Sentences

Is there a gentlemen's hair-dresser near here?	fíih ḥalláaʕ l-irrigáal ʕuráyyib hína ?
How do you want it, sir?	ʕaɣmíllak ʕéeh fi ʃáɣrak ?
A haircut, please, trim back and sides.	ʕuẓẓíli ʃáɣri, min faḍlak, wi ʕaggarhúuli m-iggawáanib wi min wára.
Not too short, please.	ma-tʕaggarúuʃ ʕáwi, min faḍlak.
A two-days-old beard.	dáʕni baʕálha yoméen min. ɣéer ḥiláaʕa.

[1] A feminine noun.

Please trim my moustache.	min ʃáḍlak, wáḍḍab ʃánabi.
I should like a shampoo.	ʕana ɣáawiz ʃampúu, min faḍlak.
You can give me a shave, too.	ʕiḥláʕli dáʕni kamáan, min faḍlak.
Does this shaving-cream give a good lather?	maɣgúun ilḥiláaʕa da-byiɣmil ráɣwa-kwayyísa?
Here is a hot towel, sir.	ʕitfáḍḍal fúuṭa súxna-(a)héh !
He is getting bald.	huwwa-byiʃlaɣ.
He is turning grey.	ʃáɣru biyʃíib.
Have you a hair-restorer?	ɣándak ḥáaga ma-txallíiʃ iʃʃáɣri yiʃɣaṭ?
Have you any good hair-oil?	ɣándak zéet ʃáɣri-kwáyyis?
Should I leave a tip for the assistant?	láazim aslíib baʃʃíiʃ ɣaʃan iṣṣábi?
I would like to make an appointment with my usual assistant for to-morrow at eleven.	ʕana ɣáawz(a)-áḥgiz maɣáad maɣa-lḥalláaʕa-btáɣti búkra-ssaɣa-ḥḍáaʃar.
Everything is booked up for to-morrow, I am sorry.	ʕiḥna maʃɣulíin búkra, ʕana ʕáasif.
Can I come for a perm on Monday?	ʕáʕdar áagi ɣaʃan amáwwig ʃáɣri yóom litnéen?
Don't cut off too much, please.	ma-tʕaṣṣárʃi ʃáɣri ʕáwi, min faḍlak.
I should like to try a new hair-style.	ʕana ɣáawz(a)-aɣáyyar listáyl bitaɣ ʃáɣri.
What colour do you want your hair dyed?	ɣáwza tisbúɣi ʃáɣrik bi ʕáyyi lóon?
I should like a dark brown shade.	ʕana ɣáwza lóon búnni ɣáamiʕ.
Do you sell lipsticks and nail varnish to match?	ʕíntu bitbíiɣu ʕáḥmar ʃafáayif wi-dháan ḍawáaʃir yiwáfʕu(h)?
For your make-up we have cream and face powder, eyebrow pencils and rouge.	ɣandína-kríim wi búdra l-ilwíʃʃ w-iʕláam l-ilḥawáagib wi ʕáḥ-mar ɣaʃan ittuwalítt.
Have you a manicure service?	ɣandúkum manikéer hína?
Have you any toilet soap?	ɣandúkum ṣabúun wíʃʃ?

CLOTHING [1]

Vocabulary

men's clothing	miláabis l-irrigáal
pyjamas	bijáama, bijamáat
dressing-gown	roob, ʕirwáab
slippers	ʃibʃib, ʃabáaʃib

---

[1] Only European-style clothing is dealt with in this section.

socks	ʃaráab, ʃarabáat
shoes	gázma (pair) : fárdit gázma (one)
suspenders	ḥammaláatʃarabáat : ḥammáalitʃaráab (one)
garters	ʕasáatik ʃarabáat ; ʕástik ʃaráab (one)
drawers, pants	libáas, ʕilbísa
vest	fanílla, fanilláat
shirt	ʕamíiʃ, ʕumʃáan
braces	ḥammáalit banṭalóon
belt	ḥizáam, ʕiḥzíma
collar	yáaʕa, yaʕáat ; liyáaʕa, liyaʕáat
stud	zuráar liyáaʕa, zaráayir liyaʕáat
cuff-links	zaráayir ʕasáawir ilʕamíiʃ
tie	garafíṭṭa, gurafiṭṭáat ; karafítta, karafittáat ; karaváṭṭa, karavaṭṭáat
suit, lounge-suit	bádla, bídal
jacket	jakétta, jakettáat
trousers	banṭalóon, banṭalonáat
waistcoat	sidéeri, sadáari
evening-dress	bádlit issáhra
overcoat	bálṭu, baláaṭi (or balṭuwáat)
cap	kaskítta, kaskittáat
hat	barníiṭa (or burnéeṭa), baraníiṭ
beret	birée(h), bireháat
gloves	gawánti, gawantiyyáat ; fárdit gawánti (one)
stick	ʑáʑa, ʑuʑy
umbrella, parasol	ʃamsíyya, ʃamsiyyáat
scarf	talfíiḥa, talafíiḥ ; kuʃíyya, kuʃiyyáat
handkerchief	mandíil, manadíil
raincoat	bálṭu máṭar, baláaṭi máṭar
suit material	ʕumáaʃ bádla
sports wear	maláabis irriyáaḍa
cardigan	kardigáan, kardiganáat
pullover	bilóovar, bilovráat
stockings	ʃarabáat
underwear	maláabis daxilíyya
brassiere	sutiyáan, sutiyanáat
slip	ʕamíiʃ, ʕumʃáan
briefs	kalsúun, kalsunáat
night-dress	ʕamíiʃ nóom
girdle, roll-on	kursée(h), kurseháat
dress, gown	fustáan, fasatíin
blouse	bilóoza (or bilúuza), bilozáat
suit, costume	tayyéer, tayyeráat
apron	ʕéeprun (or ʕáprun), ʕeprunáat

fur coat	bálṭu fárw, baláaṭi fárw
veil	búrʃuẓ, baráaʃiẓ ; béeʃa, beʃáat (on hat)
square, headkerchief	ʃiʃáarb, ʃiʃarbáat
shawl	ʃaal, ʃiláan
high-heeled shoe	gázma-b káẓbi ẓáali
walking-shoe	gázma-b káẓbi wáaṭi
sole (of shoe)	naẓl
fashion	móoḍa, moḍáat
design	tafṣiila, tafṣiláat
material	ʃumáaʃ, ʃumaʃáat
silk	ḥariir
velvet	vílvit
wool	ṣuuf
linen	kittáan
jewels, jewellery	migawharáat
ring	xáatim, xawáatim
necklace	ẓuʃḍ, ẓuʃúud
bracelet	ʃiswíra, ʃasáawir
ear-rings	ḥálaʃ (pair), ḥulʃáan (pairs) ; fárdit ḥálaʃ (one)
tailor	xayyáaṭ, xayyaṭíin
dressmaker	xayyáaṭa
coat-hanger	ʃammáaẓa, ʃammaẓáat
red	ʃáḥmar, ḥámra, ḥumr
blue	ʃázraʃ, zárʃa, zurʃ
green	ʃáxḍar, xáḍra, xuḍr
yellow	ʃáṣfar, ṣáfra, ṣufr
brown	búnni [1]
grey	ruṣáaṣi
black	ʃíswid, sóoda, suud
white	ʃábyaḍ, béeḍa, biiḍ
purple	banafsigi
orange	burtuʃáani
silver	fáḍḍi
golden	dáhabi
light (in colour)	fáatiḥ, fátḥa, fatḥíin
dark	ɣáamiʃ, ɣámʃa, ɣamʃíin
to dress	libis, yílbis ; lábbis, yilábbis (transitive)
to undress	ʃálaẓ, yíʃlaẓ
to put on	libis, yílbis (e.g. iggázma)
to take off	ʃálaẓ, yíʃlaẓ (e.g. ilbarnííṭa)

[1] Also " coffee-coloured ".

to sew   xáyyaṭ, yixáyyaṭ
to mend   ṣáilaḥ, yiṣállaḥ
to darn   ráfa, yírfi

Sentences

Do you know a good tailor?   tiɛraf xayyáaṭ kuwáyyis?
I want a suit made to measure.   ɛáawiz afáṣṣal bádla.
I prefer a suit made to measure   ɛan-afáddạl ilbádḯa-ttaḟɡḯil ɛan
   to a ready-made one.   iggáhza.
What sort of material do you   ʿéeh nóoɛ ilʿumáaṣ illi
   stock?   ɛandúkum?
I want a lounge suit.   ɛana ɛáawiz bádla, min faḏlak.
Single-breasted or double-   bi ṣáffi wáaḥid walla-b ṣafféen?
   breasted?
Do you wear a belt or braces?   ʿinta-btilbis ḥizáam walla
                                        ḥammaláat?

The sleeves are too short.   ʿilʿikmáam ṣuɛayyára ʿáwi.
The trousers are too long.   ʿilbanṭalóon ṭawfil ʿáwi.
The lapels are too wide.   tányit ijjakétta ɛarfiḏa ʿáwi.
The jacket does not fit.   ʿijjakétta mif ɛala ʿáddi.
To-morrow is your first fitting.   ʿilburúuva-lʿawwalaníyya búkra.
I should like a dark sports jacket   ɛáawiz jakétta lónha yáamiʿ wi
   and a pair of light grey flannel   banṭalóon fanílla-rɡáaɡi fáatiḥ.
   trousers.
The suit is well cut.   ʿilbádla maẓbúuṭa.
Show me some check shirts,   warríini-lʿumɡáan ilmurabbaɡáat
   please.   illi ɛándak, min faḏlak.
Six starched collars.   sitti yaʿáat minaffíyya.
Have you a blue silk tie?   ɛándak karaváṭṭa ḥarfir zárʿa?
Half a dozen coloured and a   núṣṣi dástit manadfil milawwṃna
   dozen white handkerchiefs.   wi dástit manadfil béeḏa.
The hat is too big for me.   ʿilbarnfiṭa wásɛa ʿáwi ɛaláyya.
I must send my grey hat to be   ɛana láazim ʿábɛat barnfiṭti-
   cleaned.   rmáadi titnáḏḏaf.
This suit must be repaired, the   ʿilbadláadi láazim tiṣṣállaḥ,
   lining is torn.   ʿilbiṭáaṇa mitʿaṭṭáɡa.
Please send these shoes to be   wáddi-ggazmáadi yiḥuṭṭúlha
   half-soled.   núṣṣi náɡl.
The slippers need new heels.   ʿiffíbfib ɛáawiz náɡli-gdfid.
I like plain socks.   ʿiffarabáat issáada tiɛgíbni.
The woollen socks have shrunk.   ʿiffarabáat iṣṣúuf káffu.
The colours have run.   ʿilʿalwáan báhatit.
Do you prefer brown or black   tifáḏḏal gázma búnni walla gázma
   shoes?   sóoda?

The shoes are too tight.	ʕiggázma dayyáʕa.
The toes of these boots pinch.	ʕiggázma dayyáʕa min ʕuddáam.
A pair of brown laces, please.	rubáaṭ gázma ʕásmar, min faḍlak.
Which lasts longer, silk or nylon clothes ?	ʕilhudúum ilḥariir tiṭiiṣ ʕáktar walla-lhudúum innáylun ?
Have you any pink slips which are not too expensive ?	ṭándak ʕumṣáan lábani ma-tkúnʃi ɣálya ʕáwi ?
Where can I get the ladders in my stockings repaired ?	ʕáʕdar aṣállaḥ ilʕáṭẓ illi-f ʃaráabi féen ?
The stockings are laddered and holed.	ʕiʃʃaráab maʕṭúuẓ wi-mxárraʕ.
I want a blue-striped blouse with long sleeves.	ʕana ṭáwza-blóoza zárʕa-mxaṭṭáṭa bi-kmáam ṭawfiila.
The brown skirt is very smart.	ʕiggunílla-lbúnni gamiila ʕáwi.
It is too large for me.	di wásʕa ṭaláyya ʕáwi.
You can have it altered/taken in/let out.	múmkin tiṣςállaḥ/tiddáyyaʕ/titwássaẓ.
I need a light woollen winter dress.	ʕana ṭáwza fustáan ṣúuf xafiif l-iʃʃíta.
Have you any low-necked evening dresses ?	ṭandúku fustáan sáḥra-b sídra makʃúuf ?
I want a black-lace veil.	ʕana ṭáwza béeʃa dantilla sámra.
This green dress really does suit you.	ʕilfustáan láxḍar da láayiʕ ṭaléeki ʕáwi.
This cardigan is nice and warm.	ʕilkardigáan da biydáffi-kwáyyis.
You can find leather goods in that shop.	tiláaʕi-f maḥálli da baḍáayiẓ gild.
I need a handbag and purse.	lazímni ʃánṭit yáddi-w maḥfáẓa.
I am looking for a pair of shoes size five.	ʕana badáwwar ṭala gázma maʕáas xámsa.
I am sorry, madam, in Egypt sizes are numbered differently. I should say yours is (number) 35.	ʕáasif, ya ḥáanim, ʕiggízam mitnammára-b ʃáklі táani hína-f máṣr. ʕaẓúnni maʕáasik yibʕa xámsa-w talatíin.
The hat with the black feathers does not match your brown coat.	ʕilbarnúiṭa di ʕúmmi ríyaʃ sámra miʃ máʃya maʕa-lbálṭu-lbúnni-btáaẓik.
I will take this silver watch with the leather strap.	ʕana ḥáaxud issáaẓa-lfáḍḍa di ʕúmmi ʕástik gild.
Have you any small gold ear-rings ?	ṭandúkum ḥulʕáan dáhab ṣuɣayyára ?

ENTERTAINMENTS, PASTIMES, SPORTS

THE THEATRE

Vocabulary

the theatre and other entertainments	ʕilmásraḥ w-almaláahi [1]-lʕáxra
the Opera House	dáar ilʕúpra
concert hall	qáaʒit ilmusíiqa
entertainment guide	dalíil ilmaláahi
play	riwáaya, riwayáat
comedy	kummídya; malháah
tragedy	tira(a)ʒíidya; maʕsáah
drama	diráama; qíṣṣa
variety show	másraḥ mutanawwaʒáat
show	ʒarḍ; ʒárḍi nímar; tamsíil
concert	musíiqa sinfuníyya; ḥáfla musiqíyya
circus	sark
folk songs	yúna báladi
musical instrument	ʕáala musiqíyya
public, audience	ʕinnáas
seating capacity	ʒádad ikkaráasi
late-night performance	ʕilḥáfla-lʕaxíira; ʕissuwarée(h)
early evening performance	ʕilḥáfla-lʕawwalaníyya (or -lʕúula)
matinée	ʕilmatinée(h) [2]
foyer	mádxal
cloakroom, toilet	dó(o)rt ilmáyya
refreshment room	bufée(h)
auditorium	ʒáala
box	looj; buks
circle	balkóon
gallery	ʕáʒla-lmásraḥ
stage	másraḥ
footlights	ʕanwáar ilmásraḥ
wings	kawalíis
dressing-room	ʕúgrit tayyíir ilmaláabis
national theatre	ʕilmásraḥ ilqáwmi
scenery	manáaẓir
background	mánẓar xálfi; báakgirawnd
prompter	muláqqin
props-man	mutaʒáḥhid ilmaláabis

[1] The form (ʕ)al of the article marks what is essentially a literary form.

[2] Often a morning performance in cinemas.

company (theatrical)	gamɛíyyit ilʃanniyyíin ; ʃittiḥáad
producer	múxrig
author; composer	muʃállif
playwright	riwáaɡi
poet	ʃáaɡir, ʃúɡara
cast	ʃilmumassiliin
actor	mumássil (-a, -iin, -aat) [1]
leading man	báṭal, ṣabṭáal
leading lady	báṭala, baṭaláat
ballet	balée(h)
dancer (male)	ráaqiṣ, raqṣiin
dancer (female)	ra(a)qíṣa, raqṣáat (or raqqáaṣa, raqqaṣáat)
ballerina	ra(a)qíṣat ilbalée(h) [2]
understudy	ʃilbádal
scene	mánẓar, manáaẓir
part	door, ʃidwáar
song	ʃuɣníya, ʃaɣáani
interval	ʃistiráaḥa
curtain	sitáara
safety curtain	sitáarit ilʃamáan
singer	muɣánni, muɣanníyya, muɣanniyyíin, muɣanniyyáat [1]
acrobat	ʃaragóoz, ʃaragozáat
conjurer	ḥáawi, ḥuwáah
clown	muhárrig, muharrigíin
tamer	muráwwiḍ, murawwiḍíin
finale	niháayit ilɣárḍ
applause	taṣfíiq (or tasʃíif)
booing	tahzíiʃ
to tour (the provinces)	laff, yilíff (f-ilmudiriyyáat)
to watch a performance	ḥáḍar, yíḥḍar ittamsíil
to bow	ʃinḥána, yinḥíni (or yinḥáni)
to play the piano	llɛíb, yílɛab ɛa-lbiyáanu

Sentences

What's on at the theatre tonight ?	fíih ʃéeh f-ilmásraḥ illéela ?
There's a drama by a modern author at the State Theatre.	fíih riwáaya katíbha muʃállif ḥadíiθ f-ilmásraḥ ilwáṭani.

[1] See footnote on p. 192.
[2] The form ra(a)qíṣat is marked as literary in many ways, including -at for -it.

We shan't get any tickets.	míſ ḥanláaſi tazáakir.
The house is sold out.	ſittazáakir xílẓit (or xúluẓit).
Can I order tickets by telephone ?	ſáſdar áḥgiz tazáakir b-ittilifóon ?
Can you see all right from that seat ?	ſáayiſ kuwáyyis min ikkúrsi da ?
I need some opera-glasses.	ſana ẓáawiz tiliskóop.
I'd like some coffee in the interval.	ẓáawiz áſrab ſáhwa fi listiráaḥa.
You can only have it in the refreshment room.	láazim tiráuḥ ilbuféeḥ ẓalaſan tiſrábḥá.
The curtain's going up/coming down.	ſissitáara-btirtáfaẓ/btínzil.
What a marvellous setting !	manáaẓir ilmásraḥ gamíila gíddan.
The lead hasn't learned his part very well.	ſilbáṭal míſ ḥáafiẓ dóoru-kwáyyis.
The play was enthralling/boring/amusing.	ſirriwáaya kanit mumtáaza/báyxa/laṭíifa.
The footlights are too bright.	ſanwáar ilmásraḥ qawíyya (or ſidíida) ſáwi.
There was a lot of/very little applause.	ſittasſíif kan ḥá(a)ddl/baẓíiẓ gíddan.
Have you seen the new show at the Rihani Theatre ?	ſúft irriwáaya-ggidíida-f másraḥ irriḥáani ?
The songs are by a well-known composer.	ſilſayáani-btáaẓit wáaḥid maſhúur.
I don't understand Arab/Eastern music, and I don't always like what I hear.	ſana ma baſhámſ ilmusíiqa-lẓarabíyya/ſſarqíyya wi mabtiẓgibníiſ ilḥagáat illi basmáẓha [1] mínha.
Have you been to Umm Kalsuum's [2] recital this month ?	rúḥti ḥáflit ſúmmi kalsúum bitaẓt iſſáhri da ?
I'd like to take the children to the circus.	ſana ẓáawiz awáddi-lſawláad issárk.
Did they enjoy the performance ?	ſittamsíil ẓagábhum ?

---

[1] Pronounced -ḥha.
[2] A popular woman singer.

CINEMA

Vocabulary

cinema	sínima, sinimáat
local cinema	ʕissínima-lmaḥallíyya
film	film, ʕafláam
screen	ʃáaʃa, ʃaʃáat
talking film	fílmī náuṭiʕ
silent film	fílmī ṣáamiṭ
plot	qíṣṣa, qíṣaṣ
cartoon	kartúun
newsreel	fílm ilʕaxbáar
Western	fílmī kawbóoyz
detective film	fílmī bulíisi
comedy	fílmī kóomdi
documentary	fílmī wa(a)qíʕi
film studio	ʕistúdyu, ʕistudyuwáat (or ʕistudyuháat)
projector	ʕáalit ʑárḍ
slides	siláaydz
dubbing	dubláaj
subtitles, translation	targáma
cut	ʕaṭ̣ʕ, ʕuṭúuʕ
sound-track	mágra-ṣṣóoṭ
script	riwáaya
script writer	káatib riwáaya, kuttáab riwayáat; riwáaʕi, riwaʕiyyíin
director	múntig, muntigíin; mudíir ilʕintáag
producer	múxrig, muxrigíin
revival	ʑárḍi táani
re-make	ʕixráag gidíid
cinema-goers	ruwwáad issínima [1]
cinema programme	birnáamig [2] issínima
supporting programme	ʕilbaráamig iθθanawíyya
U-certificate film	fílmī l-ilgamíʕ
X-certificate (adults only)	fílmī l-ilkibáar fáqaṭ
continuous performance	ʑárḍi mustamírr
separate performances	ʑárḍi ʑáadi
doorman	bawwáab
cash-desk, cashier	kays
booking office, box office	ʃibbáak ittazáakir

[1] The corresponding singular requires the particle **min**, i.e. **fuláan** ("so-and-so") **min ruwwáad issínima.**

[2] Plural **baráamig.**

usher	ɣáamil issínima, ɣummáal issínima
usherette	ɣa(a)míɩat issínima, ɣa(a)miláat issínima
operator	ɣáamil mákanit ilɣárḍ
choc-ice	ʃáays kiríim bi ʃukuláaʈa
sweets	ḥalawiyyáat
film-fan	múɣram b-issínima
cast	ʃilmumassilíin
hero	báʈal, ʃabʈáal
heroine	báʈala, baʈaláat
male star	nágmi sinimáaʃi
female star	nágma sinimaʃíyya
villain	ʃirríir
colour film	fílmi-mláwwin ; fílmi b-ilʃalwáan
the end	ʃinniháaya
anthem	ʃissaláam ilwáʈani
to film, shoot, photograph	ṣáwwar, yiṣúwwar
to go to the pictures	ráaḥ, yirúuḥ issínima

Sentences

When does the next performance start ?	ʃilɣárḍ ittáani ḥayibtídi-ssaɣa káam ?
The news-reel is shown at 3.30.	ʃilʃaxbáar ḥatúɣraḍ [1] f-issínima-ssáaɣa taláata-w núṣṣ.
Is it a continuous performance ?	da ɣárḍi mustamírr ?
When is the film's first night going to be ?	ʃilɣárḍ ilʃáwwal l-ilfilmída yóom ʃéeh ?
Look at the programmes in the evening papers.	ʃúuf ilbaráamig f-iggaráayid ilmasaʃíyya.
Two stalls for the last perform-ance, please.	tazkartéen ṣáala l-ilɣárḍ ilʃaxíir, min faḍlak.
We had better sit at the back.	ʃáḥsan núṣɣud f-ilʃáaxir.
Is there any emergency exit ?	fíih báab maxṣúuṣ l-ilxuráug ɣánd ilxáʈar ?
Can tickets be booked in advance ?	múmkin ḥágzi tazáakir muʃad-dáman ?
I know you know the plot, but please don't tell me.	ʃana ɣáarif innak ɣáarif ilqíṣṣa láakin ma-tʃullíiʃ, min faḍlak.
A new film is being shown.	fíih fílmi-gdíid biyúɣraḍ.
I've seen this film before.	ʃana ʃúft ilfilmída ʃabli kída.

[1] -tuɣraḍ exhibits the shape of the Classical passive but is commonly used in educated colloquial.

It's only a revival.	da bássï tagdïid l-ilfïlm.
Don't miss it !	ma-yfutákʃ ilfilmïda !
Did you read the review ?	ʕaréet ittaɤlïiq ɤa-lfïlm ?
It's a slow-moving film.	ʕilfïlmï da-yzáhhaʕ.
It's a thriller [1]—very exciting.	da fïlmï bulïisi múrɤib gíddan.
The criminal is always the last one you suspect.	ʕilmúgrim húwwa-lli-nta dáyman tiftíkir innu ʕáhsan wáahid.

BROADCASTING

Vocabulary

broadcasting	ʕizáaɤa
broadcasting station	mahátťit ʕizáaɤa
transmission	ʕizáaɤa
reception	ʕistaqbáal
radio	rádyu, radyuwáat
loudspeaker	mukábbir iʂʂóoť
earphone(s)	sammáaɤa, sammaɤáat
battery set	rádyu batťaríyya
valve	lámbit rádyu, lúmaḍ rádyu [2]
condenser	kundánsa (or kundánsar) ; mukáθθif, mukaθθifáat
volume	ʃíddit iʂʂóoť
cabinet	sandúuʕ irrádyu
knob	muftáah, maʃatíih
mains	kahrába
power-point	fíiʃa, fiʃáat
aerial	ʕéeryal
frame aerial	ʕéeryal ʕiťáari
inside aerial	ʕéeryal da(a)xíli
flex, wire	silk
adjustment	ẓabť
direct current	tayyáar mustamírr
alternating current	tayyáar mutaqátťiɤ
disturbances, " atmospherics "	ʕittiráab gáwwi, ʕittirabáat gawwíyya
interference	tadáxxul
short wave	móoga ʕuɠayyára
medium wave	móoga mutawaʂʂíťa
long wave	móoga ťawíila

[1] Or " detective story ".

[2] Notice the unexpected plural form. lambáat also occurs ; so, too, do the singular/plural forms lánḍa/lúnaḍ (or lanḍáat).

selectivity	ḥasa(a)síya
microphone	mikrufóon
announcer	mu(u)zííɡ, muziɡíin
programme parade	birnáamig ilⱾizáaɡa
disc, record	Ⱦisṭuwáana, Ⱦisṭuwanáat
news	ȾilⱾaxbáar
weather forecast	Ⱦinnáʃra-lgawwíyya
talk	muḥáḍra, muḥaḍráat ; ḥadíiθ, Ⱦaḥadíiθ
serial	silsíla ; qíṣṣa musalsála
listener	mustámiɡ, mustámiɡa, mustamiɡíin, mustamiɡáat [1]
television set	tilivizyóon, tilivizyonáat
screen	ʃáaʃa
tape-recorder	giháaz tasgíil, Ⱦaghízit tasgíil
to switch on	wállaɡ, yiwállaɡ irrádyu ; ṭáⱾa, yiṭⱾi irrádyu
to tune in	dáwwar, yidáwwar irrádyu
to listen in	símiɡ, yísmaɡ irrádyu
to earth	wáṣṣal, yiwáṣṣal b-ilⱾárḍ

Sentences

Can you pick up foreign stations with your set ?	tiⱾdar tigíib ilmaḥaṭṭáat ilⱾagnabíyya b-irrádyu-btáaɡak ?
My set is out of order.	Ⱦirrádyu-btáaɡi mitɡáṭṭal.
There's a lot of disturbance and fading on my set.	Ⱦirrádyu-btáaɡi fíih xarwáʃa-w laxbáṭa f-iṣṣóoṭ kitíir.
Reception is poor.	Ⱦilmaḥáṭṭa di ḍaɡíifa.
Can you recommend a good wireless repair shop ?	tíɡraf maḥálli-kwáyyis li tagllíḥ irradyuwáat ?
Can you send someone round to have a look at it ?	tiⱾdar tíbɡat ḥáddī-yʃúufu(h) ?
The valves want renewing.	Ⱦillúmaḍ bitaɡ irrádyu lazim tiggáddid.
Where do I take out a licence for my set ?	Ⱦagíib rúxṣa l-irrádyu-mnéen ?
You can get the licence at the (local) telegraph office.	tiⱾdar táaxud irrúxṣa min máktab ittiliyráaf.
Do you often listen in ?	Ⱦinta-btísmaɡ irrádyu-ktíir ?
Only when they broadcast concerts.	lamma biyzíiɡu mu(u)síiqa sinfuníyya báss.
Is there a talk on the radio this evening ?	fíih muḥáḍra f-irrádyu-lléela ?

---

[1] The series is borrowed from the written language, whence a gender distinction between plural forms.

My neighbours' wireless disturbs me.	rádyu-ggiráan biyiʕliʕni.
I like listening to music programmes.	ʕana baḥíbb ásmaʕ ilmuxta(a)ráat ilmu(u)si(i)qíyya (or birnáamig ilmutanawwiʕáat ilmu(u)si(i)-qíyya).
Did you hear the news?	simiʕt ilʕaxbáar?
There's a play on the radio to-night at eight.	fíih riwáaya f-irrádyu-lleláadi-ssáaʕa tamánya.
What was the weather forecast?	ʕalu ʕéeh f-innáʃra-ggawwiyya?
Did you buy your set on hire-purchase?	ʕiʃtaréet irrádyu-btáaʕak b-iʈʈaʕsíiʈ?
Our neighbours come to us to hear the children's programmes.	ʕiggiráan biyíigu ʕandína yismáʕu birnáamig ilʕaʈfáal.
Would you like to hear the gondola-song of Abd al-Wahhaab?	ʒáawiz tísmaʕ ʕuyníyit ilgundúul bitaʒit ʒábd ilwahháab?
The station has closed down.	ʕilmaḥáʈʈa di xalláʃit ʕizáaʒa.
They always close down with the national anthem.	biyínhu-lʕizáaʒa dáyman b-issaláam ilwáʈani.

PHOTOGRAPHY

Vocabulary

photography	taṣwíir
camera	futuʊráfya, futuʊraʊyáat
box camera	kámira búks
folding camera	kámira bi munʈáax
miniature camera	kámira ṣuʊayyára
ciné camera	kámira sinimaʕíyya
film	film, ʕafláam
plate	looḥ, ʕalwáaḥ
lens	ʒádasa, ʒadasáat
spool	bákara, bakaráat
aperture	fátḥa
diaphragm	ḥáagib innúur
shutter	ḥáagib ilʒádasa
filter	fíltar, fíltaráat
flash	nuur
self-timer	kámira biṣṣáwwar bi nafsáha
exposure meter	maʕáas innúur
leather case	ʃánʈa gild
tripod	ḥáamil

photograph	ṣúura, ṣúwar
snapshot	láṣṭa, laṣṭáat
slow motion	taṣwíir baṭíiʕ
light	nuur
focus	búʃra
stereoscopic picture	ṣúura mugassáma
three-dimensional film	fílmi-b tálat ʕabʕáad
negative	ẓafríita, ẓafaríit
positive	ṣúura, ṣúwar
developer	ḥáamiḍ
fixer	ṣáaṣil muθábbit
print	ṭábʕa, ṭabʕáat
printing paper	wáraʕ ṭibáaʕa
dark room	ʕilṣóoḍa-ḍḍálma
cameraman, photographer	muṣawwaráati, muṣawwaratíyya
street photographer	muṣawwaráati ʃ-iʃʃáariʕ
under-exposed	(ṣúura) miḍallíma ; (ṣúura) náʃṣa núur
over-exposed	(ʕiṣṣúura) xádit núur ; (ṣúura) minaw-wára ʕáktar m-illáazim
to expose	ẓárraḍ, yiẓárraḍ
to focus	ẓábaṭ, yiẓbuṭ ilẓádasa
to develop	ḥámmaḍ, yiḥámmaḍ
to enlarge	kábbar, yikábbar
to retouch	wáḍḍab, yiwáḍḍab
to make copies	ẓámal, yiẓmil núsax

Sentences

May I take a photograph here ?	ʕáʕdar áaxud ṣúura hína ?
You must hand in your camera.	láazim tisállim ilkámira-btáʕtak
Where can I get photographic materials ?	ʕáʕdar aʃtíri ʕadawáat [1] taṣwíir mináen ?
I want a roll film, size 6 by 9 cm.	ʕana ẓáawiz fílmi maʕáas sitta-tísẓa, min faḍlak.
Could you put it in for me ?	tíʕdar tirakkibúuli, min fáḍlak.
Do you develop plates and films ?	bitḥámmaḍ ʕalwáaḥ taṣwíir w ʕafláam ?
Please let me have a proof.	ẓáawiz aʃúuf biráuva, min faḍlak
These photos are under-exposed.	ʕiṣṣúwar di-mḍallíma-ʃwayya.
Could you intensify them ?	tíʕdar tiwaḍḍáḥhum ?
Is the light too bright ?	tiftíkir innúur ʃidíid ʕáwi ?
I should like to have this snap enlarged.	ʕana ẓáawiz iẓṣúura di titkábbar

[1] Sing. ʕadáah.

How much would an enlargement cost ?	ʕittakbíir yikállif káam ?
This portrait is out of focus.	ʕiṣṣúura di miʃ maẓbúuṭa.
Can you recommend a good photographer ?	tiʕdar tiʕúlli ẓala-mṣawwaráati-kwáyyis ?
I am going to have my photo taken.	ʕana ḥaṣṣáwwar.
I shall keep the photographs in an album.	ʕana ḥálfaẓ iṣṣúwar fi ʕalbúum.
Are you a keen photographer ?	ʕinta múyram b-ittaṣwíir (ór ʕinta bitḥibb ittaṣwíir or ʕinta ɣáawi taṣwíir) ?

FOOTBALL

Vocabulary

football	kúrat ilʕádam
match	liẓb ; mu(u)ba(a)ráah, maaba(a)ra(a)yáat
team	fírʕa, fíraʕ ; farííʕ
the backs	ʕilbakáat
the half-backs	ʕilhafbakáat
the forwards	ʕilʕamamiyyfíin
goalkeeper	goon, ʕigwáan
(right/left) back	ʕilbáak (ilyimíin/iʃʃimáal)
(right/left/centre) half	ʕilháafbaak (ilyimíin/iʃʃimáal/ilwiṣṭáani)
forward line	ʕilxáṭṭ ilʕamáami
home team	ʕilfírʕa-lmaḥallíyya
away team	ʕilfírʕa-lyaríiba
ground	málẓab, maláaẓib
shot, free kick, penalty	ʃóoṭa, ʃotáat
corner	kóornar, kornaráat
cup	kaas
classification, league	tartíib
football association	ʕittiḥáad kúrat ilʕádam
first half	ʕilháaf táɑyim ilʕawwaláani
second half	ʕilháaf táɑyim ittáani
final	ʕinniháaʕi
semi-final	ʕábl inniháaʕi
referee	riff ; ḥákam, ḥukkáam
side-lines	ʕilxuṭúuṭ ilga(a)nibíyya
half-way line	ʕilxáṭṭ ilwiṣṭáani
goal	goon, ʕigwáan
crossbar	ɣárdit iggóon
goalpost	ɣamúud iggóon, ɣimdáan iggóon

net	ʃábaka
ball	kóora, kúwar
shin-pad	rúkba, rúkab
score-board	táxtit innatíiga
to shoot	ʃaat, yiʃúut
to kick	ḍárab, yíḍrab ; ʃaat, yiʃúut
to kick off, start	ʕibtáda, yibtídi
to dribble	dáḥrag, yidáḥrag ikkóora
to pass	báaṣa, yibáaṣi
to score	dáxxal, yidáxxal góon ; gaab, yigíib góon
to be on top	báʕa, yíbʕa ʕáḥsan
to draw	ʕitẓáadil, yitẓáadil
to win, to beat	ɣálab, yíɣlib
to lose	ʕityálab, yityílib

Sentences

Shall we go to the football match next Sunday afternoon ?	tíigi níḥḍar muba(a)ráat ikkóora yóom ilḥádd illi gáay baẓd idḍúhr ?
It's an international match.	di muba(a)ráah dawlíyya.
Are they well-known teams ?	ʕilfíraʕ illi ḥatílẓab maʃhúura ?
Everybody was cheering.	kullí wáaḥid kan biyíhtif.
What a terrific shot !	ʕamma ʃóota faẓíiẓa ʕáwi !
The crowd doesn't seem to agree with the referee.	yíẓhar inn iggumhúur miʃ mittífiʕ maẓa-rríff.
Why is the referee blowing his whistle now ?	ʕirríffi biyṣáffar léeh dilwaʕti ?
He handled.	lámas ikkóora-b ʕíidu.
That's a foul !	di yálṭa !
The home team is two up.	faríiʕ ilbaladíyya ɣáalib b-itnéen.
Our team was leading at half-time.	ʕilfaríiʕ bitáẓna káan kasbáan f-ilḥáaf táẓyim ilʕawwaláani.
What was the score ?	gáabu káam góon ?
We drew.	ṭiláẓna diróon.
Did Tirsana beat Al-Ahli ?	ʕittirsáana ɣálab ilʕáhli ?
Tirsana won 3—2.	ʕittirsáana ɣálab taláata l-itnéen.
The right back is playing well.	ʕilbáak ilyimíin biyílẓab kuwáyyis.
It was a wonderful goal.	káan góon háayil.
Is your team playing in the next round of the Cup ?	firʕítkum ḥatílẓab ẓa-kkáas f-iddóora-ggáyya ?
How many teams take part in the Cup ?	fiih káam faríiʕ ḥayilẓábu ẓa-kkáas ?
How many does the ground hold ?	ʕilmálẓab yisáaẓi káam ?

TENNIS

Vocabulary

tennis	tínis
tennis match	mu(u)ba(a)ráah f-ittínis
tennis court	málɣab tínis
game	geem
set	sett ; magmúuɣa
point	líɣba
singles	mu(u)ba(a)ráah fárdi
doubles	mu(u)ba(a)ráah záwgi
mixed doubles	muxtálaṭ záwgi
racket	máḍrab (tínis), maḍáarib
tennis ball	kóorit tínis
net	ʃábaka
base-line	ʕilxáṭṭ ilxa(a)rígi
service-line	xáṭṭ isséerv
server	ráami-sséerv
umpire	ḥákam, ḥukkáam
linesman	muláaḥiz, mulaḥzíin
slice	katt
lob	ʃóota ṭawíila ɣálya
cannon-ball ; drive	ʃóota qawíyya
forehand	ʃóota ʕamamíyya
backhand	ʃóota xalfíyya
professional (player)	láaɣib muḥtárif
to volley	ʕáṭaɣ, yiʕṭaɣ iʃʃóota
to serve	ráma, yírmi (-sséerv)
to spin	dáwwar, yidáwwar (ikkóora)
to return	ṣaḍḍ, yiṣúḍḍ

Sentences

Do you play tennis ?	bitilɣab tínis ?
I am not a good player.	ʕana ma balɣábʃi-kwáyyis.
Are there any courts in the neighbourhood ?	fíih maláaɣib ʕuráyyib ?
You can join our tennis club, if you like.	tíʕdar tinḍámmi-l náadi-ttínis bitáɣna, ʕiza ḥabbéet.
The subscription is very high.	liʃtiráak ɣáali ʕáwi.
Have you brought your racket with you ?	gibtī maḍrábak maɣáak ?
I need new tennis shoes and half a dozen balls.	ʕana ɣáawiz gázmit tínis gidíida-w núṣṣi dástit kúwar.

Throw that ball away, it doesn't bounce any more.	ʕírmi-kkóora di-bʕíid, ma ɣadítʃi bitnúṭṭi-kwáyyis.
I must have my racket restrung.	láazim aɣállaḥ ilmáḍrab bitáɣni.
Let's start with a singles and we can fix some doubles later.	xallíina nibtídi-lʕáwwil b-ilmu(u)-ba(a)ráah ilfárdi-w baɣdéen nibʕa-nwáffaʕ záwgi.
Your service !	ʕisséervi-bṭáaɣak ! (or ʕínta-llihatibtídi).
That was a fault ! Fault !	di kanit[1] ɣálṭa ! ɣálṭa !
The ball touched the net.	ʕikkóora lámasit iʃʃábaka.
You should let the ball bounce.	láazim tisíib ikkóora-tnúṭṭ.
I only play for fun.	ʕana bálɣab l-ittasáali (or l-ittaslíya) bass.
Fifteen-love.	xamaṣṭáaʃar — láa ʃéeʕ.

RIDING AND RACING

Vocabulary

riding	rukúub ilxéel
racing	sibáaʕ
riding hack	ḥuṣáan irrukúub
racehorse	ḥuṣáan issibáaʕ
thoroughbred	ḥuṣáan ʕaṣíil
thoroughbred mare	fáras ʕaṣíila
stallion	ḥuṣáan, ḥiṣína ; xeel
mare	fáras, ʕafráas
foal	muhr
bay	ʕáʃʕar, ʃáʕra, ʃuʕr
dapple grey	rumáadi-mnáʕʕaṭ
white, grey (horse)	ḥuṣáan ábyaḍ
black (horse)	ḥuṣáan íswid
chestnut (horse)	ḥuṣáan ághab
rider	ráakib, rákba, rakbíin
jockey	júki (or jóoki)
stud-owner	ṣáaḥib ilxéel
stable-owner	ṣáaḥib liṣṭábl
riding outfit	bádlit rukúub ilxéel
reins	ligáam
stirrup	rikáab, rikabáat
spur	mihmáaz, mahamíiz
saddle	sarg
saddle girth	ḥizáam

[1] Pronounced kat in quick speech.

riding-school	madrásit rukúub ilxéel
race-course	ḥálabit issibáaς
groom	sáayis, sayslin
trot	rakḍ
gallop	ẕadw
canter	ḥarwála
flat race	sibáaς
steeplechase	sibáaς ilḥawáagiz
trotting-race	sibáaς irrákḍ
winning post	ẕaláamit ςáaxir issibáaς
totalisator	riháan mutabáadal
winner	kasbáan
betting	riháan
the front legs	ςirrigléen ilςuddamaníyya
the hind legs	ςirrigléen ilwarraníyya
horse-shoe	ḥidw
by a length	bi ṭúul
to ride, mount	ríkib, yírkab
to dismount	nízil, yínzil
to kick	ráfaṣ, yúrfuṣ
to buck	ςitbáaha, yitbáaha
to shy	gámaḥ, yígmaḥ
to bolt	ʃárad, yíʃrid
to back a horse	ráahin, yiráahin (ẕa-lḥuṣáan)
to neigh	ṣáhal, yiṣhal
to stamp	daas, yidúus
to harness	sárrag, yisárrag

Sentences

Is there a riding-school in the town?	ḟiih madrásit rukúub ilxéel f-ilbálad di?
I should like to hire a horse.	ςana ẕáawiz aςággar ḥuṣáan.
I need some riding-lessons.	ςana ẕáawiz áaxud durúus fi-rkúub ilxéel.
A course of riding-lessons costs a lot of money.	magmúuẕit durúus rukúub ilxéel bitkállif (filúus) kitíir.
Where can I hire a riding-outfit?	ςáςdar aςággar bádlit rukúub xéel minéen?
Have you any riding-breeches?	ẕándak banṭalonáat rukúub xéel?
Where is my whip?	ḟeen ilkurbáag bitáaẕi?
The horse is vicious.	ςilḥuṣáan ʃíris.
The mare is lame.	ςilfáras ẕárga.
Do you like going to the races?	bitḥíbbi titfárrag ẕala-sbáaς ilxéel?

Where is the entrance to the race-course?	téen báab málɛab issábaɛ ?
The nearest I was to a win was when I backed the second.	ɛáɛrub márra kuttí háksab tíiha lamma rahíntí ɛa-lhusáan illi tíliɛ ittáani.
My horse was scratched just before the start.	ɛilhusáan illi rahíntí ɛaléeh tallaɛúuh m-issábaɛ ɛablíma yibtídi.
Have you any idea which horse will win?	tíɛdar tixámmin ɛáyyl-hsáan hayíksab ?
I have an idea the French horse will win.	ɛithayyáali-nn-ilhusáan ilfaransáawi húwwa-lli hayíksab.
Whose is the winner?	ɛilhusáan illi kísib bitaɛ míin ?
Who trained the winner?	míin illi márran ilhusáan illi kísib ?
Did you back the favourite?	ɛinta rahíntí ɛa-lhusáan ilmufáddal ?
Where is the totalisator?	téen makáan ilmurúhna ?
There are two race-courses in Alexandria, one called the Sporting, the other Sumuha.	tíih malɛabéen li-sbáaɛ ilxéel f-iskindiríyya, wáahid ismu " spóorting " w-ittáani-smu " sumúuha ".

SHOOTING

Vocabulary

shooting	ɛiṣṣéed
marksman, hunter	ṣayyáad, ṣuyyadíin
shooting-party	tagámmuɛ iṣṣayyadíin
bird shooting	ṣéed iṭṭuyúur
fox	táɛlab, taɛáalib
deer, gazelle	yazáal, yizláan
rabbit	ɛárnab, ɛaráanib
hare	ɛárnab bárri, ɛaráanib barríyya
game	ṭuyúur or hayawanáat iṣṣéed
partridge	hágal, hiyáal
siluki, greyhound	kálbi-slúuɛi; kiláab silúɛiyya
gun-dog	kálbi ṣéed
the bag	haṣílit iṣṣéed
rifle	bunduɛíyya, banáadiɛ
shotgun	bunduɛíyyit ráṣṣ, banáadiɛ ráṣṣ
butt	yárad, ɛayráad
barrel	masúurit bunduɛíyya
trigger	zináad, ɛiznída
shot	ṭálɛa, ṭalɛáat

sight	niʃinkáah, niʃinkaháat
cartridge	xartúuʃ, xaratʃíʃ
snare	ʃábaka, ʃabakáat
trap	maʃyáda, maʃáayid
hunting grounds	ʃárḍ iʃʃéed
to shoot	ḍárab, yíḍrab b-ilbunduʃíyya
to hit	ʃaab, yiʃíib
to miss	ʃittálʃa xayyíbit [1]
to stalk	ʃitráʃʃab, yitráʃʃab
to hunt, go shooting	ʃaad, yiʃíid

Sentences

Is there any chance of going shooting hereabouts ?	fíih ḥitta múmkin ilwáaḥid yiʃíid fíiha hína ?
Would you like to go shooting hares with me ?	tiḥíbbi tíigi-tʃíid ʃaráanib barríyya-mʃáaya ?
This ground is reserved for shooting.	ʃilʃárḍi di maḥgáuza l-iʃʃéed.
Is the shooting season for birds open ?	múusim ʃéed ittéer ibtáda ?
A brace of partridges and two rabbits.	góoz ḥágal wi ʃarnabéen.
Are you a good shot ?	ʃinta-btíʃraf tiʃíid kuwáyyis ?
I have practised target shooting.	ʃana-tmarránti ʃala ʃiʃá(a)b(i)t ilḥádaf.
Did you clean your gun ?	ʃinta naḍḍáfti bunduʃiyyítak ?
I've been shooting in Manzala.[2]	kuntí baʃíid ṭéer f-ilmanzála.
Where can I buy a rifle ?	ʃáʃdar aʃtíri bunduʃíyya-mnéen ?
Can you let me have some cartridges ?	múmkin tiddíini-ʃwáyyit xaratʃíʃ, min faḍlak ?
There are foxes and hares in the desert.	fíih taʃáalib wi ʃaráanib barríyya f-iʃʃáḥra.
We mostly go shooting birds in Egypt.	ʃíḥna-f ʃáylab ilʃaḥwáal binʃíid ṭuyúur fi máʃr.

FISHING

Vocabulary

fishing	ʃéed issámak
fisherman	ʃayyáad issámak
fishing-boat	ʃáarib ʃéed

[1] Lit. " the shot missed ".
[2] In the north of the Delta.

fishing-fleet	ʕawáarib ǵeeḍ
fishing-tackle	ʕadawáat ǵeeḍ issámak
net	ʃábaka, ʃabakáat
harpoon	ḥárbit iṣǵeed
angler	ṣayyáad b-issinnáara
fishing-rod	bóoṣit (or ɣaṣáayit) issinnáara, boṣáat iṣṣananíir
fishing-line	xéeṭ issinnáara
float, bob	ɣawwáama, ɣawwamáat
fish-hook	sinnáara, sananíir
bait	ṭuɣm
worm	dúuda, didáan
fly	dibbáana, dibbanáat
salt-water fish	ṣámaka m-ilmáyya-lmálḥa
herring	rínga, ringáat
cod	sámak bakaláa
sole	sámak múusa
tunny	tóona or sámak tóona
sardine	sardíin
red mullet	búuri ʕáḥmar
grey mullet	búuri
shell-fish	sámak bi maḥáara
octopus	ʕuxṭubúuṭ
crab	ʕábu galámbu
prawns	gambári
lobster	lubístar
salmon	sálamun
fresh-water fish	sámak níili
carp	ʃabbúuṭ
pike	ʕábu ḥárba
eel	tiɣbáan sámak, taɣabíin sámak
fish-bone	gáfa (c.), gafáaya, gafayáat
fish-scale	ʕiʃr (c.), ʕiʃráaya, ʕiʃrayáat
sea	baḥr, buḥúur
lake	buḥáyra, buḥayráat
river	nahr, ʕánhur
stream	tírɣa, tíraɣ
fishpond	bírkit sámak
to fish	ṣáad, yiṣíid sámak
to angle	ṣáad, yiṣíid b-issinnáara
to bite	kal, yáakul

Sentences

Do you like fishing?	bithíbbī ṣéed issámak?
Do I need a licence to fish here?	láazim yikúun maẓáaya rúxṣa ẓaʃan aṣṭid hína?
Where can I buy fishing-tackle?	ʃáʃdar aʃtíri ʃadawáat ṣéed issámak minéen?
I've forgotten to bring my fishing-rod.	nislit aglib ẓaṣáayit issinnáara-btáẓti.
The bait is no good.	ʃiṭṭúẓmī miʃ kuwáyyis.
Have you had a good catch?	ṣídti ¹-ktīr?
Can one go out with the fishing-fleet?	ʃilwáaḥid yíʃdar yíṭlaẓ maẓa ʃawáarib iṣṣéed?
What bait do you use?	ʃéeh iṭṭúẓm illi bitṣtid bíih?
Is angling popular in Egypt?	ʃinnáas biyhíbbu ṣéed issámak b-issinnáara-ʃ máẓr?
Did you fry the fish we caught this morning?	ʃaléet issámak illi ṣidnáah innahárda-ṣṣúbḥ?
There is a great variety of shell-fish on the Egyptian coast.	fíih ʃanwáaẓ kitíira min issámak ʃábu maḥáara ẓala-ʃʃawáaṭiʃ ilmaṣríyya.

SWIMMING

Vocabulary

swimming	sibáaha ˙
seaside-resort	piláaj, pilajáat; máẓyaʃ, maẓáayiʃ
swimming-pool	ḥammáam sibáaha
(lady's) bathing-costume	mayóo(h) ḥarīimi, mayoháat ḥarīimi
swimming-trunks	mayóo(h) rigáali
bath-towel	fúuṭit ḥammáam
bathing-cap	ṭaʃíyyit ḥúma
cabin	kabíina, kabáayin
attendant	yaʃíir, ɣúfara
lifebelt	ḥizáam innagáah
artificial respiration	tanáffus ṣináaẓi
cramp	taʃánnug
diving-board, spring-board	mináṭṭa
swimmer	sabbáaḥ, sabbáaḥs, sabbaḥíin
breast stroke	ẓúum sídr
back stroke	ẓúum ḍáhr
butterfly stroke	ẓúum faráaʃa

¹ Pronounced ṣíttī.

crawl	ɣúum báṭn
dive	ɣáṭsa, ɣaṭsáat
beach	piláaj, pilajáat
sunbathing	ḥammáam ʃáms
wave	moog, Ɛamwáag
shower	duʃʃ, Ɛidʃáaʃ
to swim	ɣaam, yiɣúum
to dive	yíṭiṣ, yíɣṭoṣ
to plunge	naṭṭ, yinúṭṭ
to crawl	ɣáam, yiɣúum ɣala báṭnu(h)
to shiver	Ɛirtáɣaʃ, yirtíɣiʃ
to dry	náʃʃif, yináʃʃif ; Ɛitnáʃʃif, yitnáʃʃif
to float	ɣaam, yiɣúum
to drown	yíriɛ, yíɣraɛ
to bathe	Ɛistaḥámma, yistaḥámma

Sentences

Shall we go for a swim (bathe) ?	tíigi nistaḥámma ?
Can we bathe in the river ?	níʃdar nistaḥámma f-innáhr ?
No, you must go to the swimming-pool.	láɛ, láazim tirúuḥu ḥammáam issibáaḥa.
No bathing !	mamnúuɣ listiḥmáam !
Are you a good swimmer ?	Ɛinta bitɣúum kuwáyyis ?
Let's swim to the opposite bank.	yálla-nɣúum l-iʃʃáṭṭ ittáani.
The current is very strong.	Ɛittayyáar ʃidíid Ɛáwi.
Can you swim on your back ?	tíʃdar tiɣúum ɣala ḍáhrak ?
He is floating.	huwwa ɣáayim.
Can you do the crawl ?	tíʃdar tiɣúum ḍárbī-ḍráaɣ ?
I've got cramp.	ḥaɣálli taʃánnug.
Swim and help him, he's gone under.	ɣúum wi sá(a)ɣdu(h), láḥsan da yíṭiṣ.
He was nearly drowned.	huwwa káan ḥayíɣraɛ.
Stay in the shallow water.	xallíik f-ilmáyya-lli míʃ ɣarfíɛa.
Hang on to the life-line.	Ɛimsik fi ḥábli-lɛamáan !
Don't swim beyond the danger sign.	ma-tɣúmʃi baɣdi ɣalámt ilxáṭar.
This part is for swimmers only.	Ɛilḥítta di l-ílli-byiɣráfu-yɣúumu báss.
Is there a vacant hut ?	fíih kabíina fáḍya ?
Can you recommend a nice seaside-resort ?	ma tiɣráfʃi máṣyaf kuwáyyis ?
The yellow flag means there is no undertow.	Ɛilɣálam láṣfar maɣnáah inni ma fíiʃ dawwáama.

Who won yesterday's water-polo match ?	míin illi kísib líʒbit ilpúululma(a)ʕíyya-mbáariḥ ?
There is an open-air swimming-pool in the town.	fíih ḥammáam sibáaḥa makʃúuf f-ilbálad di.

ROWING AND BOATING

Vocabulary

rowing	tagdíif
boating	ʕittanázzuh f-ilʕawáarib
boat	ʕáarib, ʕawáarib
steamship, launch	ʕáarib buxxáari, ʕawáarib buxxaríyya
rowing boat	ʕáarib tagdíif
punt	pant, pantáat
houseboat	ʒawwáama, ʒawwamáat
rubber boat	ʕáarib maṭṭáaṭ
motor-boat	lanʃ, lanʃáat
skiff	ʕiskíff
oar	migdáaf, magadíif
paddle	bádal, bidáal
rudder	dáffa, daffáat
sliding seat	kúrsi mutaḥárrik
oarsman	mugáddif, mugaddifíin
cox	mudíir iddáffa
crew	baḥḥáara
plank	looḥ, ʕilwáaḥ
starboard	yimíin
port	ʃimáal
to row, paddle	gáddif, yigáddif
to steer	wággiḥ, yiwággiḥ
to float	ʒaam, yiʒúum

Sentences

Boats for hire.	ʕawáarib l-ilʕigáar.
Come to the jetty.	taʒáala ʒa-lmársa.
You can hire a boat for ten piastres an hour.	tiʕdar tiʕággar ʕáarib bi ʒáʃara sáay f-issáaʒa.
There's a strong head wind.	fíih ríiḥ ʃidíid muwagháana.[1]
The boat leaks.	ʕilmáyya-btúdxul ilʕáarib.
Let's go and watch the boat-race.	yálla nitfárrag ʒala-sbáaʕ ilʕawáarib.

[1] muwa(a)g(i)ha + na.

Our club won by two lengths.	nadíina sábaʕ bi ṭuléen.
Are you a member of the Rowing Club?	ʕinta ɣáḍwi-ʃ náadi-ttagdíif ?
I should like to join your club.	ʕana ɣáawiz aʃtárik fi nadíiku(m).
I bought a small rubber boat.	ʃiʃtaréet ʕáarib maṭṭáaṭ ɣuɣáyyar.

SAILING

Vocabulary

sailing boat	ʕáarib ʃiráaɣi
sail	ʕalɣ, ʕulúuɣ
yacht	yaxt, yuxúut
mast	ɣáari, ɣawáari
boom	ʕárya, ʕawáari
keel	ʕáɣdit issafíina or qa(a)ɣídit issafíina
flag	ɣálam, ʕaɣláam
lighthouse	fannáara, fannaráat
barge	márkib náʕl, maráakib náʕl
buoy	ʃamandúura, ʃamanduráat
anchor	mírsa (or mársa), maráasi
breeze	riiḥ, ʕaryáaḥ (or riyáaḥ) ; nasíim, nasáayim
dead calm	háadi [1] gíddan
yachting season	fá ṣli-rkúub ilyuxúut
regatta	sibáaʕ ilʕawáarib
course	ṭarlíʕ, ṭúruʕ
to sail	ríkib, yírkab ʕáarib ʃiráaɣi
to strike	ráxa, yírxi (-lʕalɣ)
to manoeuvre	ɣámal, yíɣmil munawráat
to cruise	ṭaaf, yiṭáuf ilbáḥr
to reef	ṭáwa, yíṭwi (-lʕalɣ)
to drift	ʕingáraf, yingírif maɣa-ttayyáar
to put into harbour	rása, yírsi ; rássa, yirássi
to reach port	wíṣil, yíwṣal ilbárr

Sentences

There's a sailing boat anchored in the harbour.	fíih ʕáarib ʃiráaʕi ráasi f-ilmíina.
There's a fresh breeze to-day; it's good sailing weather.	fíh ríiḥ kuwayyísa-nnahárda ; da gáwwi-kwáyyis ɣaʃan rukúub ilʕáarib.

[1] Adjectival form, as in ʕilbáḥri háadi gíddan "the sea is dead calm".

Weigh the anchor.	ʃíil ilmársa !
Help me hoist the sails.	saɣídn(i)-áfrid ilʕulúuɣ.
Let's spend the day on the water.	yálla-nʕáḍḍi-lyóom f-ilmáyya.
Have you enough to eat with you?	maɣáak ʕáklī-kfáaya ?
Do you know anything about sailing?	tíɣraf ḥáaga ɣan rukúub ilʕawáarib iʃʃiraɣíyya ?
We've often cruised in the Mediterranean.	ʕíhna lafféena-ktíir b-ilʕáarib f-ilbáḥr ilʕábyaḍ.
Is this yacht seaworthy?	ʕilyáxtī da yistáḥmil ilbáḥr ?
We were overtaken by the storm.	ʕilɣaʕífa fagaʕítna.
The boat's heeling over.	ʕilʕáarib máayil ɣala gámbu(h).
The yacht has capsized.	ʕilyáxt inʕálab.
There's a regatta out at sea this afternoon.	fíih sibáaʕ ʕawáarib f-ilbáḥr innahárda baɣd iḍḍúhr.
Set the course north, we've drifted too far west.	xálli ṭaríʕna ɣala-nnáḥya-lbaḥaríyya, ʕíhna-nḥaráfna ʕáwi náḥyit ilɣárb.

INDOOR GAMES

Vocabulary

indoor games	ʕalɣáab manzilíyya
draughts	ḍáama ; síiga [1]
draughtboard	lóoḥit iḍḍáama
king	málik, mulúuk
man, piece	wáraʕ (c.), wáraʕa, waraʕáat ; kalb, kiláab [2]
chess	ʃaṭaráng
chess-board	lóoḥit iʃʃaṭaráng
queen	ʕilwazíir
king	ʕilmálik
knight	ʕilḥuṣáan
rook, castle	ʕiṭṭábya
bishop	ʕilfíil [3]
pawn	ɣaskári, ɣasáakir
dice	zahr (generic) ; wáḥda min izzáhr (a die)
dice-box	sandúuʕ izzáhr
roulette	rulítt

[1] Kind of draughts played on the ground with pieces of stone in the countryside.

[2] In síiga only.

[3] Lit. " elephant ".

lottery	lutaríyya
skittles	kiil
billiards	bilyárdu
cannon	karambóola, karamboláat
chalk	tabaʃír
cue	ʒáʒa ¹-lbilyárdu
pocket	geeb, giyúub
dominoes	dúmina
pack of cards	kutʃéena, kataʃíin
player	láaʒib, láʒba, laʒbíin
suit	ʕilli záyyi báʒd ; loon
spades	baʂtóoni
hearts	kúuba
diamonds	dináari
clubs	subáati
ace	ʕaas, ʕasáat
ace of spades	ʕáas baʂtóoni
king	ʃáayib, ʃuyyáab
queen	bint, banáat
jack, knáve	wálad, wiláad
joker	jóokar
ten	ʕilʒáʃara
deucé	ʕilʕitnéen
trump	wáraʕa rábħa
dummy	ḍámi or moor or máyyit
to play	líʒib, yílʒab
to gamble	líʒib, yílʒab ʕumáar
to play cards	líʒib, yílʒab kutʃéena
to shuffle	fánnaṭ, yifánnaṭ ikkutʃéena
to deal	fárraʕ, yifárraʕ
to cut	ʕáṭaʒ, yíʃṭaʒ
to ruff, trump	yálab bi wáraʕa rábħa
to take a trick	kísib, yíksab iddóor
to follow suit	wáafiʕ, yiwáafiʕ ; líʒib, yílʒab zayy ilwáraʕa-lʕawwalaníyya
to take a piece (chess)	kál, yáakul wáraʕa
to protect the king	ħáma, yíħmi-lmálik
to check	káʃʃ, yikíʃʃ ilmálik
to mate	máwwit, yimáwwit ilmálik
to cast dice	ráma, yírmi-zzáhr

¹ Or ʒáʒat.

Sentences

Do you often play draughts ?	ʕinta-btilʕab dáama-ktiir ?
No, I'm more interested in chess.	láa, ʕana baḥíbb iʃʃaṭaráng áktar.
It's your move.	ʕiddóor ʐaléek.
I castle the king.	ʕana ḥáḥmi-lmálik, ḥaḥúṭṭu makáan iṭṭábya.
I wonder if I can exchange that knight for a rook.	ya tára (a)ɣáyyar ilḥuṣáan da bi ṭábya.
Whites to play.	lábyaḍ yilʐab.
If you move that pawn your queen is in danger.	ʕiza ḥarrákt ilʐaskári da-lwazíir bitáaʐak ḥayinkíʃif.
Check !	kíʃʃ i ¹ málik !
Check and mate !	ʕilmálik máat, xaláaṣ !
Will you play me a game of table-tennis ?	tilaʐíbni bíngi búng (or kóoraṭ iṭṭáwla).
He's good at billiards.	huwwa-byilʐab bilyárdu-kwáyyis.
Have you ever seen a pool game ?	ʐumrákʃi ʃúfti liʐbit bilyárdu ʕamrikáani ?
I'll give you ten cannons.	ḥaddíilak ʐáʃar karamboláat.
We can play at three cushions.	níʕdar nilʐab fi tálatt irkáau báss.
Shall we play billiards or cards ?	tiḥíbbi nilʐab bilyárdu walla kutʃéena ?
Have you a new pack ?	maʐáak kutʃéena-gdíida ?
I've shuffled, you cut.	ʕana fannáṭṭ, xúd iʕʐaʐ.
You deal.	ʃárraʕ.
Who will score ?	miin ḥayʐídd ?
Whose call (or turn) is it ?	ʕiddóor ʐala miin ?
Diamonds are trumps.	ʕilʕawráaʕ iddinaríyya ḥíyya-lli rábḥa.
Your play, your turn.	ʕilʐab, ʕiddóor ʐaléek.
You must follow suit.	ʕinta láazim tilʐab wáraʕamwáʕʕa.
This is my trick.	dí liʕbíti.
I must discard.	ʕana magbúur ármi wáraʕa muxtálifa.
Don't look at my cards.	ma-tbúṣṣiʃ fi wáraʕi.
Lay the cards on the table.	ḥúṭṭ ilwáraʕ ʐa-ṭṭarabéeʐa.
I've lost a pound at cards.	ʕana-xṣúrti-gnéeh fi liʐbit ikkutʃéena.
He's won the kitty.	huwwa kísib kúlli ḥáaga.
I've five spades in my hand.	ʕana-mʐáaya xámas baṣtonáat.

¹ The expression, like the game, comes from Persia, and i here is the Persian so-called " ezafe ".

THE TIME

Vocabulary

time	Sizzáman
watch	sáaɣa, saɣáat
wrist-watch	saɣit yádd
sundial	mizwála, mazáawil
clock	saɣit ḥéeṭ (wall); saɣit máktab (mantelpiece, etc.)
alarm clock	munábbih, munabbiháat
hand	ɣáSrab, ɣaSáarib
dial, face	míina
second-hand	ɣáSrab issawáani
minute-hand	ɣáSrab iddaSáayiS
hour-hand	ɣáSrab issaɣáat
watchmaker	saɣɣáati, saɣatíyya
second	sánya, sawáani
minute	daSíiSa, daSáayiS
hour	sáaɣa, saɣáat
day	yoom, Sayyáam (or Siyyáam)
Sunday	yóom ilḥádd
Monday	yóom litnéen
Tuesday	yóom ittaláat
Wednesday	yóom lárbaɣ
Thursday	yóom ilxamíis
Friday	yóom iggúmɣa
Saturday	yóom issábt
week	Susbúuɣ, Sasabíiɣ
month	ʃahr, Súʃhur (or ʃuhúur)
January	yanáayir [1]
February	fibráayir
March	máaris
April	Sabríil
May	máayu
June	yúnya (or yúnyu)
July	yúlya (or yúlyu)
August	Saɣúʃṭuṣ
September	sibtámbir (or sibtímbir)
October	Suktóobar
November	nufímbir (or nufámbir)
December	disímbir (or disámbir)

[1] It is unlikely that the user of this book will require the different names of the lunar months of the Muslim year.

season	faşl, fuşúul
spring	rabíiɛ
summer	şeef
autumn	xaríif
winter	ſíta
year	sána, siniín (or sanawáat)
leap year	sána kabíisa
century	qarn, qurúun
working days, week-days	Sayyáam ilɛámal ; Sayyáam ilSusbúuɛ
public holiday	ɛúţla, ɛuţláat
holiday(s)	Sagáaza, Sagazáat ; fúsḥa
Qurban Bairam [1]	ɛíid iddiḥíyya or Silɛíid ikkibíir
Ramadan Bairam [2]	ɛíid ilfíţr or Silɛíid işşuɛáyyar
New (lunar) year	ɛíid ráɛs issána-lhijríyya
10 days after New Year	ɛaſúura
the Prophet's birthday	ɛíid máwlid innábi
Easter	ɛíid ilfíşḥ or ɛíid ilqiyáama
Christmas	ɛíid miláad ilmasíiḥ
morning	şubḥ
every morning	kúlli yóom işşúbḥ
noon, midday	ḍuhr
afternoon	báɛd iddúhr
evening	mísa or mása
every evening	kúlli yóom f-ilmísa
night	leel (c.), léela, layáali
midnight	núşş illéel
to-night	Silléela or Silleláadi
last night	Silléela-lli fáatit
the night before last	Silléelạ-lli Sábl illi fáatit
to-day	Sinnahárda
yesterday	Simbáariḥ
the day before yesterday	Sáwwil imbáariḥ
three days ago	Sáwwil áwwil imbáariḥ
some days ago	díik innaháar
this year	Sissanáadi
last year	Sissána-lli fáatit or ɛáamin áwwil
the year before last	Sissána-lli Sábl illi fáatit or Sáwwil ɛáamin áwwil
three years ago	Sáwwil áwwil ɛáamin áwwil

[1] The feast occurring after the pilgrimage in the Muslim month of pilgrimage.

[2] The feast which takes place immediately after the fasting period of the month of Ramadan.

some years ago	díik issána
moon	ςámar, ςiςmáar
star	nígma or nagm, nugúum
sun	ʃams [1]
calendar	natíigá, natáʃyig
sunrise	ʃurúuς iʃʃáms
sunset	yurúub iʃʃáms
eclipse	xusúuf ilqámar (moon); kusúuf iʃʃáms (sun)
full moon	ςámar arbaʒtáaʃar; badr; ςámar káamil
new moon	hiláal [2]
first quarter	ςirrúbς ilςawwaláani
third quarter	ςirrúbς íttáalit
the modern age	ςilʒáʃr ilḥadíis
the Middle Ages	ςilʒuʃúur ilwúʃṭa
the pre-Islamic period	ςilʒáʃr ilja(s)híli
time of the Prophet	fátrit innubúwwa
time of the three Caliphates	ʒáʃr ilxulaʃáaς irru(a)ʃidíin
time of the Umayyad dynasty	ʒáʃr iddáwla-lςumawíyya
time of the Abbasid dynasty	ʒáʃr iddáwla-lʒabbasíyya
in olden times	ςayyáam zamáan; ʃ-ilʒuʃúur ilqadíima
nowadays, the present day	ςilwáςt ilḥáaḍir; liyyámdi
the past	ςilςayyáam illi fáatit
the future	ςilmustáqbal
summer-time	ςittawςíit iggéeſ
early	(min) bádri
punctual	ʃ-ilmaʒáad
late	mitςáxxar, mitςaxxára, mitςaxxaríin
in good time	bádri
in advance	ςabl
to wind up (watch)	mála, yímla
to repair	ʃállaḥ, yiʃállaḥ
to wake up, get up	ʃáḥa, yíʃḥa
to wake (someone) up	ʃáḥḥa, yiʃáḥḥi
to go to bed, go to sleep	naam, yináam; dáxal, yídxul ʃ-issiríir
to get up early	ʃáḥa, yíʃḥa bádri
to go to bed late	náam, yináam mitςáxxar

[1] A feminine noun.
[2] Egyptian terms for " moon " in relation to size are : hiláal (new), badr (full), maḥáaq (no moon). ςámar implies no specific reference to size.

Sentences

Can you tell me the right time ?	tiṢdar tiṢúlli-ssaẓa káam b-izzábṭ, min faḍlak ?
Is your watch right ?	sáẓtak maẓbúuṭa ?
It is ten minutes fast.	miṢaddíma ẓáṣar daṢáayiṢ.
It is a quarter of an hour slow.	miṢaxxára rúbẓi sáaẓa.
It always keeps good time.	dáyman maẓbúuṭa.
What time is it ?	Ṣissáaẓa káam ?
It's exactly eight o'clock.	Ṣissáaẓa tamánya b-izzábṭ.
It's five past eight.	Ṣissáaẓa tamánya-w xámsa.
It's a quarter-past eight.	Ṣissáaẓa tamánya-w rúbẓ.
It's half-past eight.	Ṣissáaẓa tamánya-w núṣṣ.
A quarter to nine.	Ṣissáaẓa tísẓa-illa rúbẓ.
One a.m.	Ṣissáaẓa wáḥda ṣabáaḥan.
Eight a:m.	Ṣissáaẓa tamánya ṣabáaḥan.
Three p.m.	Ṣissáaẓa taláata masáaṢan.
Eleven p.m.	Ṣissáaẓa-ḥḍáaṣar masáaṢan.
It is noon.	Ṣissáaẓa-ṭnáaṣar.
The train leaves at 2.30.	ṢilṢáṭrì biyṢúum issáaẓa-tnéon wi núṣṣ.
You'll have to be at the station half an hour beforehand.	láazim tikúun f-ilmaḥáṭṭa Ṣábl ilmaẓáad bi núṣṣi sáaẓa.
Don't be late.	ma titṢaxxárṣ.
I shall be in time/on time.	ḥáagi f-ilmaẓáad.
It's time to get up/to go to bed.	láazim tiṢúum báṢa/tináam báṢa.
Hurry up, it's half-past seven.	bi súrẓa, Ṣissáaẓa sábẓa-w núṣṣ.
My alarm clock has stopped.	Ṣilmunábbih bitáaẓi wíṢif.
I must take my watch to the watchmaker.	Ṣana láazim awáddi sáẓti l-issaẓáati.
It needs cleaning.	ẓáwza titmásaḥ.
The glass is cracked.	ṢilṢizáaz maflúuṢ.
Set your watch by the station clock.	Ṣiẓbuṭ sáẓtak ẓala sáaẓit ilmaḥáṭṭa.
There'll be a concert next month.	(ḥaykun) fíih ḥáfla musiqíyya-ṣṣáhr iggáyy.
I shall be back in a week.	Ṣana ḥárgaẓ báẓdi Ṣusbúuẓ.
A fortnight ago I was in London.	Ṣana kúttì-f lándan min Ṣus-buẓéen.
It gets dark early.	Ṣiddínya bitḍállim [1] bádri.
What is the date to-day ?	Ṣinnahárda káam (f-iṣṣáhr) ?
To-day is the fifteenth of September.	Ṣinnahárda xamastáaṣar sibtímbir.

---

[1] Pronounced biḍḍ-.

My birthday is on the tenth of October.	ǧlid miláadi yóom ɛáſara ɛuktóobar.
Are you going away this year?	ɛinta ḥatsáafir búrra-ssanáadi?
I came back the day before yesterday.	ɛana-rgíɛt áwwil imbáariḥ.
I shall be leaving again to-morrow (the day after to-morrow, next week).	ɛana ḥasáafir táani búkra (báɛdi búkra, ilɛusbúuɛ iggáay).
Don't arrive at the last minute.	ma-tgíiſ fi ɛáaxir daɛíiɛa.
One moment, please.	daɛíiɛa, min fáḍlak.
At dawn.	ɛilfágr.
At dusk.	ɛilmáyrib.
Last year was a leap year.	ɛissána-lli fáatit kanit[1] sána kabíisa.
Can you spare me a moment?	tismaḥ daɛíiɛa.
I have no time.	ma ɛandíiſ wáɛt.
It's getting late.	ɛitɛaxxárna.
Please call for me early.	taɛáala bádri, min faḍlak.
He left long ago.	míſi min bádri.
This building is two centuries old.	ɛilmábna da ɛúmru qarnéen (or baɛáalu qarnéen).
How old are you?	ɛúmrak kam sána?
I was thirty-six last January.	kutti sítta-w talatíin yanáayir illi fáat.
He is in his forties.	húwwa f-ilɛarbiɛináat.
She is an old lady.	hiyya sítti ɛagúuza.
He is older than his brother.	huwwa ɛákbar min axúuh.
She is younger than her sister.	hiyya ɛáɛyar min uxtáha.

THE WEATHER

Vocabulary

the weather	ɛiggáww
climate	manáax
weather	ſaɛs
air	háwa
heat	ḥaráar
warmth	dáfa
cold	bard
rain	máṭar

[1] Pronounced kat in quick speech.

snow	talg [1]
sun(shine)	ʃams
thunderstorm	zawbáȝa, zawáabiȝ
thunder	raȝd
lightning	barʕ
thunderbolt	ȝa(a)ȝíqa, ȝawáaȝiq
hail	bárad [1]
ice	galíid [1]
thaw	dawabáan ittálg [1]
sky	sáma
cloud	saháab (c.), saháaba, súhub
wind	riih, ʕaryáah
gale, tempest	ȝa(a)sífa, ȝawáaȝif
hurricane	ʕiȝȝáar, ʕaȝaȝíir
breeze	nasíim
fog	dabáab
mist	dabáab xafíif
dew	náda
frost	tilíig [1]
horizon	ʕúfuq
rainbow	qáwsu qúzah
cardinal points	ʕilgiháat ilʕaȝlíyya
North	ʃimáal ; báhari
East	ʃarʕ
South	ganúub ; ʕíbli
West	yarb
compass	búȝla, buȝláat
tide	madd
ebb	gazr
flow	madd
sea, ocean	bahr, buhúur
flood	fayadáan
atmosphere	gaww
fine weather	gáwwi-kwáyyis
bad weather	gáwwi wíhiʃ
cold	bard ; saȝȝ
chilly	bard
warm	dáafi ; harr
hot	harr
it is freezing	ʕiddínya tálg
it is snowing	ʕiddínya bitmáṭṭar tálg

[1] The term is included as useful for talking about weather conditions outside Egypt.

it is raining	ſiddínya bitmáṭṭar
the sun is coming out	ſiſſámsi ḥaṭíṭlaẓ ahé(h)
the sun rises at six	ſiſſámsi-btíṭlaẓ issaẓa sítta
the sun sets at five	ſiſſámsi-btúẓrub issaẓa xámsa
the sky is overcast	ſissáma-myayyíma

Sentences

What is the weather like ?	ſiggáww izzáyyu-nnaharda ?
It is fine.	ſiggáwwi-kwáyyis.
It's a lovely day.	ſinnahárda yóom laṭíf.
The weather is beautiful/dull.	ſiggáwwi gamíil/miyáyyim.
The weather is changeable.	ſiggáwwi mutaqállib.
The weather is settled.	ſiggáwwi ṣáuft.
It's hot/cold.	ſiddínya ḥárr/bárd.
It's rainy.	ſiddínya bitmáṭṭar.
It's foggy.	ſiddínya malyáana ḍabáab.
It's very slippery, be careful.	ſiddínya zuḥléeſa, xud báalak.
It's a nice evening.	ſiggáww illeláadi-kwáyyis.
It's close, sultry.	ſiddínya kátma.
Do you think the weather will stay fine ?	tiftíkir inn iggáwwi ḥaytínni-kwáyyis ?
The north wind is cold.	ſirríiḥ ilbáḥari báarid.
It's stormy, windy.	ſiddínya ríiḥ.
The wind has dropped.	ſirríiḥ báṭṭal.
It's raining cats and dogs.	ſilmáṭar séel.
It's pouring.	ſilmáṭar ſidíid ſáwi.
I am wet through.	ſana mablúul xáaliṣ.
Where is my umbrella ?	féen ſamsiyyíti ? [1]
Take a raincoat with you.	xúd maẓáak báltu máṭar.
Will there be a thunderstorm ?	ḥaykúun ſíih zawbáẓa ?
It's thundering and lightning.	ſiddínya-btúbruſ wi tírẓid. [2]
The sky is completely overcast.	ſissáma-myayyíma tamáam.
The sky is clear.	ſissáma ſáfya.
It's clearing up.	ſiddínya bitnáwwar ; ſilyéem biyrúuḥ.
It's too sunny here, let's sit in the shade.	ſiſſámsi ḥámya ſáwi hína, taẓáala núſẓud ſ-iḍḍíll.

---

[1] ſamsíyya is " parasol " rather than " umbrella " ; most of this " bad weather " Arabic will not be required in relation to conditions on the spot, but one needs to be able to talk about weather conditions in general.

[2] Notice the different order in comparison with the English.

It's getting chilly.	ςiddínya bitbárrad.
Are you cold?	ςínta bardáan ?
I feel hot.	ςana ḥarráan.
It's warm in here.	ςiddínya dáfa hina.
I can't stand the heat.	ςana miʃ ςáadir ɣa-lḥárr.
It's a warm day.	ςinnahárda dáfa.
It's a warm climate.	ςiggáwwï dáafï.
What's the temperature?	dáragit ilḥaráara káam ?
It has gone up to 22° (Centigrade).	báςit ςitnéen wi ςiʃríin miςawïyya.
The glass is rising/falling.	ςiddáyt iggáwwi-byirtáfiɣ/ -byinxáfiḍ.
The meteorological station is up on that hill.	maḥáṭṭit ilςarɣáad iggawwïyya fóoς ittallída.
They broadcast the weather report every day.	biyzíɣu-nnáʃra-ggawwïyya kúlli yóom.
The atmosphere is clear.	ςiggáwwï ɣáafï.

SOCIAL LIFE

Vocabulary

social life	ςilḥayáah ligtimaɣíyya
visit, call	ziyáara, ziyaráat
invitation	dáɣwa, daɣawáat
party	ḥáfla, ḥafaláat
appointment	miɣáad, mawaɣíid
meeting	muςábla, muςabláat
chat	dardáʃa
reception	ςistaςbáal, ςistaςbaláat
visiting-card	biṭáaςit ziyáara, biṭaςáat ziyáara
acquaintance	maɣrífa, maɣáarif
friend	ṣáaḥib, ςaṣḥáab ; gadíiq, ςaɣdiqáaς
neighbour	gaar, giráan
to invite	dáɣa, yídɣi
to visit, call on	ẓaar, yizúur
to ring the bell	dáςς, yidúςς iggáras ; ḍárab, yíḍrab iggáras
to arrive	wiṣil, yíwṣal
to be punctual	wiṣil, yíwṣal f-ilmaɣáad
to be late	ςitςáxxar, yitςáxxar
to welcome	ráḥḥab, yiráḥḥab (bi)
to take leave	xárag, yúxrug

to expect, wait for	ʕistánna, yistánna ; ʕintáẓar, yintíẓir
to meet (a friend in the street)	ʕáabil, yiʕáabil (gadíiʕ ɪ̄-iʃʃáariʕ)
to introduce	ʕáddim, yiʕáddim
to say good-bye	wáddaʕ, yiwáddaʕ (long journey) ; ʕáal maʕa-ssaláama (in the street)
to make an appointment (with)	wáaʕid, yiwáaʕid ·
to make conversation, to converse	ʕikkállim, yikkállim
to push the door	dáfaʕ, yídfaʕ ilbáab
to pull the door	sáḥab, yisḥab ilbáab

PAYING A CALL

Sentences

Did you ring the bell ?	ʕinta ḍaráḥt iggáras ?
Is Miss (or Mrs.) Aziza at home ?	ʕaziiza háanim ɪ̄-ilbéet ?
Please come in.	ʕitfáḍḍal ídxul.
Mrs. Ali would like to speak to you.	ḥáram ilʕustáaz ʕáli ʕáwzatkallímak.
Show the visitor in.	dáxxal izzáayir.
Very pleased to see you.	fúrṣa saʕíida.
It's a great pleasure to me.	ʕana saʕíid gíddan.
The pleasure is mine.	ʕana ʕásʕad.
Thank you for your kind invitation or It was kind of you to invite me.	mutaʃákkir gíddan ʕala daʕwitak iṭṭayyíba.
Make yourself at home.	da béetak, xúd ráḥtak.
You are very kind.	ʕinta kariim ʕáwi.
My parents send their regards.	wáldi-w waldíti biysállim ʕaléek.
Am I late (early) ?	ʕana-tʕaxxárti walla ʕéeh ? (ʕana gáyyī bádri ?)
May I introduce my husband ?	ʕaʕáddim lúkum zóogi ?
May I introduce my friend Hasan ?	ʕaʕaddímlak gadíiʕi ḥásan ?
Here are my son and daughter.	da ʕíbni wí di bínti.
Please sit down.	ʕitfáḍḍal úʕgud.
Have some tea and cake.	ʕitfáḍḍal ʃáay wi xúd káḥki kamáan.
Please help yourself.	ʕitfáḍḍal.[1]

[1] The form is an imperative one ; the corresponding feminine form is ʕitfaḍḍáli and the plural ʕitfaḍḍálu.

Do stay to dinner.	xallíik maɣáana l-ilɣáʃa.
Next time you must stay with us.	ɛilmárra-ggáaya láazim tistánna-mɣáana.
Can you put me up for to-night ?	ɛáʃdar abáat hína-lléela ?
I'm sorry but I must go.	ɛana ɛáasif, ɛana láazim ámʃi.
Do stay a little longer.	xallíik maɣáana kamáan ʃuwáyya.
I have to meet a friend.	láazim aɛáabil wáahid ɡáhbi.
I mustn't miss my train.	láazim álhaɛ ilɛátr.
I hope you'll come again soon.	ɛahíbb aʃúufak táani-ɛráyyib.
Come whenever you like.	ɛitɛáddal fi ɛáyyi wáɛt ithíbb (or tiɡíbak).
Many thanks for your hospitality.	mutʃákkir ɡiddan ɣala kúramak.
Could we meet for lunch to-morrow ?	niɛdar nitɛáabil ɡa-lɣáda búkra ?
Sorry, I have an engagement.	ɛáasif, ɛana maʃɣúul f-ilwaɛtída.
I've nothing on the day after to-morrow.	ma ɣandíiʃ háaga (or ɛana fáadi) báɣdi búkra.

N.B. We most of us say what is expected of us in given circumstances. This not only involves a host, for example, in the expression of typical greetings but his guest also in appropriate responses. Such exchanges tend to be even more ritualistic and closely bound together in Arabic than in European languages. The following are examples of typical Egyptian exchange between friends or acquaintances, host and guest, etc.

Lit. " Peace be on you " (said by newcomer).	ɛissaláamu ɣaléekum.[1]
Peace be on you, the mercy of God and His blessings.	ɣaléekumu-ssaláam wi rahmátu-lláah wi barakáatu(h).
Greetings (by host).	ɛáhlan wi sáhlan.[2]
Greetings.	ɛáhlan wi sáhlan bíik.
Greetings (by non-Muslim host).	saɣíida.[3]
Greetings.	saɣíida-mbáarak (or -mbárka).
Do sit down. How are you ?	ɛitɛáddal istaráyyah. ɛizzáyyi hadrítak/ɛizzáyyi sihhítak/ɛizzáyy ilháal/ɛizzáyyak ? [4].

[1] This general greeting between Muslims or Christian and Muslim is not used by women. Notice the plural suffix -kum, a common feature of the language of personal address.

[2] Less formal than ɛissaláamu ɣaléekum, it may be used when passing an acquaintance in the street and translates " hullo "; ɛáhlan alone is even less formal.

[3] saɣíida and the reply are not used between Muslims.

[4] The alternatives are given in descending order of formality.

Very well, thank you.[1] How are you ?	Silḥámdu li-lláah, Salláah yiḥfáẓak (or ṣiḥḥíti-kwayyísa). Sizzáyyi ḥaḍritak ínta ?
Very well, thank you.	Silḥámdu li-lláah.
How is the family ?	Sizzáyy ilṛéela ?
Very well, thank you.	Silḥámdu ii-lláah, kuwayyisíin.
Lit. " You have honoured us " (i.e. I'm very pleased to see you).	ſarraftína.
Lit. " May God honour you ".	Salláah yiſárraf ſádrak (or Salláah yiſarráfak).
Lit. " You have given us light ".[2]	nawwárti bétna (or nawwartína).
Lit. " God give you light ".	Salláah yináwwar ṛaléek.
Lit. " You have cheered us ".[3]	Sanistína.
Lit. " May God cheer you ".	Salláah yiſánsak.
Lit. " Blessing has come ".[3]	ḥáṣalit ilbáraka.
Lit. " God bless you ".	Salláah yibáarik fíik.
Do have a cup of coffee.	Sitfáḍḍal fingáan Sáhwa.
Lit. " May you always have coffee ".[4]	Sáhwa dáyman.
Lit. " May your life be ever-lasting ".	dáamit ḥayáatak.
Please excuse me, I've an appointment.	Saḥíbb astáSzin/SastáSzin baSa/ Sismáḥli, ṛándi maṛáad.
Stay a while, it's still early.	xallíik ſuwáyya, líssa bádri.
Thank you (but I must go).	Saſkúrak.
Remember me to the children.	sallímli ṛala-lSawláad.
Thank you, I will (lit. " God give you peace ").	Salláah yisallímak.
Good-bye.	maṛa-ssaláama.
Good-bye.	Salláah yisallímak.

The following examples, for which there is usually no very appro-priate English translation, relate to occasions as indicated.

Good wishes on the occasion of the big feast ṛíid iḍḍiḥíyya or Qurban Bairam.	Sin ſáaS alláah issána-ggáyya-tkun ṛala gábal ṛarafáat.[5]

.[1] The literal translation is " Praise be to God, may God protect you ".

[2] An alternative to ſarraftína.

[3] A further alternative to ſarraftína, but also commonly used at the end of a visit.

[4] Said after the coffee has been drunk.

[5] Lit. " If God wills, may you be at Mount Arafat next year ".

Response.	(ḥna w-íntu) gámzan, ʿin ʃáaʕ alláah.[1]
On other festival occasions, including the important Ramadan Bairam.	kúlli sána w-inta ṭáyyib/kúlli ʿáam w-antum bi xéer.
Response.	w-ínta ṭáyyib/w-ínta b-iṣṣíḥḥa w-issaláama.
To pilgrim returning from Mecca.	ḥággi mabrúuk (or mabrúur) or ḥággi mabrúur wi zámbi mayfúur.
Response by pilgrim.	zuʕbáal zandúkum or ʿalláah yibáarik ffik.
Congratulations to groom or bride after wedding.	mabrúuk, zuʕbáal ilbakáari or mabrúuk, ʿin ʃáaʕ alláah zurríyya ṣálḥa.
Response.	ʿalláah yibáarik ffik.
Bon voyage !	ʿin ʃáaʕ alláah tikun ríḥla-kwayyísa.
Response.	ʿin ʃáaʕ alláah, wi-nʃúuf wiʃʃúkum bi xéer.
Welcome to one returning from a journey.	ḥamdílla b-issaláama (or za-ssaláama).
Response by traveller.	ʿalláah yisallímak.
When visiting a sick person.	salámtak.
Response by invalid.	ʿalláah yisallímak.
Invitation to join you (eating, drinking, etc.).	ʿitfáḍḍal.
Declining the invitation.	láʕ, mutaʃákkir or ziʃt.
Congratulations !	mabrúuk.
Thank you.	ʿalláah yibáarik ffik.
Congratulations on your success.	ʿahanníik bi nagáaḥak.
Thank you.	ʿaʃkúrak.
Beggar's request for alms.	ḥásana li-lláah.
Refusal.	ʿalláah yizṭíik or zal-alláah or zal-álla.

[1] Lit. " we and you (sc. you and I) together, I hope ".

PASSING THE TIME OF DAY,¹ ETC.

Good morning.	ṣabáaḥ ilxéer or ṣabáaḥ innúur.
Good morning (reply).	ṣabáaḥ ilxéer (or innúur) ɣaléek or ṣalláah yiṣabbáḥak b-ilxéer.²
Good day.	naháarak saɣíid.³
Good day (reply).	naháarak saɣíid mubáarak.
Good evening.	misáaʕ ilxéer (or mísa-lxéer).⁴
Good evening (reply).	misáaʕ ilxéer (or mísa-lxéer) ɣaléek or ṣalláah yimasṣ̌ik b-ilxéer.
Good evening.	léltak saɣíida.⁵
Good evening (reply).	léltak saʕíida-mbáarak (or mbárka).
Good night (on parting at night).	tíṣbaḥ ɣala xéer.
Good night (reply).	ṣalláah yiṣabbáḥak b-ilxéer or w-ínta min ʕáhl ilxéer or w-ínta min ʕáhlu(h).
Haven't seen you for a long time.	ma ʃuftákʃi baʕáali (or min) múdda ṭawíila.
What a pleasant surprise to see you.	ɣúdfa ṭayyíba gíddan inn aʃúufak.
Pleased to see you.	kuwáyyis inn aʃúufak.
Delighted (to meet you).	mabṣúuṭ.
We must keep in touch with each other.	láazim niṭṭíṣil bi baɣḍína.
Good-bye, see you again soon.	maɣa-ssaláama, ʕaʃúufak ʕuráyyib.
Pleasant journey.	ríḥla saɣíida.
Good luck. All the best.	maɣa-ssaláama. ʕatmannáalak kúlli xéer.
Keep well; look after yourself.	xud báalak bi náfsak.
Cheerio.	maɣa-ssaláama.
Don't forget us.	ma tinsanáaʃ.

---

¹ ʕissaláamu ɣaléekum, ʕáhlan wi sáhlan, and saɣíida, together with their appropriate responses, are used as general greetings at any time of day.
² ṣabáaḥ innúur may also be used as a somewhat less formal response to ṣabáaḥ ilxéer.
³ This exchange is used between Christians, or between Christian and Muslim.
⁴ ʕásɣad alláahu misáak, with the reply ṣalláah yimasslik b-ilxéer, is also in use.
⁵ Again, unlikely to be used by Muslims.

REQUESTS

Please ...	min fáḍlak ... ʕiꜩmil maꜩrúuf ... walláahi tiꜩmílli-lxídma di ... walláahi tixdímni ... ʕargúuk ...
A cup of coffee, please.	fingáan ʕáhwa, min fáḍlak.
May I trouble you for a match (a light)?	maꜩáak kabríit, min fáḍlak ? or tísmaḥ tiwalláꜩli.
May I ask you to do me a favour ?	múmkin tiꜩmílli xídma, min fáḍlak ?
I've a favour to ask you.	ʕana líyya ꜩándak rága.
Excuse me.	ꜩan íznak or ʕismáḥli.
Would you be good enough to post this letter for me ?	tísmaḥ tírmi-ggawábda f-ilbúꜩṭa ?
I've a request to make.	ʕana ꜩáawiz mínnak ḥáaga.
I don't want to be disturbed.	ʕana miʃ ꜩáawiz ḥáddï yiʕlíʕni (if sleeping)/yiꜩaṭṭálni (if working).
Can you help me ?	múmkin tisaꜩídni ?
Your request will be granted.	ṭalabáatak maqḍíyya or ṭalabáatak.
Have you applied for your passport ?	ʕaddímtï ṭálab ꜩaʃan paꜱpóorak ?
May I open the window ?	múmkin áftaḥ iʃʃibbáak ?
Do you mind if I close the door ?	tísmaḥ áʕfil ilbáab ?
May I apply for the job ?	múmkin aʕáddim ṭálab l-ilwaꜩíifa di ?
I should like to hear your opinion.	ꜩáawiz áꜩraf ráʕyak.
What do you want ?	ꜩáawiz éeh ?
Can I help you ?	ʕáyyï xídma ?
Don't bother.	miʃ muhímm or ma tiꜩꜩíbʃï náfꜱak

THANKS

Thank you.	ʃúkran/maꜩa-ʃʃúkr/ʕaʃkúrak/ mutaʃákkir/mutaʃakkiríin/ káttar xéerak.
Don't mention it.	ʕilꜩáfw.
Many thanks.	mutaʃákkir gíddan/ʕálfï ʃúkr.
I'm very grateful (to you).	mamnúun gíddan.
Much obliged.	maꜩa-ʃʃúkr.
I am deeply indebted to you.	da fáḍli-kbíir mínnak.
You are very kind.	xéerak ꜩaléena (or ꜩaláyya).
You've done me a great favour.	ʕafḍáalak ꜩaláyya-ktíir.

I wish I could repay you.

nixdímak f-ilʕafráah or rabbína yiɤaddárni ɤala ráddi maɤrúufak (or gamîilak).

Please accept my sincere thanks.[1]

wa tafaḍḍálu bi qabúul fáaʕiq ittahiyyáat.[1]

Thank you very much for the present.

mutaʃákkir gíddan ɤa-lhadíyya.

REGRETS, APOLOGIES

I am sorry you are not well.

la báʕsï ɤaléek.

I am sorry for you.

ʕana zaɤláan ɤaʃáanak.

I am sorry about the misunderstanding.

ʕana ʕáasif ɤala súuʔ ittafáahum da.

May I express my regrets.

ʕana ʕuqáddim ʕiɤtiza(a)ráati.[2]

It is very regrettable.

háaga muʕsifa gíddan.

Let me express my condolences.

ʕáxlag ittaɤáazi[2]; ʕilbaʕíyya-f hayáatak.

Pardon. Sorry.

ʕáasif. la muʕáxza.

I beg your pardon.

la muʕáxza.

Excuse me a minute.

ɤan ʕíznak.

Please forgive me.

ʕigzúrni, min faḍlak.

I didn't want to hurt your feelings.

ʕana ma ʕagádttiʃ[3] aʕxlik.

It was not my fault.

ma kanítʃi[4] ɤalíti.

I didn't do it on purpose.

ʕana ma kúntiʃ[5] ʕáaɤid.

Don't be angry.

ma tizɤálʃ.

Please don't take offence.

ma tifhamnîiʃ ɤálat.

Don't think me impolite.

ma tiʃtikirʃ inn ána ʕaliil izzóoʕ.

Please put it down to my ignorance.

ʕáɤl ana ma kúntiʃ[5] fáahim.

INQUIRIES

Where is the station?

ʕilmahátta féen?

Can you direct me to the post-office?

tiʕdar tiwarríini máktab ilbaríid/ ilbúsṭa?

Is this the way to the theatre?

ʕilmásrah innahyáadi?

Is there any bus-stop near here?

ʃíih máwʕaf ʕutubfis hína- ʕráyyib?

---

[1] Written language only.
[2] May be said or written (e.g. in telegram).
[3] Pronounced ʕaɤáttiʃ.
[4] Pronounced ma katʃi in rapid speech.
[5] Pronounced ma kúttiʃ.

Where is the booking-office ?	féen ʃibbáak ittazáakir ?
Where can I change money ?	ʕaláaʕi fákka féen ?
Where can I leave my luggage ?	ʕasíib ʒáfʃi féen ?
Can you get me a taxi ?	tiʕdar tigíbli táksi, min fáḍlak ?
Which is the best hotel in this town ?	ʕéeh ʕáḥsan lukánda f-ilbálad di ?
Can I have a room for one night ?	ʒáawiz áḥgiz ʕóoḍa l-illéela ?
Where is the lift ?	ʕilʕaṣanʒéer féen ?
Are there any letters for me ?	fíih gawabáat ʒaʃáani ?
Where does Mr. Usman live ?	ʕilʕustáaz ʒusmáan sáakin féen ?
Does Dr. Tammam live here ?	ʕidduktúur tammáam sáakin hína ?
Has anybody called ?	fíih ḥáddī sáʕal ʒaláyya ?
Was there any telephone message for me ?	ḥáddī ḍarábli tilifóon ?
Could you tell me about/recommend me . . . ?	tiʕdar tiʕúlli ʒala . . . ?

PUBLIC NOTICES

Caution !	xáṭar !
Look out !	ʕíḥðar ! [1]
Danger ! Do not touch !	xáṭar ! mamnúuʒ illáms !
Danger of death !	xáṭar mumʃit !
Private ! No entry !	xaaṣṣ ! mamnúuʒ idduxúul !
Keep off the grass.	mamnúuʒ lmáʃy ʒala-lḥaʃíiʃ.
Trespassers will be prosecuted.	mamnúuʒ idduxúul.
Wet paint.	ʕíḥðar ilbúuya.
Stick no bills.	mamnúuʒ láṣq ilʕiʒla(a)náat.
Beware of the dogs.	ʕíḥðar ilkiláab.
Beware of pickpockets.	ʕíḥðar innaʃʃa(a)líin.
No hawkers.	mamnúuʒ ilbéeʒ hína.
You may telephone from here.	tilifonáat ʒumumíyya.
Entrance ; way in.	duxúul ; mádxal.
Exit ; way out.	xurúug ; báab ilxurúug.
Emergency exit.	báab ilxáṭar.
Toilet.	dáwrat miyáah ; mara(a)ḥíiḍ.
Vacant.	xáali.
Engaged.	maʃyúul.
Road up.	taṣlíiḥ.
Keep to the right (left).	yamíin (ʃimáal) ṭáqaṭ.
Drive slowly.	ḥáddiʕ issúrʒa.

[1] ð as th in " the ".

Diversion.	Sittariis maʃyúul.
No thoroughfare.	Sittariis masdúud.
One-way street.	Sittigáah wáaḥid.
Main road ahead.	Saṭṭariiq almuqáaṭiɛ raʃíisi.
Pedestrians only.	l-ilmuʃáah ɬáqaṭ.
No traffic.	mamnúuɛ murúur issayya(a)ráat.
No parking.	mamnúuɛ wuqúuf issayya(a)ráaṭ.
Red.	Sáḥmar.
Amber.	Súṣfar.
Green.	Sáxḍar.
Traffic lights.	Siʃa(a)ráat ilmurúur.
No smoking.	mamnúuɛ ittadxíin.
Private.	xaaṣṣ.
Open from 8 to 2.	mawaɛíid ilɛámal min tamánya l-itnéen.
For hire.	l-ilSi(i)gáar.
No bathing.	mamnúuɛ listiḥmáam.

BOOKS, NEWSPAPERS, AND MAGAZINES

Vocabulary

books, newspapers, and magazines	kútub wi súḥuf wi magalláat
bookshop	maktába, maktabáat
public library	maktába ɛáamma, makáatib ɛáamma
volume	mugállad, mugalladáat
edition	ṭábɛa, ṭabɛáat
binding	taglíida, taglidáat
guide-book	kitáab siyáaḥi, kútub siyaḥíyya
novel, story	qíṣṣa, qíṣaṣ
bookstall	kúʃk iggaráayid
press	Siggiḥáaɬa
newspaper	garíida, garáayid ; gurnáal, garaníil [1]
daily	garíida yawmíyya, garáayid yawmíyya
weekly	garíida (magálla) Susbuɛíyya
monthly	magálla ʃahríyya, magalláat ʃahríyya
illustrated paper	garíida (magálla) muṣawwára
technical (professional) journal	gurnáal ɬánni, garaníil ɬanníyya
trade journal	gurnáal tugáari, garaníil tugaríyya
official bulletin	náʃra rasmíyya, naʃaráat rasmíyya

[1] Sometimes gurnáan, garaníin.

comic paper	magálla mudḥíka or magálla fuka(a)híyya
fashion magazine	magállit ilʕazyáaʕ ¹
review, periodical	magálla, magalláat
leader	ʕilmaʕáal irraʕíisi
news	ʕilʕaxbáar
short story	qíṣṣa qaṣíira
column	ɣamúud, ɣawamíid
cartoon	karikatéer
review (book, film, theatre)	naqd ; taɣlíiq
headlines	ɣanawíin
advertisement	ʕiɣláan, ʕiɣlanáat
publisher	náaʃir, na(a)ʃiríin
editor	muḥárrir, muḥarriríin
journalist	ṣáḥafi, ṣaḥafiyyíin
reader	qáariʕ, qurráaʕ
printer	ɣáamil iṭṭibáaɣa, ɣummáal iṭṭibáaɣa
print	maṭbúuɣ ; ṭibáaɣa
bookseller	bayyáaɣ kútub, bayyaɣíin kútub ; ṣáaḥib maktába, ʕaṣḥáab makáatib
newspaper vendor	bayyáaɣ garáayid
to publish	náʃar, yínʃur (or yun-)
to print	ṭábaɣ, yíṭbaɣ
to read	ʕára, yíʕra
to skim through	ʕiɣɣáffaḥ, yiɣɣáffaḥ

Sentences

Have you any modern literature ?	ɣándak kútub f-ilʕádab ilḥadíiθ ? ²
Can you recommend a good guide-book ?	tiʕdar tiʕúlli ɣala kitáab siyáaḥikwáyyis ?
Please show me some illustrated books on Egyptian architecture.	warríini min fáḍlak báɣḍi kútub muṣawwára ɣan fánn ilɣimáaralmáṣri.
Haven't you a bound copy of this novel ?	ma ɣandákʃi núsxa-mgallída min ilqíṣṣa di ?
I want a good Arabic–English pocket dictionary.	ʕana ɣáawiz qamúus géeb ingilíizi ɣárabi-kwáyyis.
Is there a good library here ?	fíih maktába-kwayyísa hína ?
Please bring me the morning paper.	min fáḍlak hátli-ggaríidaṣṣabaḥíyya.

---

¹ A written form ; sing. ziyy.
² θ as *th* in English " think ".

Have the evening papers come out ?	Siggaráayid ilmasaSíyya `ílʒit P
Are these the latest periodicals on economic matters ?	Silmagallátdi Sáaxir magalláat ẓáharit f-ilSiqtiṣáad P
Have you read the leader ?	Saréet ilmaSáal irraSíisi (or ilmaSáal liftitáaḥi) P
What's the news ?	Séeh ilSaxbáar P
The late news is at the bottom of the first page in Al-Ahram.	Sáaxir xábar fi Sásfal iẓẓáḷḥa-lSúula f-ilSahráam.
Please let me have a weekly paper.	Sana ẓáawiz garíida Susbuʒíyya, min faḍlak.
Let me have a comic paper, please.	min fáḍlak Siddíini magálla faka(a)híyya.
Do you stock English papers ?	ẓandúku garáayid ingilíizi P
Could I borrow your paper for a minute ?	múmkin astílif garídtak daSíiSa P
Have you read the advertise-ments ?	Saréet ilSiʒlanáat P
I've read the " Situations Va-cant " (" Situations Wanted ") section.	Saréet qism " wazáayif xálya " (" wazáayif maṭlúuba ").
Which is the best fashion maga-zine ?	Séeh Sáḥsan magálla l-ilSazyáaS P
Have you a map of Cairo ?	ẓándak xaríiṭa l-ilqahíra P
The bookstall at the corner has them.	tilaSíihum f-ilmaktába-lli ʒa-lSímma.
Do you read the national and international Press ?	bitíSra-ggaráayid ilmaḥallíyya w-iggaráayid ilʒa(a)lamíyya P

THE HOUSE

Vocabulary

house	beet, biyúut
building	mábna, mabáani ; ʒimáara, ʒimaráat
flat	ʃáSSa, ʃúSaS
storey	door, Sadwáar
basement	badróom, badromáat
cellar	máxzan táḥt ilSárḍ, maxáazin táḥt ilSárḍ
attic	Sódt [1] issuṭúuḥ
roof	saṭḥ, suṭúuḥ
wall	ḥéeṭa,`ḥeṭáan
window	ʃibbáak, ʃababíik

[1] Pronounced Soṭṭ.

balcony	balkóona, balkonáat
glass-covered balcony	varúnda ʕizáaz, varandáat ʕizáaz
door	baab, bibáan
key	muftáaḥ, mafatíiḥ
room	ʕóoḍa, ʕiwaḍ
floor	ʕarḍ ; door, ʕadwáar (storey)
ceiling	saʕf, ʕúsʕuf
drawing-room	ʕóḍt [1] iggulúus
dining-room	ʕóḍt [1] iṣṣúfra
bedroom	ʕóḍt [1] innóom
dressing-room	ʕóḍt [1] ittasríiḥa
study	ʕóḍt [1] ilmáktab
nursery	ʕóḍt [1] ilʕiyáal
hall	ṣáala, ṣaláat
bathroom ; bath(-tub)	ḥammáam, ḥammamáat
wash-basin	ḥooḍ, ʕiḥwáaḍ
lavatory	kabinée(h), kabineháat
stairs	síllim, saláalim
banisters	darabzéen
furniture	ʕafʃ
stove	furn, ʕifráan
air-conditioning	takyíif háwa
radiator	raḍyéetar, raḍyetaráat
curtain	sitáara, satáayir
blind, shutter	ʃiiʃ
sunblind	tánda, tandáat
brazier	mánʕad, manáaʕid
switch	muftáaḥ innúur ; kubs,[2] kubsáat
lamp	lámba, lambáat ; lánḍa, lanḍáat
carpet	siggáada, sagagíid
table	ṭarabéeẓa, ṭarabeẓáat
chair	kúrsi, karáasi
easy-chair	futáyy, futiyyáat
mirror	miráaya, mirayáat
sideboard	bufée(h), bufeháat
cupboard	duláab, dawalíib
bed	siríir, saráayir
couch	kánaba, kanabáat
bedside table	ṭarabéeẓa-ṣyayyára ; kumudlíinu, kumudináat
pillow	mixádda, mixaddáat
blanket	baṭṭaníyya, baṭṭaniyyáat

---

[1] Pronounced ʕoṭṭ.

[2] Pronounced kups.

sheet	miláaya, milayáat
eiderdown	liḥáaf, Ɛilḥifa
bedspread	máfraʃ siríir
kitchen	mátbax, matáabix
kitchen range	wabúur ittábx, bawabíir ittábx
cooker	(gas) fúrnI b-ilɣáaz; (electric) fúrnI kahrabáaƐi [1] (or fúrnI b-ikkahrába)
shelf	raff, rufúuf
coal fire	náar fáḥm
pan	ḥálla, ḥílal
saucepan	kasaróola, kasaroláat
frying-pan	máƐla, maƐlayáat; táaʒa, tuʒáat
pots and pans	Ɛadawáat ilmátbax
cutlery, silver	faddíyya
crockery, china	ʃíini
teapot	barráad ʃáay, barariid ʃáay
coffee-pot	barráad Ɛáhwa, barariid Ɛáhwa
gas (electricity, water) meter	ɣaddáad ɣáaz (kahrúba, máyya)
pantry	(Ɛódt ik)karáar
to cook	tábax, yútbux
to live	síkin,[2] yúskun; ɛaaʃ, yiɛíiʃ
to move in (out)	náƐal, yinƐil fi (min)
to lease, to rent	Ɛággar, yiƐággar

Sentences

Flats to let.	ʃúƐaƐ l-ilƐi(i)gáar.
Have you taken a furnished flat ?	Ɛaggárti ʃáƐƐa b-ilɣáfʃ (or bi ɣafʃáha) ?
I want a room with service.	ɣáawiz Ɛóoḍa maɣa-lxídma.
I want full board.	Ɛana ɣáawiz Ɛóoḍa b-ilƐákl.
I want to buy a house with a garden.	ɣáawiz aʃtíri béet bi-gnéena.
Where do you live ?	Ɛinta sáakin féen ?
I live on the second floor, to the right.	Ɛana sáakin f-iddóor ittáani, ɣa-lyimíin.
I live on the top floor.	Ɛana sáakin f-iddóor ilƐaxráani.
The stairs have (just) been painted.	Ɛissaláalim madhúuna búhya.
Is your friend upstairs ?	ɣáḥbak fóoƐ ?

---

[1] Or kahrabáaƐi.
[2] Or sákan.

He's downstairs in the dining-room.	huwwa táḥti-f Ṣóḍt iṣṣúfra.
I want a large, airy room.	Ṣaña ẓáawiz Ṣóoḍa háwya-w wásẓa.
This room looks on to the park.	ṢilṢóoḍa di bitṭúlli ẓa-lmuntáza.
This building has a lot of floors with four flats on each.	Ṣilẓimáara di ffiha-dwáar kitlíra, wi kúlli dóor ffih Ṣárbaẓ fúṢaṢ.
I need a writing-desk and book-cases.	yilzámni máktab wi dawallíb kútub.
Is the bed comfortable?	Ṣissiríir murlíḥ ?
It is too hard (soft).	gáamid (láyyin) Ṣáwi.
Switch on (off) the light.	wállaẓ (ṭáffi) innúur.
The lamp on the bedside table has no bulb.	ṢilṢabajóora-lli gámb issiríir ma fiháaf lámba.
Can I have a bath?	múmkin áaxud ḥammáam ?
There's no hot water to-day.	ma fíif máyya súxna-nnaharda.
Where is the maid?	féen ilxaddáama ?
The boy (sc. servant) is nowhere to be found.	Ṣana mif láaṢi-lfarráaf (or Ṣilfarráaf mif mawgúud).
The table is laid for lunch.	Ṣiṣṣúfra gáḥza l-ilyáda.
The knives, forks, teaspoons, and tablespoons are in the side-board drawer.	Ṣissakakíin, Ṣiffíwak, maẓáaliṢ iffáay w-ilmaẓáaliṢ fi dúrg ilbuféeh.
This crockery is chinaware.	ṢilṢiṭbáaṢ di ṣíini.
This flat is air-conditioned.	ṢiffáṢṢa di ffiha takyíif háwa.
Bring another chair to this corner.	háat kúrsi táani f-irruknída.
This door needs a new lock.	Ṣilbáab da ẓáawiz ṭábla-gdíida.
The key is lost.	Ṣilmuftáaḥ ḍáaẓ.
There's an iron bolt on the front door.	ffih tirbáas ḥadíid ẓa-lbáab ilbarráani.
What's the monthly rent for this flat?	ṢiffaṢṢáadi-b káam f-iffáhr ?
Must I pay in advance?	láazim ádfaẓ muṢáddam ?
Could I move in next month?	múmkin ánṢil hína-ffáhr iggáay ?
When did you move out of your old flat?	naṢálti Ṣímta min faṢṢítak ilṢadíima ?
Are you the owner of this house?	Ṣinta gáaḥib ilbéet da ?
I've only a lease for one year.	Ṣana-mṢaggáru sána wáḥda báss.[1]

[1] Lit. " I've leased it (sc. house), etc.".

GEOGRAPHICAL DIVISIONS

COUNTRIES AND NATIONS

Vocabulary

countries and nations	ſaddúwal w-alſúmam [1]
Africa	ſafríiqya
African	ſafríiqi, ſafriqíyya, ſafriqiyyíin
Albania	ſalbá(a)nya
Albanian	ſalbáani, ſalbaníyya, ſalbaniyyíin
America	ſamríika
American	ſamrikáani, ſamrikaníyya, ſamrikáan or ſamríiki, ſamrikíyya, ſamrikiyyíin [2]
Arabia	ſilmamláka-lⱬarabíyya-ssuⱬudíyya
Arabian	suⱬúudi, suⱬudíyya, suⱬudiyyíin
Argentine	ſilſarjantíin
Argentinian	ſarjantíini, ſarjantiníyya, ſarjantiniyyíin
Asia	ſásya
Asian, Asiatic	ſasyáawi, ſasyawíyya, ſasyawiyyíin
Australia	ſusturálya
Australian	ſusturáali, ſusturalíyya, ſusturaliyyíin
Austria	ſinnímsa
Austrian	nimsáawi, nimsawíyya, nimsawiyyíin
Belgium	baljíika
Belgian	baljíiki, baljikíyya, baljikiyyíin
Brazil	barazíil
Brazilian	barazíili, barazilíyya, baraziliyyíin
Bulgaria	bilɣárya
Bulgar, Bulgarian	bilɣáari, bilɣaríyya, bilɣariyyíin
Canada	kánada
Canadian	kánadi, kanadíyya, kanadiyyíin
Chile	ſíili
Chilean	ſíili, ſilíyya, ſiliyyíin
China	ſiṣṣíin
Chinese	ṣíini, ṣiníyya, ṣiniyyíin
Czechoslovakia	tʃikusluvákya
Czech	ráagil, ḥáaga, etc., min (or bitáaⱬ) tʃikusluvákya
Denmark	ſiddinimárk
Dane, Danish	dinimárki, dinimarkíyya, dinimarkiyyíin

---

[1] Written form.
[2] Ṣálam ſamrikáani " American pen(cil) " but either ráagil ſamrikáani or ráagil ſamríiki.

Egypt	maṣr [1]; bárri máṣr; ſilqúṭr ilmáṣri
Egyptian	máṣri, maṣríyya, maṣriyyíin
England	ſingiltíra
Englishman, English	ſingilíizi, ſingilizíyya, ſingiliziyyíin, ſingilíiz
Eritrea	ſaritríya
Eritrean	ráagil, ḥáaga, etc., min ſaritríya
Ethiopia	ſilḥábaſa
Ethiopian	ḥábaſi, ḥabaſíyya, ſaḥbáaſ
Europe	ſurúbba
European	ſurúbbi, ſurubbíyya, ſurubbiyyíin
Finland	fillánda
Finn, Finnish	fillándi, fillandíyya, fillandiyyíin
France	faránsa
Frenchman, French	faransáawi, faransawíyya, faransawiyyíin
Germany	ſalmánya
German	ſalmáani, ſalmaníyya, ſalmáan
Ghana	γáana
Ghanaian	ráagil, etc., min γáana
Great Britain	biriṭáanya-lγúzma
Briton, British	biriṭáani, biriṭaníyya, biriṭaniyyíin
Greece	ſilyunáan
Greek	yunáani, yunaníyya, yunáan
Holland	hulánda
Dutchman, Dutch	hulándi, hulandíyya, hulandiyyíin
Hungary	ſilmágar
Hungarian	mágari, magaríyya, magariyyíin
Iceland	ſayislánda
Icelander, Icelandic	ráagil, etc., min ſayislánda
India	ſilhínd
Indian	híndi, hindíyya, hanádwa
Ireland	ſayirlánda
Irishman, Irish	ſayirlándi, ſayirlandíyya, ſayirlandiyyíin
Israel	ſisraſíil
Israeli	ſisraſíili, ſisraſilíyya, ſisraſiliyyíin
Italy	ſiṭá(a)lya
Italian	ṭalyáani (or ṭul-), ṭalyaníyya, ṭaláyna or ſiṭáali, ſiṭalíyya, ſiṭaliyyíin
Japan	ſilyabáan
Japanese	yabáani, yabaníyya, yabaniyyíin
Jugoslavia	yuγusláfya
Jugoslav	yuγusláafi, yuγuslafíyya, yuγuslafiyyíin

[1] **maṣr** is generally used in Egypt itself in the sense of " Cairo ".

Kenya	kínya
Kenyan	ráagil, etc., min kínya
Luxemburg	luksumbúrg
Luxemburger	ráagil, etc., min luksumbúrg
Mexico	ſilmaksíik
Mexican	maksíiki, maksikíyya, maksikiyyíin
New Zealand	niwzi(i)lánda
New Zealander	niwzilándi, niwzilandíyya, niwzilandiyyíin
Norway	ſinnurwéeg
Norwegian	nurwéegi, nurwegíyya, nurwegiyyíin
Pakistan	pakistáan
Pakistani	pakistáani, pakistaníyya, pakistaniyyíin
Persia	ſáaris or ſi(i)ráan
Persian	ſa(a)rísi, farisíyya, farisiyyíin or ſársi, farsíyya, farsiyyíin or ſi(i)ráani, ſiraníyya, ſiraniyyíin
Poland	bulánda
Pole, Polish	bulándi, bulandíyya, bulandiyyíin
Portugal	ſilburtuſáal
Portuguese	burtuſáali, burtuſalíyya, burtuſaliyyíin
Roumania	rumánya
Roumanian	rumáani, rumaníyya, rumaniyyíin
Russia	rú(u)sya
Russian	ráusi, rusíyya, ruus
Scotland	(ſi)skutlánda
Scotsman, Scottish	ſiskutlándi, ſiskutlandíyya, ſiskutlandiyyíin
Spain	ſasbánya
Spaniard, Spanish	ſasbáani, ſasbaníyya, ſasbaniyyíin
Sweden	ſissuwéed
Swede, Swedish	suwéedi, suwedíyya, suwediyyíin
Switzerland	suwísra
Swiss	suwísri, suwisríyya, suwisriyyíin
Turkey	turkíya
Turk, Turkish	túrki, turkíyya, ſatráak (or tarákwa)
United States of America	ſilwilayáat ilmuttáḥida-lſamrikíyya
North American	ráagil, etc., min ſamríika-ſſamalíyya
South America	ſamríika-lganubíyya
South American	ráagil, etc., min ſamríika-lganubíyya
Wales	weelz
Welshman, Welsh	ráagil, etc., min wéelz

REGIONS, TOWNS, ISLANDS

Vocabulary

regions, islands, towns	ʕalʕaqalíim, ʕalgúzur, ʕalmúdun
Ankara	ʕanqára
Athens	ʕaθíina
Balearic Isles	gúzur ilbilyáar
Bavaria	bavárya
Bethlehem	béet láḥm
Biscay	biskáay
Bordeaux	burdóo
Bombay	bumbáay
Brussels	birúksil
Burgundy	birgándi
Canary Islands	gúzur ilkanáari
Ceylon	sayaláan
Corsica	kursíika
Crete	kiríit
Cyprus	qúbruṣ or ʕúbruṣ
Dunkirk	dankírk
Edinburgh	ʕadímb(i)ra
Genoa	jíniwa
Geneva	jinéev
Greenland	girínland
(the) Hague	la(a) háay
Haifa	ḥíifa
Istanbul	ʕistambúul
Jerusalem	ʕurʃalíim or ʕilqúds
Karachi	kará(a)tʃi
London	lándan
Malta	málṭa
Marseilles	marsílya
Mediterranean (Sea)	ʕilbáḥr ilʕábyaḍ ilmutawássiṭ
Moscow	músku
Naples	náapuli
Netherlands	ʕilʕaráaḍi-lmunxáfḍa
Newfoundland	niwfáwndland
New York	niwyóork
Nairobi	nayrúubi
Nice	niis
Pekin	pikíin
Philippine Islands	gúzur ilfiliplín
Pyrenees	ʕilpiriníiz
Rhodes	róodis

Rome	róoma
Sardinia	sardínya
Scandinavia	Ṣiskandinéevya
Sicily	ṣiqilíyya
Teheran	ṭahráan
Tel Aviv	tálli ṣabíib
Thames	ṣittéemz
United Kingdom	Ṣilmamláka-lmuttáḥida
Venice	viníis
Vienna	viyánna
Warsaw	wársu
Zanzibar	zangibáar

COUNTRIES AND CAPITALS OF THE ARAB WORLD [1]

Vocabulary

Aden (protectorate and town)	Ṣádan
Algeria	ṢilgazáaṢir
Bahrein	baḥréen or Ṣilbaḥréen
Hadramaut	ḥaḍramóot
Iraq	Ṣilɛiráaq or ṢilɛiráaṢ
Jordan	ṢilṢúrdun
Kuwait	Ṣikkuwéet
Lebanon	libnáan
Libya	lí(i)bya
Cyrenaica	bárqa
Tripolitania	ṭaráablus
Morocco	murráakiʃ
Oman	ɛumáan
Persian Gulf	xaliig ilfa(a)rísi
Sudan	Ṣissudáan
Syria	súrya
Tunisia	túunis
United Arabic Republic	Ṣilgumhuríyya-lɛarabíyya-lmuttáḥida
Yemen	Ṣilyáman
Algiers	ṢilgazáaṢir
Aden	ɛádan
Aleppo	ḥálam
Amman	ɛammáan
Baghdad	baydáad
Basra	Ṣilbáṣra

---

[1] Ṣilbiláad ilɛarabíyya-w ɛawaṣímha.

Beyrut	bayrúut
Benghasi	báni ɣáazi
Casablanca	ʕiddáar ilbayḑáaʕ
Damascus	dimáʃq
Fez	faas
Homs	ḥims
Khartoum	ʕilxarṭúum
Kuwait	ʕikkuwéet
Marrakesh	murráakiʃ
Mecca	mákka
Medina	ʕilmadíina
Mosul	ʕilmáwṣil
Muscat	másqaṭ
Port Sudan	bursudáan
Oran	ʕu(u)ráan
Rabat	ʕirrabáaṭ
Riyadh	ʕirriyáaḑ
Tangier	ṭánja
Tetuan	taṭwáan
Tripoli (Libya)	ṭaráablus (ilɣárb)
Tunis	túunis
the Arab League	ga(a)míʕit iddúwal ilɣarabíyya
the Arab world	ʕilʕáalam ilɣárabi
the Maghrib	ʕilmáɣrib
the Near East	ʕiʃʃárq ilʕádna
the Middle East	ʕiʃʃárq ilʕáwsaṭ

REGIONS AND TOWNS OF EGYPT [1]

Vocabulary

administrative divisions	ʕilʕaqalíim ilʕidaríyya
governorate	muḥáfẓa, muḥafẓáat (or mi-)
province	mudiríyya, mudiriyyáat
Eastern Province	mudiríyyit iʃʃarʕíyya
Western Province	mudiríyyit ilɣarbíyya
Munufiyya Province	mudiríyyit ilmunufíyya
district	márkaz, maráakiz
Ashmun District	márkaz ʕaʃmúun
geographical divisions	ʕilʕaqalíim ilguɣrafíyya
Lower Egypt or the Delta	ʕilwágh ilbáḥari or ʕiddílta
Upper Egypt	ʕilwágh ilʕíbli or ʕiṣṣiʕíid
Western Desert	ʕiṣṣaḥráaʕ ilɣarbíyya

[1] ʕaqsáam wi múdun máṣr.

Eastern Desert	ʕiṣṣaḥráaʕ iʃʃarqíyya
Sinai	síina or ṣaḥráaʕ síina
Qattara Depression	munxáfaḍ ilqaṭṭáara
Gulf of Suez	xalíig issuwées
Gulf of Aqaba	xalíig ilʕáqaba
Red Sea	ʕilbáḥr ilʕáḥmar
Nile	ʕinníil
Rashid branch (of the Nile)	fárʕi raʃíid
Damietta branch (of the Nile)	fárʕi dumyáaṭ
Siwa Oasis	wáaḥit síiwa
Suez Canal	qanáat issuwées
Lower Egyptian	baḥráawi, baḥrawíyya, baḥárwa [1]
Upper Egyptian	ṣiʕíidi, ṣiʕidíyya, ṣaʕáyda
Bedouin	bádawi, badawíyya, badw
countryside	ʕilʕaryáaf
town	bálad, biláad ; madíina, múdun
Cairo	ʕilqa(a)híra ; maṣr
Alexandria	ʕiskindiríyya
Damietta	dumyáaṭ
Port Said	burṣaʕíid
Suez	ʕissuwées
Fayoum	ʕilfayyúum
Asyut	ʕasyúuṭ [2]
Qena	qína
Luxor	lúʕṣur
Aswan	ʕaṣwáan
Giza	ʕiggíiza
Marsa Matruh	mársa matrúuḥ
quarter (of town)	ḥayy, ʕaḥyáaʕ
Old Cairo	máṣr ilʕadíima
New Cairo	máṣr iggidíida
the Citadel	ʕilʕálʕa
Azhar Mosque	ʕilʕázhar
places of interest	ʕamáakin muhímma
the Pyramids	ʕilʕahráam
the Sphinx	ʕabu-lhóol
Pharaonic remains	ʕaṣáar ilfaráʕna
Muhammad Ali Mosque	gáamiʕ muḥámmad ʕáli
Ibn Talun Mosque	gáamiʕ íbni ṭulúun
Amr Ibn al-As Mosque	gáamiʕ ʕámr ibn ilʕáaṣ
the Antiquities Museum	dáar ilʕaṣáar ilmaṣríyya or ʕilʕantikxáana

[1] Or baḥárwa.
[2] Or ʕasyúuṭ.

Karnak	kárnak
the High Dam	ʕissádd ilɣáali
Sakkara	saʕʕáara
the Barrages	ʕilʕanáaṭir [1] ilxayríyya
the Zoo	ginént ilḥayawanáat
Literary Museum	dáar ikkútub or ʕikkutubxáana
the Muski	xáan ilxalíili
St. Catherine's Monastery	dîir san(ta) katríin
the Bitter Lakes	ʕilbuḥayráat ilmúrra

Sentences

What is your nationality?	ʕínta min ʕáyyi ʕúṭr?
I am English (Egyptian, French, German, Ghanaian).	ʕana-ngilíizi (máɣri, faransáawi, ʕalmáani, min ɣáana).
Have you any identification papers?	maʕáak ʕawráaʕ taḥʕíiʕ ʃaxṣíyya?
I have a British passport.	ʕana-mɣáaya paspóor (or gawáaz sáfar) ingilíizi.
How long have you been here?	baʕáalak hína ʕaddéeh?
Here is my identity card.	biṭáaʕit taḥʕíiʕ iʃʃaxṣíyya-btaʕt(i ʕ)ahéh.
I am Egyptian by birth.	ʕana mawlúud fi máɣr.
I am English by marriage.	ʕana góozi-ngilíizi.[2]
I am stateless.	ʕana maliyyáaʃ wáṭan.
I am a refugee.	ʕana muháagir.
Can I claim British nationality?	ʕáʕdar áṭlub ilʕinsíyya-lbiriṭaníyya?
Are you a naturalized Britisher?	ʕínta xádt ilʕinsíyya-lbiriṭaníyya?
I want to travel to Iraq.	ʕana ɣáawiz asáafir ilɣiráaʕ.
Can I enter Italy without a special visa?	múmkin ádxul ʕiṭálya min ɣéer víiza?
My mother tongue is French.	lúɣati-lʕaɣlíyya faransáawi (or ʕilfaransáawi lúɣati-lʕaɣlíyya).
Are you a foreigner?	ʕínta ʕaɣnábi?
I've been through Egypt (sc. without stopping).	ʕana ɣaddéet ɣala máɣri w-ɣna-msáafir.
I've been down the Nile.	ʕana safîrti f-innîil.
He has just returned from Syria.	ya dóob rígiɣ min súrya or huwwa líssa ráagiɣ min súrya dilwaʕti.
Do you speak English (Arabic)?	bitikkállim ingilíizi (ɣárabi)?

[1] Or ʕanáaṭir.

[2] Lit. "my husband is English".

I only speak a little Arabic.

ſana bakkállim ɤárabi baſliſ (or ſuwáyya).

I can read Arabic but I cannot speak it fluently.

ſan-áſdar áſra ɤárabi ſinnáma ma (ſa)ſdárſ akkállim kuwáyyis.

I shall have to take Arabic lessons.

ſana láazim áaxud duráus ɤárabi.

Can you recommend a good Egyptian teacher?

tiſdar tiſúlli ɤala mudárris máɤri-kwáyyis?

Can you understand me?

ſinta fa(a)hímni (or ſinta fáahim)?

You have an accent in Arabic.

ſilɤárabi-btáaɤak mikássar ſuwayya.

Do you understand the Sa'idi dialect?

ſinta-btífham kaláam iɤɤaɤáyda?

Do you speak colloquial Arabic?

ſinta-btikkállim ɤárabi dáarig?

Do you know Classical Arabic?

bitíɤraf ɤárabi faſſiħ?

I've studied Arabic.

ſana-tɤallímti ɤárabi.

I don't understand (you).

ſana miſ fáahim.

I don't understand your meaning.

ſana miſ fáahim ſáɤdak.

Please speak (more) slowly.

ſikkállim ɤala máhlak, min faɖlak.

What does that word mean?

ſikkilmáadi maɤnáaha ſéeh?

Could you please translate this sentence for me?

múmkin titargímli-ggumláadi?

How do you spell this word?

bitistahágga-kkilmáadi-zzáay?

I'll spell it (out) for you.

ſana ħastahaggáalak.

You have a good (bad) pronunciation.

núſſak kuwáyyis (wíħiſ).

They have their own dialect.

biyikkallímu láhga maxɤúuɤa.

Would you act as interpreter for me with this gentleman?

múmkin titargímli kaláam issáyyid?